"I DO NOT HAVE A DISABILITY, I HAVE A GIFT! OTHERS MAY SEE IT AS A DISABILITY, BUT I SEE IT AS A CHALLENGE. THIS CHALLENGE IS A GIFT BECAUSE I HAVE TO BECOME STRONGER TO GET AROUND IT, AND SMARTER TO FIGURE OUT HOW TO USE IT; OTHERS SHOULD BE SO LUCKY."

—SHANE E. BRYAN

"WE CAN'T HAVE ONLY JEWS CRY FOR ANTI-SEMITISM, AND MUSLIMS CRY FOR ISLAMOPHOBIA. WE CAN ONLY WIN THIS IF WE SEE IT AS ONE BIG FIGHT."

—IMAM ABDULLAH ANTEPLI

"HISTORY IS SO SUBJECTIVE. THE TELLER OF IT DETERMINES IT."

—LIN-MANUEL MIRANDA

"WHEN OUR ELDERS PRESENTED SCHOOL TO US, THEY DID NOT PRESENT IT AS A PLACE OF HIGHER LEARNING BUT AS A MEANS TO ESCAPE DEATH AND PENAL WAREHOUSING. FULLY 60% OF ALL YOUNG BLACK MEN WHO DROP OUT OF HIGH SCHOOL WILL GO TO JAIL. THIS SHOULD DISGRACE THE COUNTRY. BUT IT DOES NOT."

—TA-NEHISI COATES

"FACEBOOK LIVE HAS BECOME OUR NEW GLOBAL DISTRESS SIGNAL."

—CASEY NEWTON

"MY JOB AS A PROSECUTOR IS TO DO JUSTICE. AND JUSTICE IS SERVED WHEN A GUILTY MAN IS CONVICTED AND AN INNOCENT MAN IS NOT."

—SUPREME COURT JUSTICE SONIA SOTOMAYOR

"IF YOU CAN CONVINCE THE LOWEST WHITE MAN HE'S BETTER THAN THE BEST COLORED MAN, HE WON'T NOTICE YOU'RE PICKING HIS POCKET. HELL, GIVE HIM SOMEONE TO LOOK DOWN ON AND HE'LL EMPTY HIS POCKETS FOR YOU."

—PRESIDENT LYNDON JOHNSON

"THE WORLD IS TOO DANGEROUS TO LIVE IN— NOT BECAUSE OF THE PEOPLE WHO DO EVIL, BUT BECAUSE OF THE PEOPLE WHO SIT AND LET IT HAPPEN."

—ALBERT EINSTEIN

"AMERICA STANDS U... WORLD, THE ONLY... FOUNDED ON RAC... AN IDEAL."

—PRESIDENT RONALD REAGAN

Dear Reader,

This book was hatched, like so many good ideas, over a meal.

Last year, two of us—one a photojournalist, film producer, and curator; the other an innovator and entrepreneur—had dinner together to catch up on our lives and compare notes on the state of the world. Jonathan had recently wrapped up a stint at the White House where he served as Special Assistant to President Barack Obama and Director of the Office of Social Innovation and Civic Participation. Rick had just finished *The Human Face of Big Data*, a PBS TV special and large-format illustrated book exploring the impact of our increasingly connected technological world on civilization.

Jonathan was about to embark on a new job as CEO of the Anti-Defamation League (ADL), a nonprofit with a 100-year history of fighting anti-Semitism and discrimination in all its forms. As we discussed the enormous strides that the United States has made against intolerance over the past century, we realized that neither of us could recall a book dedicated to celebrating, in words and photographs, the many Americans who had fought for the right to be treated equally, with dignity and respect, despite differences such as race, faith, national origin, or sexual orientation. That evening, we envisioned *THE GOOD FIGHT*, a book aimed at reminding us how far we had come over the past century.

By the following summer, the project was well underway, and we were confident that the book's message was in tune with the times. But as the 2016 presidential race legitimized long-simmering hatreds and bigotries, we realized that this book needed to be more than simply a retrospective. With so many of the nation's achievements against injustice potentially in jeopardy, we expanded the scope of the project to encompass the many challenges that America faces today and to serve as a call to action.

As you are about to discover, this is no ordinary book. *THE GOOD FIGHT: AMERICA'S ONGOING STRUGGLE FOR JUSTICE* is a visual time machine illustrating many of the courageous struggles that so many Americans have fought to bring us all closer to the ideal enshrined in our Constitution: "Freedom for All". The book communicates its message in multiple ways—through evocative photographs, thought-provoking essays, and bold infographics, plus a unique smartphone app that invites readers to dive deeper via dozens of videos. Our hope is that you will spend time exploring and sharing the stories here. You might not agree with every point of view found in these pages, but we hope this book will prompt readers to appreciate both how much work remains to be done and how quickly our nation's hard-fought-for progress can be undone if we do not remain vigilant.

We invite you to join us in carrying on *THE GOOD FIGHT*.

Sincerely,

Rick Smolan
CEO, *Against All Odds Productions*

Jonathan Greenblatt
CEO, *Anti-Defamation League*

ADL
Anti-Defamation League®

NEW YORK, NEW YORK c. 1930. A newly arrived immigrant family looks out from Ellis Island across New York Harbor at the Statue of Liberty and the land they will soon call home. From 1892 to 1954, millions of people from Europe and Russia entered the United States through the federal immigration station at Ellis Island in search of safety and the opportunity to live a better life. Today, nearly half of all U.S. citizens have at least one ancestor who came through Ellis Island.

SEE **PAGE 25** ON HOW TO USE YOUR PHONE TO VIEW

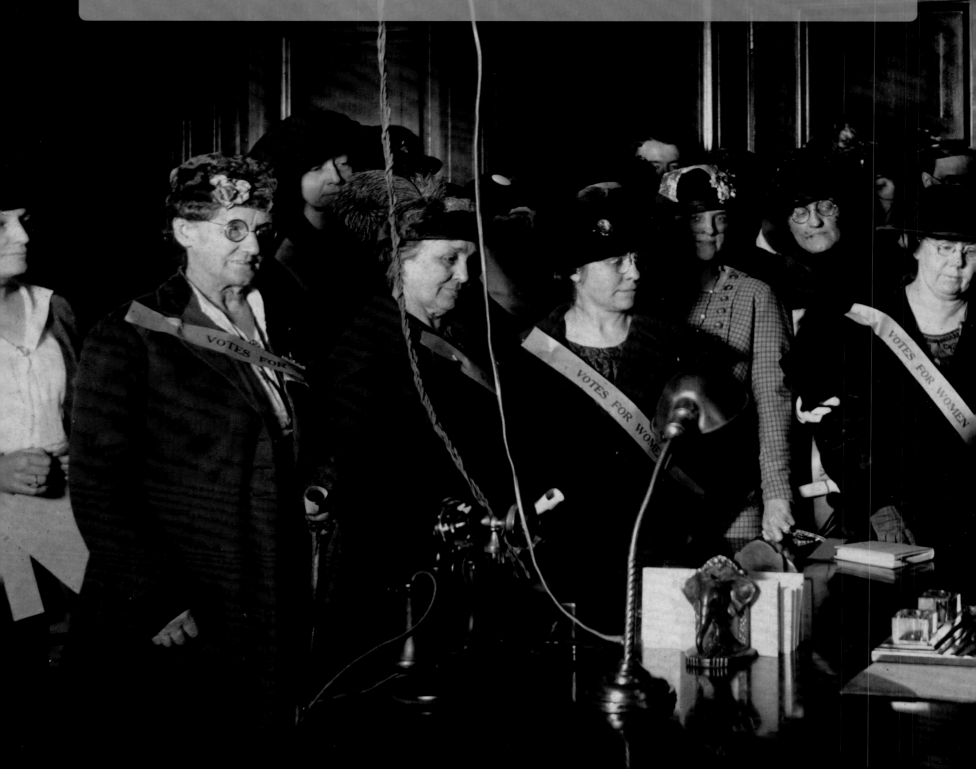

In 1920, after a decades-long struggle, women gained the right to vote. But still, unmarried **women were forbidden** from using contraceptives, abortion was a punishable crime, and getting pregnant led to being immediately fired.

FRANKFORT, KENTUCKY, JANUARY 6, 1920. As a group of women suffragists looks on, Kentucky Governor Edwin P. Morrow signs the Nineteenth Amendment to the U.S. Constitution, guaranteeing the right to vote. The amendment, which had already been approved by the U.S. Congress, went on to win approval from three-fourths of the country's state legislatures and was ratified that August. The amendment represented a major milestone, after more than 70 years of struggle for women's rights.

More than **25,000 protesters** from a variety of backgrounds joined Martin Luther King Jr. and other civil rights activists in the march from Selma to Montgomery in 1965. Three months later, federal legislation was passed to protect voting rights for African Americans.

SELMA, ALABAMA, 1965. Americans from around the country joined together for the historic civil rights march from Selma to Montgomery, the Alabama state capital. Led by Martin Luther King Jr., the marchers were attacked and beaten back twice by state and local police, drawing attention to their demand for enforcement of African American voting rights. In response to the violence, President Lyndon Johnson dispatched National Guard troops to protect the protesters. On their third attempt, the marchers finally reached Montgomery. © STEVE SCHAPIRO

The 2016 Dakota Pipeline protest was the largest unified gathering of Native Americans in U.S. history, with more than 300 tribes and 10,000 supporters, including thousands of veterans.

CANNON BALL, NORTH DAKOTA, SEPTEMBER 9, 2016. Native Americans and supporters march along a road near the Standing Rock Sioux Reservation to protest construction of the 1,200 mile long, $3.8 billion Dakota Access Pipeline. Indian and environmental opponents of the underground oil pipeline noted the construction company's long history of leaks and voiced their concerns that the pipeline would disturb sacred tribal burial grounds and endanger the water supply for millions of people living downstream. 📷 ALYSSA SCHUKAR

Reaffirming the rights of all Americans to their own faith, **Air Force cadets** now participate in training that reinforces separation of church and state.

COLORADO SPRINGS, MAY 2016. U.S. Air Force Academy cadets in Colorado Springs joyously celebrate their graduation. A decade prior, things were not so happy. A scandal erupted at the Academy when it emerged that senior officers, Christian faculty and staff members were openly proselytizing, calling on cadets to embrace Jesus Christ. Once Air Force authorities became aware of the problem, they worked with the Anti-Defamation League to create a training program that reinforced the constitutional requirement to separate church and state. Since 2007, every incoming class of 1,400 cadets has participated in role-playing scenarios involving respect for religion at the school. To date, more than 14,000 cadets have benefited from the training. 📷 LIZ COPAN

NEW YORK, NEW YORK, JULY 9, 2016. Playwright, composer, and actor Lin-Manuel Miranda (foreground) acknowledges applause after his final performance as Alexander Hamilton in his Emmy- and Pulitzer Prize-winning musical *Hamilton* on Broadway. In addition to Miranda, who is Latino, in the title role, African American, Latino, and other minority actors play the parts of George Washington, Thomas Jefferson, and the other Founding Fathers, a device that underscores the timelessness of the American immigrant experience. Although the cast wears costumes of the eighteenth century, the music and lyrics represent a contemporary combination of hip-hop, R&B, and classic Broadway styles, making the story of the nation's birth even more relevant to modern audiences.
📷 BRUCE GLIKAS

Hamilton **broke new ground** with a diverse racial cast portraying the Founding Fathers. It was nominated for 16 Tony Awards.

More than 11,000 women were motivated to run for political office in 2017, up from 800 in 2016.

WASHINGTON, D.C., JANUARY 21, 2017. The Women's March was the largest single-day demonstration in U.S. history. A thinly veiled protest against the inauguration of President Donald Trump the day before, the March inspired millions of people around the country who gathered in support of women's rights. The largest demonstration was in Washington, where participants paraded down Pennsylvania Avenue. But more than 600 women's rights protests, involving almost 5 million people, were held the same day in over 30 countries. 📷 JESSICA RINALDI

CHARLOTTE, NORTH CAROLINA, JUNE 30, 2016. Shaquille Vance (left) lunges across the finish line in the men's 200-meter dash, just ahead of Regas Woods (far left) at the U.S. Paralympic Trials. International athletes with disabilities ranging from amputated limbs and quadriplegia to visual and intellectual impairment have competed in the Paralympic Games since 1988. The Games, which grew from a small gathering of British World War II veterans to become one of the world's largest sporting events, are held immediately following the summer and winter Olympic Games. ◎ BOB LEVERONE

Until 1974, "ugly laws" were used to prevent people with disabilities from appearing in public view. In 2016, 4.1 billion watched the Paralympic Games, which celebrated the athletes' achievements.

CHICAGO, ILLINOIS, JANUARY 30, 2017. Meryem Yildirim (left), a 7-year-old Muslim American girl sitting on her father's shoulders, encounters Adin Bendat-Appell, a 9-year-old Jewish American held aloft by his father. The children met as their parents joined a demonstration at Chicago's O'Hare International Airport to protest President Donald Trump's ban on travelers from 6 Muslim-majority countries, even those with valid U.S. visas and residence permits. The executive order, which appeared to be unconstitutionally targeting Muslims, was hastily announced and badly planned, throwing airports into turmoil. Protests erupted in a dozen cities across the country, while immigration lawyers rushed to airports, volunteering their services to those who had been detained. Federal courts blocked the order and a second attempt as well, branding both as discriminatory and unconstitutional. NUCCIO DINUZZO

Reflecting on their own persecution during World War II, Jewish Americans banded together with their Muslim brethren to combat President Trump's hastily implemented travel ban in January 2017.

WASHINGTON, D.C., JUNE 26, 2015. A delighted Pooja Mandagere (left) receives a kiss from Natalie Thompson in front of the Supreme Court as they celebrate the historic ruling legalizing same-sex marriages in the United States. 📷 DOUG MILLS

In June 2015, the Court ruled that same-sex marriages be recognized equally in every state. This historic ruling resulted in more than **123,000 same-sex marriages** in the following 12 months.

MONTGOMERY, ALABAMA, MARCH 1965. Protesting conditions that had effectively disenfranchised black voters throughout Alabama, civil rights activists set out to march the 54-mile route from Selma to the state capital of Montgomery, and press their case. Their first attempt resulted in "Bloody Sunday," when police attacked the marchers with truncheons and tear gas at Selma's Edmund Pettus Bridge. But after a federal judge ruled that the demonstration was protected by the First Amendment, the march began anew, providing an iconic picture (below) that memorialized the protesters' dignity and purpose. Congress passed the Voting Rights Act later that year.
JAMES KARALES

THE GOOD FIGHT

AMERICA'S ONGOING STRUGGLE FOR JUSTICE

BY RICK SMOLAN AND JENNIFER ERWITT

THIS BOOK WAS MADE POSSIBLE BY A GENEROUS GRANT FROM ERIC AND LINDA HORODAS

STERLING PUBLISHERS | AGAINST ALL ODDS PRODUCTIONS

WE GO BACK TO THE WELL
BY BRET STEPHENS

"**THERE IS NOTHING WRONG** with America that cannot be cured by what is right with America."

These words, spoken by President Clinton at his first inauguration in 1993, precisely capture what it is, really, that makes the United States exceptional.

Not economic wealth. Not military might. Not geographic advantages. Rather, the unique power of national regeneration and moral renewal that flow from our foundational principle: "created equal."

What is it that we do as Americans when our social fabric needs repair? We go back to the well. The well is the Declaration of Independence—a document that makes a timeless claim, even if it was written and signed by men who were creatures of their time.

If we are created equal, then neither religious beliefs nor property requirements can determine who gets to vote.

If we are created equal, then skin color must never again be a license for human bondage or second-class citizenship.

If we are created equal, then gender should be no bar to the ballot—or to the boardroom.

If we are created equal, then sexual orientation cannot be an obstacle to an individual's pursuit of happiness.

If we are created equal, then any freshly sworn-in *immigrant* from the poorest country stands on equal footing with every descendant of the Mayflower.

In 1963, from the steps of the Lincoln Memorial, Martin Luther King Jr. called the Declaration "a promissory note to which every American was to fall heir." The United States in the time of Jim Crow racial segregation fell well short of the promise of the Declaration. But even if the promise had been betrayed, it had not been forsaken. It is what made the realization of King's dream possible.

Students today are taught a great deal about the history of prejudice, as well as exclusion and oppression, in the United States. It is important to teach that history, but it is not enough.

U.S. history is also a story of liberation. There is wrongdoing but also rectification, guilt but also conscience, bigotry but also enlightenment.

Above all, there is civic courage. We are familiar with the storybook examples of courage, from Harriet Tubman to the Freedom Riders. But what makes *The Good Fight* an important addition to the literature on civil rights is its powerful reminder that American civic courage is not simply the story of a few heroes. On the contrary, it is the story of millions of Americans who took the Founders at their word and demanded that the promise be redeemed. As Thomas Jefferson said, "The earth belongs in usufruct to the living."

Nearly 70 years ago, a Jewish refugee arrived in this country, almost penniless, with her 10-year-old daughter. Like 80 million others, they immigrated because they believed America's promise was worth the journey and, if necessary, the fight. As the son of that daughter, what a privilege it is to be asked to be a part of this beautiful book. ■

Bret Stephens is an Op-Ed columnist for *The New York Times* and winner of the 2013 Pulitzer Prize for Commentary. He was raised in Mexico City and is a former editor in chief of the Jerusalem Post. 🐦 *@BretStephensNYT*

PARIS, FRANCE, c. 1876. For refugees, immigrants, and those seeking a better life, the Statue of Liberty has long been a universal symbol of freedom, equality, and opportunity. Completed in 1886, the statue was a gift from France with the chains and shackles lying at her feet designed to mark the end of American slavery. The statue's iconic torch-bearing arm (right) was built in a Paris foundry a year before the rest of the statue, and was temporarily displayed at Madison Square Park.

CONTENTS

USE *THE GOOD FIGHT* APP TO TRIGGER OVER 60 VIDEOS!

On your smart phone, download **The Good Fight Viewer** from the App Store, GooglePlay or by visiting *http://thegoodfightviewer.com*

Wherever this symbol appears, point your phone's camera at the entire photograph to view related content.

Try it now: Launch **The Good Fight Viewer** and point your phone's camera at the cover.

25

OUR TWO AMERICAS
BY TODD BREWSTER

IN A VOLUME DEDICATED to the civil rights struggles of African Americans and Native Americans and Asian Americans and every other hyphenated American, of women and gays and grays and people with disabilities, of those who identify as transgender, no gender, or multiple gender, of religious believers and nonbelievers—Jews, Christians, Muslims, atheists—and of immigrants from all corners of the world, what wisdom is there to be found buried deep in the annals of our past?

Well, it's actually pretty simple. Separated only by time and circumstances, the people who are the subject of this book were stirred by the same progressive rhythm that has beat inside all of us since our Founding, the same clash of wills that was written into our establishing documents, and they marched in pursuit of the same elemental truth that is a crucial strand of our DNA: freedom is more righteous than tyranny.

Indeed, it is our contribution to human progress that we Americans play out our national story year after year, generation after generation, struggle after struggle, learning this one truth, unlearning it, and then learning it all over

BATON ROUGE, LOUISIANA, JULY 9, 2016. A series of police shootings of African American men had already sparked protests across the United States and given energy to the nascent Black Lives Matter movement, when 28-year-old Ieshia Evans, her olive-green dress billowing in the breeze, confronted officers in riot-gear on a Baton Rouge highway. Evans and others blocked the road in protest over the police shooting of Alton Sterling that had taken place four days earlier outside a nearby convenience store. The powerful image of her arrest (right) quickly went viral, defining both the moment and the protest movement. Although the photo turned her into a national icon, Evans shunned publicity. She had traveled from her home in Pennsylvania "because she wanted to look her son in the eyes to tell him she fought for his freedom and rights." 📷 JOHNATHAN BACHMAN

again. For all too often, this push for recognition, this assertion of principle, this "good fight" that gave us our independence, is a fight we have fought—and continue to fight—with ourselves.

Think about it. In the middle of the nineteenth century, divided by the argument over the future of slavery, we engaged in a bloody Civil War—a "second" American Revolution, if you will, necessary to finish the work that was started in the first one. Early on, President Abraham Lincoln insisted that that war (or "rebellion," as he preferred to call it, not willing to recognize the secession of 11 Southern states) was a contest to preserve the union *and only to preserve the union.* Yet by 1862, he had come to see "union" as not merely some geographical concept, not only a contract between states, but also as a pledge to shared principle. To Lincoln, "union" was a vow uttered long before our Constitution, one going all the way back to our Declaration of Independence, with its reverence for both liberty *and equality.*

The decision to free the slaves followed, a bold proclamation that injected new vigor into the cause. But now think of how in the decades after that war was decisively won, after slavery had been outlawed by the Thirteenth Amendment and "equal protection of the laws" enshrined by the Fourteenth, we reverted to a new kind of racial abuse—not involuntary servitude, no, but "home rule," as it was slyly called, white supremacy encoded by law and enforced by the gun, the whip, and ultimately, the noose. "Black bodies swinging in the Southern breeze," intoned the great Billie Holiday (page 68) in her distinctively mournful timbre, "Strange fruit hanging from the poplar trees."

Then move the cursor of your imagination to a point nearly a hundred years after the Civil War, to February 1, 1960, and the story of four black college students who, in an act of deliberate provocation, chose to sit in a "whites-only" section of a Woolworth's lunch counter in Greensboro, North Carolina, demanding to be served. Years later, in an interview with NPR, one of the students, Franklin McCain, recalled the feeling of trepidation as he and the others embarked on their bold task. This was, after all, still a time when a black man passing a white man on the street was expected to lower his gaze in an act of subservience. Yet here they were—four men barely out of their teens—ready to stare down the whole sordid history of Jim Crow. Then, a mere "15 seconds" into their protest, McCain became surprised by "the most wonderful feeling … of liberation … [of] restored manhood …" There to lay claim to something that he and the others knew to be their basic human right, he entered a "natural high" that made him feel "almost invincible." The experience was so inflating, so affirming, McCain sensed that if he had died there and then, if this was to be his last act on this Earth, his life could still be said to have had meaning, he could still be said to have been *somebody*. Funny how powerful freedom can feel when you start your day on the other side of it.

The Good Fight is filled with stories like that one, tales of courage that often led to genuine, if sometimes illusory, achievement. It also contains myriad

NEW YORK, SEPTEMBER, 1924. Jeannette Rankin, a leading advocate for women's rights, was the first woman to be elected to the U.S. Congress. In 1916, she won an election in Montana, one of a handful of states that allowed women to vote. In Congress, Rankin was instrumental in initiating the legislation that eventually became the 19th Amendment to the U.S. Constitution, which granted unrestricted voting rights to women. A progressive member of the Republican Party, Rankin (above), pictured here in New York's Union Square in 1924, delivered fiery speeches in support of gender equality and civil rights. In 1940, she was elected to a second term. A lifelong pacifist, she was one of 56 lawmakers who voted against the United States' entry into World War I and the only member of Congress who voted against the declaration of war against Japan after its attack on Pearl Harbor in 1941.

IN 1882, CONGRESS passed the Chinese Exclusion Act, which, as a response to nativist appeals, banned Chinese laborers from coming to the United States and rendered all Chinese Americans already here as permanent aliens, unable to be granted US citizenship. Many, including the sitting president, Chester Arthur, found the law objectionable, but, threatened with

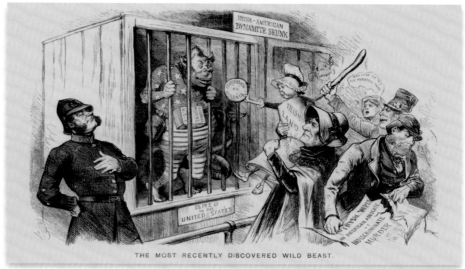

THE MOST RECENTLY DISCOVERED WILD BEAST.

a veto-proof congressional majority, Arthur signed it anyway. Chinese laborers had been arriving since the California Gold Rush in 1848 and had helped to construct the first transcontinental railroad. But by the 1880s, they were being accused of depressing wages. Proponents of the act feared a nation overrun by "coolies," a derogatory term obscure in its origins. Republican Senator George Frisbie Hoar of Massachusetts, an outspoken critic of the measure, described it as "nothing less than the legalization of racial discrimination." But the popular mood was against him as can be seen here in a detail from an advertisement for "Magic Washer" laundry soap (above), where the manufacturer declares that the quality of his product will allow Uncle Sam to boot the Chinese back to Asia. The Chinese Exclusion Act was not repealed until 1943, when Washington needed to solidify its alliance with China against Japan during World War II. It was then that President Franklin Delano Roosevelt called the law a "historic mistake."

DURING THE NINETEENTH and twentieth centuries, Irish immigrants were also the targets of widespread discrimination in the United States. Nativist Protestant groups regarded Irish laborers, like the Chinese, as undercutting wages, while the country's dominant Protestant society stereotyped the Irish as violent, alcoholic, and racially inferior to Anglo-Saxons (above, right).

examples of cowardice, suffering, and unfathomable abuse, of derogatory terms—wop, kike, wetback, mick, nigger, fag, towel-head, the list is endless—and evil that denies understanding. Think only of the brutalized corpse of the 14-year-old Emmett Till, killed in 1955 for leering at a white woman (a "crime" that turned out to have been a lie), or, in our own time, the shooting death of Srinivas Kuchibhotla, an Indian immigrant who, in February 2017, was targeted in a Kansas bar after a local, likely mistaking him for a Muslim, told Kuchibhotla to "get out of my country." Taken with the tales of heroic achievement, these stories describe a path that is not so much a straight line to progress as a scribble—a zig this way, a zag that, followed by a sudden painful reverse and, finally, a grand leap forward.

How else to mark a disjointed journey that winds through such achievements as *Brown v. Board of Education*, the successful bus boycott that followed the arrest of Rosa Parks, the forced integration of Central High School in Little Rock, Arkansas, the 1963 March on Washington, and the Civil Rights Act of 1964, as well as the 1963 firehose assault on protesters in Birmingham, the police beating of Rodney King, and the murders of Laquan McDonald, Trayvon Martin, and Freddie Gray? How do we make sense of a people who cheered the lynching of the innocent Jewish businessman Leo Frank and who fed on the anti-Semitic rants of the enormously popular Catholic "radio priest" of the 1930s—Father Charles Coughlin—and yet less than a decade later, embraced Jewish composer Irving Berlin's "God Bless America" (page 122) as their anthem of national purpose, inspiring the nation's soldiers in their quest to defeat Hitler and the Nazis? The Supreme Court's 1986 decision upholding a law that criminalized homosexual sex *and* the moment, less than 30 years later, when a majority of justices on the same court found, in *Obergefell v. Hodges*, a right to same-sex marriage fundamental to "the liberty of person," conferring on hundreds of thousands of unions the imprimatur of permanence and respect? And how, in a single lifetime, does a country go from forced sterilization of the mentally ill to the 1990 Americans With Disabilities Act?

After the young Sandra Day, daughter of Arizona cattle ranchers, graduated third in her class at Stanford Law School in 1952, more than 40 law firms greeted her application for employment with the terse response: "We don't hire women." Yet just 29 years later, Justice Sandra Day O'Connor became the first of her sex to serve on the U.S. Supreme Court. And while today we live with the shame that it is still more likely that a black man in his 30s has been in prison than that he has completed a college degree (mass incarceration, says former Ohio State Law Professor Michelle Alexander, is the "new" Jim Crow), that sad picture (page 55) shares the same historical space with the one showing our first African American president walking hand in hand with famed veteran Civil Rights leader Congressman John Lewis at the 50th anniversary of the march on Selma (page 77).

While there is no denying that the nation has made tremendous strides in the name of liberty, we should not take too much comfort in thinking that the "good fight" is a fight where right inevitably triumphs. There is, and always has been, a contradiction at the heart of our history, an incongruity between the America we aspire to be and the America we really are. You can see it in the way that the nation embraces the idea of equality, even as it still brands difference as "other." You can hear it as we school the world on the blessings of liberty, even as we consistently deny those same blessings to many of our own people, or, even worse, demonize them for no better reason than that they do not look or act or think or love the way most of the rest of us do. This, too, is America.

And yet, how often it is that our founding moment, our revolutionary creed, calls us to return to the path of virtue? In 1886, at the dedication of the Statue of Liberty, suffragists chartered a boat and shouted protests from the harbor. They recognized the paradox that "Lady Liberty" celebrated freedom in a nation where women could not even exercise the "sacred right to the elective franchise" (as the leaders of the landmark Seneca Falls convention of 1848 had reverently described it). Thirty years later, with the campaign for women's voting rights gaining new momentum, marchers co-opted the image of the Liberty Bell to further their cause, even creating a 2,000-pound bronze replica—a "Justice Bell," as they renamed it—which they paraded about on a flatbed truck, its clapper affixed inside to prevent it from being rung until the right to vote was won. When it was, in 1920, by constitutional amendment, the bell did toll, at a ceremony held, appropriately enough, in Independence Square, Philadelphia.

During World War II, the reliance on women to take the place of men in the depleted workforce—the "Rosie the Riveter" of Kay Kyser's song and Norman Rockwell's 1943 cover for *The Saturday Evening Post* (page 188)—brought a new image to counter Lady Liberty's classical purity. Here were women who were muscular, independent, and up to the task. In the postwar years, there was an expectation that women would somehow return passively to a place of dependency, and they did, but only for a brief period. In 1963, Betty Friedan was writing of "the problem that has no name," her artful phrase for the life of

IN JUNE 1964, three civil rights workers—Michael Schwerner and Andrew Goodman, both Jewish New Yorkers, and James Chaney, a local African American—disappeared in Mississippi while registering African Americans to vote. In response, Attorney General Robert F. Kennedy launched a massive investigation, code-named "Mississippi Burning," sending 200 FBI agents and scores of federal troops to comb the woods and swamps of Neshoba County. Two months later, the victims' bullet-riddled remains were discovered under an earthen dam. Nineteen men, including Sam Bowers, the Grand Wizard of the White Knights of the Ku Klux Klan of Mississippi, Cecil Price, the local deputy sheriff; and Edgar Ray Killen, a part-time Baptist minister, were implicated in their murders. Mississippi refused to prosecute them, leaving the federal government to indict the men on civil rights violations. An all-white federal jury found seven of the men guilty. Federal district court judge William Howard Cox, a notorious segregationist who referred to black Mississippi voters as "a bunch of niggers...acting like a bunch of chimpanzees," sentenced the men to light prison terms ranging from three to 10 years. Among Mississippians, the men were treated like folk heroes. None of those convicted served more than six years. But in 2005—41 years after the murders—a Mississippi court, citing fresh evidence, convicted 80-year-old Killen on three counts of manslaughter and sentenced him to 60 years in prison.

MEMPHIS, TENNESSEE, MARCH 29, 1968. With bayonets fixed, the Tennessee National Guard warily eyes a march by the city's sanitation workers and supporters. The workers had gone on strike for higher wages and better working conditions, but because their membership was predominantly black, the confrontation with the city's entrenched white power structure had a racial tone as well. The previous month, two workers had died when faulty equipment led to their being absorbed into a garbage truck compressor, an eerily symbolic event and one that led them to adopt the slogan "I Am a Man." And it was at an appearance in support of them that Martin Luther King gave his "I Have Been to the Mountaintop" speech on April 3. The next day King was shot dead by an assassin.

domesticity that, still forced upon women by both custom and law, left them unfulfilled appendages of a male power structure. By 1970, when, to mark the 50th anniversary of the women's suffrage amendment, Friedan organized a "Women's Strike for Equality," the movement she helped start had won a following so large that it appeared to eclipse in achievement the Civil Rights campaign upon which, in many ways, it was modeled. Indeed, what is now an understanding of near-national consensus—that women should rightly have careers in law, medicine, business, and politics, and that they should not only be accepted into military academies like West Point and Annapolis but also be fighting in combat right next to their male counterparts—is the result of much hard work. What followed was a move for greater rights and acceptance for gays, seniors, immigrants, and the disabled, traveling in that familiar yet undefinable rhythm, alternating between landmark triumphs and critical setbacks.

We have been fortunate that so much of this extraordinary history has played out, and continues to play out, in front of the cameras. There is no way to ignore the influence that the mass media—whether through news, entertainment, advertising, or the personal effusions that dominate expression on our modern-

day devices—has had on the evolution of social justice. Radio was the first technology to break down regional barriers, introducing a national culture and also a debate over national values, whatever those might be. But soon there were also magazines—big picture weeklies like *LIFE* and *LOOK*—that arrived through the letter slot and opened the eyes of the uninitiated to a celebrity on one page, the injustice of segregation on the next.

Television amplified Joseph McCarthy's corrosive accusations against the "sinister other" during the days of the Red Scare, but after CBS newsman Edward R. Murrow took on the Wisconsin politician in a revealing confrontation over the senator's sensational charges, it was also television that took McCarthy down. In the 1970s, Mary Tyler Moore, as Mary Richards (page 169), was enjoying a very fulfilling, charming, professional life in wholesome Minneapolis, even if that life was being lived without the steady presence of a man, thank you very much. And who knew that Norman Lear (page 126) would encourage a period of national soul-searching when Archie Bunker, Lear's creation, appeared on the small screen in *All in the Family* to show us that bigotry didn't have to wear a white sheet? No, you could find it in your living room, relaxing in a favorite chair, spouting prejudice at the pages of the *Daily News*.

The book you hold in your hands contains hundreds of sterling photographs, "still pictures" (the term seems unsatisfying to describe a medium that can so positively vibrate with meaning) that provide us with the sometimes brutal, sometimes magical, poetry of the frozen moment. Here you will find a group of undocumented immigrants in hiding, camped out in a ditch high above the Hollywood Hills (page 156); a lone black woman in Baton Rouge, Louisiana,

Castro neighborhood to San Francisco City Hall. A visionary politician who was known popularly as the "Mayor of Castro Street," Milk leveraged the growing political and economic power of the neighborhood to pass a groundbreaking gay rights ordinance in 1978. Only one member of the Board voted against it. That was Dan White, a former police officer and firefighter who represented a largely white district of San Francisco, one where there had been a growing concern about the city's identification as a gay mecca. On November 27, 1978, nine months after the photo (opposite) was taken, White climbed through a window at San Francisco's City Hall to avoid a metal detector, whereupon he shot and killed Milk and San Francisco Mayor George Moscone. Milk soon gained the status of a martyr in the gay community and was posthumously awarded the Presidential Medal of Freedom, the country's highest civilian honor, by President Barack Obama in 2009.
📷 DANIEL NICOLETTA

IN NOVEMBER 1969, a group of 89 Indian activists occupied Alcatraz Island in San Francisco Bay (right) to publicize the "trail of broken treaties" with the U.S. government. Activists demanded title to Alcatraz under the provisions of an 1868 act stating that abandoned federal land (such as Alcatraz's notorious maximum-security prison, which had been closed six years earlier) should be returned to the Native people who once occupied it. The 19-month occupation by AIM (American Indian Movement) garnered widespread public support from Bay Area residents. The dockworkers union threatened to shut down the port of Oakland if the protesters were forcefully removed. Boaters smuggled food onto the island. Doctors and lawyers volunteered their services. Celebrities including Jane Fonda, Marlon Brando, Buffy Sainte-Marie, and Dick Gregory came to the island to show their support. Although the occupation was forcibly ended, it is remembered today as a pivotal moment in the Red Power movement, a political movement that continues today to promote self-determination for all native peoples. 📷 ART KANE

clad in a beautiful flowing green dress, her face projecting a mood of peaceful meditation, approaching a battalion of police officers in moon suits of riot gear, ready to push back (page 27); and a line of passive Japanese Americans waiting for their trip to the internment camps—the *American* internment camps—of World War II (page 109). How moved are we then to turn the page and discover three veterans of those same internment camps, decades later, saluting the flag of the country that once treated them so inhumanely (page 111)?

The new media age is rapidly making its own special contribution to the record of our history. In recognition of this development, *The Good Fight* includes technology inelegantly called the "smartphone-enabled immersive visual experience" (point your device at specially marked pictures in this book and watch as videos and music are triggered). Capturing the way that music and film have pushed our story forward, it also shows how the smartphone has become perhaps history's greatest tool of criminal accountability. For surely, the recent instances of police and vigilante violence on black victims, in particular, would have gone unnoticed if cell phones had not recorded them on video. Disturbing though it may be for a jury to be told that North Charleston police officer Michael Slager shot Walter Scott eight times in the back as Scott bolted from his car and ran from a traffic stop (page 95), it is uniquely riveting to watch it, reverse it, put it in slow motion, and then watch it again and do all of that from the privacy of your cell phone. Pictures can deceive, but they deceive less than they enlighten. No, the greater worry is that we become so inured to images of such violence— so casual about the way that they pass before us on our mobile devices like the ubiquitous pop-up ads and inane memes—that we treat them as ephemeral and

commonplace, pixilated distractions undeserving of our outrage.

There are heroes of this national saga, and some are justifiably famous—Martin Luther King, Cesar Chávez, Gloria Steinem, Harvey Milk, to name just four—but for the most part, *The Good Fight* represents a narrative written by the multitude. In 1900, the American population stood at 76 million. By the time of the nation's bicentennial, in 1976, it had climbed past 200 hundred million. And as this book is published, there are approximately 316 million of us. It has long been a cliché to say that we are a nation of immigrants, but it is less of one to say that the American story is a changeable feast, that both the content and the color of our country adjust from generation to generation: A purely Anglo-Saxon nation becomes an Anglo-Euro nation, which becomes an Anglo-Euro-Asian-African-Latino-Middle Eastern nation. There is no doubt that the immigrant has been invigorated by America and that America has been invigorated by immigrants. One of the lessons the "good fight" has left us, in all its many episodes, is that when we get it right, when we extend the "blessings of liberty" to the peoples we have once maligned as "other," they not only flourish, they also add new richness to the American story.

BILLINGS, MONTANA, DECEMBER 2, 1994. A year after anti-Semitic vandals hurled a cinder block through the window of the home of a Jewish family celebrating Hanukkah, hundreds of Billings residents, representing many religions and ethnicities, posed with menorahs in a display of religious tolerance. A local newspaper also printed a full-page image of a menorah that thousands of readers clipped and pasted on their windows. The community's show of solidarity in the face of hate drew national media attention, inspiring books, a *LIFE* magazine photo spread,, and two documentary films. Town leaders were honored at the White House. In hundreds of U.S. cities, communities launched tolerance campaigns based on the Billings model. The vandals

didn't withdraw quietly, however. Using bullets and bricks, they broke scores more windows of homes, businesses, and schools that had been displaying messages of tolerance. Someone even killed the cat belonging to one such home before the harassment subsided. No one was ever caught and punished for the vandalism. Margaret MacDonald, a Billings church leader who helped orchestrate the 1993 menorah campaign, says such efforts are needed today more than ever. "We still have a lot of work to do to confront racism, homophobia, xenophobia, and anti-immigrant attitudes," she told an interviewer. Today, MacDonald is a Montana State Representative. FRÉDÉRIC BRENNER

The writer Andrew Sullivan once compared the path of racial integration to the process of "coming out." In each instance, the minority is introduced to a majority (gay to straight, black to white) and as it is, as one hand clasps the other, old assumptions fall to the realization that we are all human, a single class of people, none of us "disordered or sick or defective or evil—at least no more than our fellow humans in this vale of tears." Expanded beyond race and sexual orientation to include all manner of difference, that is the message of this book. As Sullivan writes, "We are born into family; we love; we marry; we take care of our children; we die." Let us do it together. Come here where you are accepted, here where you can flourish, here where we make mistakes and then have the courage to correct them. There is strength in such a simple epiphany, enough to urge a people forward. ◼

Todd Brewster is an award-winning journalist and historian. He has served as a senior editor at Time, Inc., and as a senior producer at ABC News. He is the co-author, with Peter Jennings, of *The New York Times* best sellers *The Century* and *In Search of America*, and has taught journalism, law, and history at Wesleyan University, Temple University, and Cooper Union. From 2008 to 2014, he was the Don E. Ackerman director of oral history at West Point. His latest book, *Lincoln's Gamble: The Tumultuous Six Months That Gave America the Emancipation Proclamation and Changed the Course of the Civil War,* was published, to critical acclaim, in 2014. He is presently Senior Lecturer in Journalism at Mount Holyoke College. *@ToddBrewster*

AMERICAN HISTORY, AMERICAN COURAGE

"History, despite its wrenching pain, cannot be unlived, but if faced with courage, need not be lived again."
—Maya Angelou

NATIVE AMERICANS

1876 Sioux victory of Crazy Horse and Sitting Bull over Custer at Little Bighorn.

1912 Jim Thorpe is first Native American to win Olympic gold medals (pentathlon and decathlon).

1920 William ("Will") Penn Adair Rogers, a Cherokee cowboy, is known as an actor, philanthropist, social commentator, and presidential candidate.

1924 Citizenship and voting rights granted to all Native Americans born in the U.S. But since the right to vote is governed by state law, some are barred from voting until 1957.

1934 Indian Reorganization Act gives tribes more control over their own destiny.

 1941 In World War II, 25,000 Native Americans serve. Navajo and Comanche Code Talkers are key. Their code was never broken.

1947 Elizabeth Marie Tallchief begins dancing with the New York City Ballet.

1982 Wilma Mankiller is first woman elected deputy chief of the Cherokee Nation. She receives the Presidential Medal of Freedom in 1998.

1992 The Mashantucket Pequot Tribe opens Foxwoods, Connecticut, the first large casino in the U.S.

1994 U.S. District Court reinforces a 1974 fishing rights decision that affirms that 60% of salmon caught in western Washington state belongs to Indian tribes.

2009 Elouise Cobell succeeds in bringing about the largest class action settlement ($3.4 billion) in history over mismanagement of federal lands held in trust for Native Americans.

2014 Keith Harper, a member of the Cherokee Nation of Oklahoma, is first Native American U.S. ambassador.

2016 Dakota Pipeline brings together diverse Native American tribes who are supported by non-Native U.S. veterans to fight against the pipeline.

AFRICAN AMERICANS

 1870 15th Amendment guarantees the right to vote, regardless of race.

1909 The National Association for the Advancement of Colored People (NAACP) founded by W.E.B. Du Bois and others.

1936 Jesse Owens is first African American athlete to compete in the modern Olympics.

1940 Hattie McDaniel is first African American woman to win an Oscar, in *Gone with the Wind*.

1947 Jackie Robinson is first African American man to play in Major League baseball.

1954 In *Brown v. Board of Education*, the Supreme Court rules that racial segregation violates the 14th Amendment.

 1963 Martin Luther King Jr. gives "I have a dream" speech to 250,000 in D.C.

1967 Thurgood Marshall is first African American Supreme Court Justice.

1975–85 *The Jeffersons* is a sitcom featuring a successful African American couple that deals with such issues as alcoholism, gun control, interracial marriage, and adult illiteracy.

1986 *The Oprah Winfrey Show* becomes highest-rated TV show. Winfrey is the first and only multi-billionaire African American woman.

2001 Colin Powell is first African American man to become secretary of state.

2004 Condoleezza Rice is first African American woman to become secretary of state.

2008 Barack Obama is elected first African American president.

2013 Black Lives Matter is launched to empower the black community.

2013 The Anti-Defamation League (ADL) joins Supreme Court case to argue that any housing discrimination violates Fair Housing Act.

2017 *Hidden Figures* movie about three African American women who help to put first men on the moon outsells new *Star Wars* movie the week it is released.

ASIAN AMERICANS

 1921 Anna May Wong is first Asian American movie star.

1943 Young-Oak Kim is first Asian American to command a combat battalion (the 100th Infantry Battalion).

 1947 Wataru Misaka is the first nonwhite person to play in the NBA.

1962 Daniel K. Inouye becomes U.S. senator and Spark Matsunaga becomes U.S. congressman from Hawaii.

1966 George Takei is one of the first Asian Americans to be featured prominently on TV (as Lt. Sulu on *Star Trek*).

1984 Haing Ngor is first Asian American to win an Oscar for supporting actor (*The Killing Fields*).

1985 Molecular biologist Flossie Wong-Staal clones the AIDS virus.

1988 David Hwang is first Asian American to win the Tony Award for best play (*M. Butterfly*).

 1993 Connie Chung is first Asian American nightly news anchor for a major network.

2001 Elaine Chao is first Asian American woman to be appointed to the president's Cabinet (secretary of labor under President George W. Bush).

2006 Ang Lee is first Asian to win an Oscar for best director (*Brokeback Mountain*).

2013 Mazie Hirono from Hawaii is first Asian American woman elected to the U.S. Senate, the first senator born in Japan, and the first Buddhist senator.

 2014 Vice Admiral Vivek H. Murthy is appointed U.S. Surgeon General, the first Asian American in this post.

JEWISH AMERICANS

1845 Lewis Charles Levin is first Jewish person elected to the House of Representatives.

1903 Oscar Straus is appointed U.S. secretary of labor and commerce, the first Jew to hold a Cabinet post.

1913 The Anti-Defamation League (ADL) is formed under the auspices of B'nai B'rith "to stop the defamation of the Jewish people and to secure fair treatment and justice for all."

1916 Justice Louis Brandeis is the first Jew appointed to the Supreme Court.

1931 George Gershwin's *Of Thee I Sing* is first musical to win a Pulitzer.

1936 Mel Blanc joins Leon Schlesinger Productions, and is the voice for Bugs Bunny, Daffy Duck, Porky Pig, Sylvester the Cat, and Woody Woodpecker, among others.

1938 Irving Berlin's *God Bless America* sweeps America as de facto national anthem.

1955 Jonas Salk discovers the vaccine to eradicate polio.

1963 Sandy Koufax, pitcher, is most valuable player for L.A. Dodgers.

1964 *Fiddler on the Roof* opens. For 10 years, holds record for longest-running musical on Broadway.

1970 Norman Lear has highest number of sitcoms on TV simultaneously, touching on many taboo subjects.

1979 Dianne Feinstein is first female Jewish mayor of a major city (San Francisco).

1987 Barney Frank comes out as first Jewish openly gay member of Congress.

1993 Ruth Bader Ginsburg is first female Jewish Supreme Court Justice.

1994 *Schindler's List* wins Oscar for best picture, directed by Steven Spielberg.

2016 Bernie Sanders is first Jewish American to win a U.S. presidential primary (New Hampshire).

MUSLIM AMERICANS

1952 U.S. Armed Forces recognize Islam as a religious affiliation.

1957 President Dwight Eisenhower gives first speech by a sitting president at a U.S. mosque.

1960s–70s Fazlur Rahman Khan is a structural engineer and architect, considered the father of tubular designs for high-rise buildings. He designed the Willis (Sears) Tower in Chicago, the tallest building in the world until 1998.

1964 Cassius Clay joins Nation of Islam, citing religious objections to the Vietnam War. He changes his name to Muhammad Ali.

1976 Famed model Iman appears on cover of *Vogue*.

1991 Imam Siraj Wahhaj is first Muslim to lead an invocation before the start of a session of the House of Representatives.

1994 The Council on American Islamic Relations (CAIR) is formed to defend the civil rights of Muslims.

1994 First lady Hillary Clinton hosts first Eid al-Fitr (celebrating the end of Ramadan) at the White House.

2002 Khalid Khannouchi wins Chicago marathon, becoming first man to break 2 minutes 6 seconds twice in one year.

2007 Keith Ellison becomes first Muslim congressman (representative for Minnesota).

2009 Farah Pandith is first special representative to Muslim communities for the U.S. Department of State.

2012 Sharmeen Obaid wins Oscar for *Saving Face*, making her first Pakistani Muslim to win an Academy Award.

2016 Ibtihaj Muhammad is first female Muslim American athlete to earn a medal (bronze) at the Olympics, in the team sabre event.

2016 The Anti-Defamation League joins CAIR to protest President Donald Trump's Muslim ban.

2017 Mahershala Ali is first Muslim to win Oscar (best supporting actor, for *Moonlight*).

LATINO AMERICANS

1919 Adolfo "Dolf" Luque is first Hispanic World Series player (relief pitcher for the Cincinnati Reds).

1947 In *Mendez v. Westminster*, Sylvia Mendez sues after being turned away from a "whites only" public school in California. The case paves the way for *Brown v. Board of Education*, playing a key role in making school segregation illegal.

1952 Desi Arnaz, in *I Love Lucy*, is first Latin star of a TV show.

1959 Severo Ochoa wins the Nobel Prize in Physiology/Medicine for the synthesis of ribonucleic acid (RNA).

1961 Rita Moreno wins Oscar for best supporting actress in *West Side Story*.

1961 Dolores Huerta and Cesar Chavez co-found National Farm Workers Association.

1981 Roberto Goizueta becomes first Latino *Fortune* 500 CEO (Coca-Cola).

1986 President Ronald Reagan signs the Immigration Reform and Control Act. Officials estimate that some 4 million illegal immigrants will apply for legal status, and about 2 million will be eligible.

1990–3 Antonia Coello Novello is first woman ever and first Hispanic to become U.S. Surgeon General.

1991 Ellen Ochoa is first female Hispanic astronaut.

1992 *The New York Times* reports that for the first time, salsa outsold ketchup in the U.S. in 1991.

1998 Carlos Santana is first Hispanic American to be inducted into the Rock and Roll Hall of Fame.

2009 Sonia Sotomayor is sworn in as first Hispanic Supreme Court Justice.

2017 Hispanics are the fastest-growing ethnic group in the U.S.

AMERICAN WOMEN

1850 Harriet Tubman leads slaves to freedom while becoming the first female spy in America.

1872 Victoria Woodhull is first woman to run for president.

1916 Margaret Sanger opens the first birth control clinic in the U.S. Nine days later, she is arrested.

1918 Sanger wins suit in New York to allow doctors to advise patients about birth control.

1920 19th Amendment: Women get the vote after 52 years of continual campaigning.

1923 Alice Paul proposes Equal Rights Amendment. It's introduced in Congress every year thereafter but still has not passed.

1928 Amelia Earhart is first female aviator to fly solo across the Atlantic.

1947 U.S. Supreme Court says women are allowed to serve on juries.

1958 Mary Jackson is NASA's first black female engineer (*Hidden Figures*).

1965 Birth control is made legal nationwide (but only for married couples).

1970-85 Mary Tyler Moore stars in first TV show about an independent, professional, unmarried, successful woman (Mary Richards). The show wins 29 Emmys and inspires the next generation of women to be themselves.

1973 *Roe v. Wade* overturns state laws restricting the right to abortion.

1981 Sandra Day O'Connor is first female Supreme Court Justice

1993 Janet Reno is first female U.S. attorney general.

1997 Madeleine Albright is first female secretary of state.

2016 Hillary Clinton is first woman nominated to be president.

2017 Women's March on D.C. is largest mass protest ever in Washington, D.C., inspiring hundreds of simultaneous marches worldwide.

LGBTQ

1922 Gertrude Stein is first to use the word "gay" in its current meaning.

1952 Christine Jorgensen is first widely known person to undergo sex reassignment surgery.

1969 Stonewall riots in NYC become known as the impetus for the gay rights movement.

1970 First Gay Pride Parade is held in Chicago (and in NYC the next day).

1977 Harvey Milk becomes San Francisco city supervisor; first openly gay man elected to political office in California. In 2009, *Milk* wins two Oscars, for Sean Penn as Harvey Milk and for the movie's screenplay.

1983 Sally Ride is first gay astronaut.

1987 The Names Project Memorial Quilt celebrates the lives of people lost to AIDS. Current weight: 54 tons.

1988 World Health Organization holds first World AIDS Day.

1992 The gay view of politics, religion, and AIDS is the subject of Tony Kushner's Pulitzer Prize-winning play *Angels in America*.

1998 Tammy Baldwin is first openly gay person elected to federal office.

2000 Vermont is first state to legalize civil unions.

2004 Massachusetts is first state to legalize same-sex marriage.

2009 President Barack Obama signs Matthew Shepard and James Byrd Jr. Hate Crimes Prevention Act with the support of ADL.

2011 "Don't Ask, Don't Tell" ban on gays and lesbians serving in the military is repealed.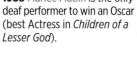

2012 Barack Obama is first sitting president to publicly support gay marriage.

2014 Tim Cook comes out as first openly gay CEO of world's most valuable company, Apple.

2015 Same-sex marriage is legalized in all 50 states.

2016 Eric Fanning is first gay secretary of the army.

2016 For the second year in a row, Jeffrey Tambor wins the leading actor Emmy for his role as a trans character in the comedy *Transparent*.

DISABLED AMERICANS

1904 Hellen Keller graduates from Radcliffe, the first deaf and blind person to earn a B.A.

1933 Franklin D. Roosevelt is first disabled president.

1963 President John F. Kennedy signs the Mental Retardation Facilities and Community Mental Health Centers Construction Act, setting aside federal funds for state development of disability assistance.

1968 The Architectural Barriers Act mandates that federally funded buildings be accessible to people with disabilities.

1968 The first International Special Olympics are held in Chicago. The event was founded by Eunice Kennedy Shriver.

1979 Geri Jewell, who has cerebral palsy, is first disabled person cast as a semi-regular in a TV series, *The Facts of Life*.

1988 Marlee Matlin is the only deaf performer to win an Oscar (best Actress in *Children of a Lesser God*).

1990 Americans With Disabilities Act is the nation's first comprehensive civil rights law addressing the needs of people with disabilities, prohibiting discrimination in employment, public services, public accommodations, and telecommunications.

1994 A deaf person, Heather Whitestone, is crowned Miss America.

2006 Due to the efforts of 20 young people in West Virginia, the first bill passes mandating K–12 students in the public school system there be taught the history of disability rights.

2013 Tammy Duckworth is elected to the House of Representatives. A former U.S. Army helicopter pilot, she lost both legs and damaged her right arm in combat.

GHOST RIDGE, SOUTH DAKOTA, 2005. During her 16-year battle with the U.S. government to obtain restitution for centuries of broken treaties, Elouise Cobell often visited Ghost Ridge for inspiration. There, during the "Starvation Winter" of 1883-1884, more than 500 Native Americans died as a result of government corruption and mismanagement. Cobell said it was her deceased ancestors who gave her the courage to keep going. "Fighting for them, fighting the same government that tried to get rid of this entire race of people" she said. 📷 KAREN KUEHN

NATIVE AMERICANS

AMONG FELLOW MEMBERS of the Blackfeet nation, she was known as Yellow Bird Woman, the great-granddaughter of a storied tribal chief. But Elouise Cobell was best known for waging a 15-year legal battle that forced the federal government to pay Native Americans $3.4 billion in compensation for more than a century of mismanaging Indian trust funds.

Cobell had graduated from business school and was working as the treasurer of the Blackfeet Nation when she began to research stories she had heard as a child about the government cheating her people. These stories, she discovered, went back to 1887, when the government parceled out tribal land to individual Indians but retained the authority to lease those lands for grazing, mining, and drilling. In exchange, the government had pledged to pay the Indian landowners from the revenues that the leases brought in.

But digging through old government records, Cobell uncovered a history of theft, diversion of funds to other accounts, and shoddy bookkeeping that left the Indians shortchanged by tens of billions of dollars. She filed a class-action suit against the government in 1996, demanding restitution.

After 7 trials and 10 appeals, a federal judge ruled in Cobell's favor in 2009, handing down the largest-ever class-action settlement against the United States. Shunning the limelight, Cobell returned to cattle ranching on her Montana reservation, where she died of cancer in 2011. In one of his last official acts, President Barack Obama recognized Cobell's work on behalf of Native Americans by posthumously awarding her the Presidential Medal of Freedom, the country's highest civilian honor. ∎

THE INDIAN WARS ARE NOT OVER
BY AARON HUEY

MANY OF YOU MAY HAVE HEARD of the Lakota, or at least the larger group of tribes called the Sioux. The Lakota are among the many tribes that were moved off their land to prisoner-of-war camps now called "reservations." The Pine Ridge Reservation is located about 75 miles southeast of the Black Hills in South Dakota. It is sometimes referred to as Prisoner of War Camp No. 344, and it is where the Lakota now live. If you have ever heard of the American Indian Movement (AIM), or of Russell Means, or Leonard Peltier, or of the standoff at Oglala, then you know that Pine Ridge has been ground zero for Native issues in the United States.

I'm a *National Geographic* photographer, and writing about my relationship with the Lakota is a very difficult one for me, because I'm white, and that is a huge barrier on a Native reservation. Despite my skin color, I've become very close with the Lakota, and they've welcomed me like family. They've called me "brother" and "uncle" and invited me to enter their lives again and again for the past decade. But on Pine Ridge, I will always be what is called *wasi'chu*, and *wasi'chu* is a Lakota word that means "non-Indian."

A less kind version of this word means "the one who takes the best meat for

TURTLE ISLAND, NORTH DAKOTA, NOVEMBER 2, 2016. When over 10,000 peaceful Native Americans, environmental "Water Protectors," and U.S. veterans gathered to object to construction of the Dakota Access Pipeline, they encountered a heavily militarized police response that included pepper spray (right), tear gas, rubber bullets, water cannons, concussion grenades, and attack dogs. Law enforcement agencies in surrounding states provided reinforcements, and a private security firm hired by the pipeline's proposed builder worked intimately and illegally with local police, adding muscle and surveillance data on the protesters, many of whom were then tied up in court on fabricated charges. Despite repeated abuses of the protesters' civil rights, the attacks went largely unseen in mainstream media. Shortly after his inauguration in January 2017, President Trump put the plan on a fast track, and by June 2017, the $3.5 billion pipeline had begun pushing oil southward to a distribution point in Illinois. ⎙ RYAN VIZZIONS

himself." It means greedy. And if we look at the lives that so many white, privileged people in this country live, we must admit that we have indeed taken the best part of the meat. My photographs capture the lives of a people who lost so that we could gain. As you look at any of my images, and as I share stories of the people that I've come to love and respect, remember that these are not just images and stories of the Lakota; they are symbolic of the struggle of all indigenous people around the world.

The following is a timeline of treaties made, treaties broken, and massacres disguised as battles. I'll begin in 1824. What is known as the Bureau of Indian Affairs (BIA) was created within the War Department, setting an early tone of aggression in our dealings with the Native Americans.

1851: The first treaty of Fort Laramie is concluded, clearly marking the boundaries of the Lakota Nation. According to the treaty, those lands constitute a sovereign nation. If the boundaries of this treaty had held—and there are legal grounds to say that they should have—the United States would look very different today. Ten years later, the Homestead Act, signed by President Abraham Lincoln, unleashes a flood of white settlers into native lands.

1862: An uprising of Santee Sioux in Minnesota ends with the hanging of 38 Sioux men, the largest mass execution in U.S. history. The execution is ordered by Lincoln, only two days after he issued the Emancipation Proclamation.

1866: The beginning of the transcontinental railroad—a new era. Our government appropriates land for trails and trains to cut through the heart of the Lakota Nation. The treaties, theoretically negotiated in good faith between our government and theirs, are thrown out the window. In response, three tribes led by the Lakota chief Red Cloud attack and defeat the U.S. Army many times. I

WOUNDED KNEE, SOUTH DAKOTA, JANUARY 1891. Historians regard the massacre at Wounded Knee Creek as one of the most shameful incidents in our national story. On December 28, 1890, U.S. troops of the Seventh Cavalry, General George Custer's old regiment, came upon a Native American party of 120 men and 230 women and children. According to contemporaneous accounts, some of these soldiers were bitter from their bloody defeat at the hands of the Sioux 14 years before, at the battle of Little Bighorn. The U.S. commander surrounded the Sioux, with 500 troops and aimed four rapid-fire Hotchkiss machine guns at them from a nearby hillside. Forced by soldiers to stand in a circle, the Sioux were ordered to surrender their weapons. They passively acquiesced, but one young warrior, Black Coyote, who was deaf, held onto his gun, and it went off during a struggle, hitting one of the officers. What happened next was not a battle, but a massacre. When the shooting stopped, as many as 300 people had been killed, half of them women and children. Twenty-five troopers also died, most of them killed in their own cross fire. Because of a blizzard, the bodies lay frozen on the ground for days and were then dumped into a mass grave (left). Although newspapers at the time characterized the carnage at Wounded Knee as an indiscriminate slaughter, the army recast the episode as a legitimate battle, and Congress awarded 20 soldiers the Medal of Honor for their "gallantry."

NORTHEAST OKLAHOMA, 1917. An elaborate plot for marrying and then murdering female members of the Osage Indian tribe led to the birth of the FBI. Mollie (above, posing with her husband, Ernest Burkhart) and her three sisters lived on a barren patch of land in northeastern Oklahoma, along with other members of her tribe. When oil was discovered under their land in the 1920s, Mollie and other tribe members became some of richest people per capita in the world, living in mansions, being driven in chauffeured cars, and sending their children to study abroad. That's when Burkhart and several other white men came courting. Posing as a suitor, Burkhart persuaded Mollie

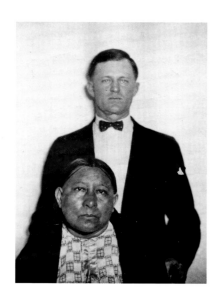

to marry him, while his accomplices courted and married Mollie's sisters and female cousins. Then, one by one, the Osage women began to die under suspicious circumstances. One was killed in an explosion; another was poisoned; a third was shot. The three sisters (above, right) pose with Mollie, second from right. In every case, the surviving husbands siphoned off their wives' wealth. Moreover, anyone attempting to investigate the deaths was also murdered. By 1924, the body count had reached two dozen. Finally, an obscure branch of the U.S. Justice Department that later became the FBI, arrested ringleaders Burkhart and his uncle, and the two received lengthy jail sentences. But according to David Grann, author of the best-selling book *Killers of the Flower Moon: The Osage Murders and the Birth of the FBI*, the other murderous husbands got away scot-free.

want to repeat that part. The Lakota defeats the U.S. Army.

1868: The second Fort Laramie Treaty clearly guarantees the sovereignty of the Great Sioux Nation and the Lakotas' ownership of the sacred Black Hills. The government also promises land and hunting rights in the surrounding states. We promise that the Powder River country will henceforth be closed to all whites. The treaty appears to be a complete victory for Red Cloud and the Sioux. Indeed, this is the only war in U.S. history in which our government negotiates a peace by conceding everything demanded by the enemy.

1869: The transcontinental railroad is completed. It begins to carry, among other things, a large number of hunters, who begin the wholesale killing of bison, eliminating a source of food, clothing, and shelter for the Sioux.

1871: The Indian Appropriation Act transforms all Indians into wards of the federal government. In addition, the military issues orders forbidding Western Indians from leaving reservations. All Western Indians at that point have effectively become prisoners of war. Also in 1871, we end the time of treaty-making. The problem with treaties is that they allow tribes to exist as sovereign nations. Those who run our government clearly have plans and realize that acknowledging the sovereignty of Native Americans is a problem—and so they change the rules yet again.

1874: General George Custer announces the discovery of gold in Lakota territory, specifically the Black Hills. The news of gold brings a massive influx of white settlers into the Lakota Nation. Custer recommends that Congress find a way to end the treaties with the Lakota as soon as possible.

1875: The Lakota War begins with the violation of the Treaty of Fort Laramie.

1876: On June 26, on the way to attack a Lakota village, Custer's Seventh Cavalry is crushed at the Battle of Little Bighorn.

1877: The great Lakota warrior and chief named Crazy Horse surrenders at Fort Robinson. He is later killed while in custody. This is also the year the government finds a way to get around the Fort Laramie treaties. A new agreement is presented to Sioux chiefs and their leading men under a campaign known as "Sell or Starve" (in which they are ordered to sign the paper, or forfeit all food for their tribe). Only 10 percent of the adult male population signs. The Treaty of Fort Laramie specifies that at least three-quarters of the tribe must sign if the land is to be given away. That clause is ignored.

1887: The Dawes Act. Communal ownership of reservation lands ends. Reservations are divided into 160-acre sections and distributed to individual Indians, with the surplus disposed of. Tribes lose millions of acres. The American dream of individual land ownership turns out to be a very clever way to divide the reservation until nothing is left. The move destroys the reservations, making it easier to further subdivide and to sell land with every passing generation. Most of the surplus land and many of the plots within reservation boundaries are now in the hands of white ranchers. Once again, the fat of the land goes to *wasi'chu*.

1890: A date I believe to be the most important in this tragic story of betrayal. This is the year of the Wounded Knee Massacre. On December 29, U.S. troops surround a Sioux encampment at Wounded Knee Creek and massacre Chief Big Foot and 300 prisoners of war, using a new rapid-fire weapon called a Hotchkiss gun that fires exploding shells. For this so-called "battle," the Seventh Cavalry receives 20 Congressional Medals of Honor for valor. To this day, this is the highest number of Medals of Honor ever awarded for a single battle. In other words, more Medals of Honor are handed out for the indiscriminate slaughter of women and children than for any battle in World War I, World War II, Korea, Vietnam, Iraq, or Afghanistan. The Wounded Knee Massacre is considered the end of the Indian Wars. Whenever I visit the site of the mass grave at Wounded Knee, I see it not just as a grave for the Lakota or for the Sioux, but as a grave for all indigenous peoples.

The holy man Black Elk said, "I did not know then how much was ended. When I look back now from this high hill of my old age, I can still see the butchered women and children lying heaped and scattered all along the crooked gulch, as plain as when I saw them with eyes still young. And I can see that something else died there in the bloody mud and was buried in the blizzard: a people's dream died there, and it was a beautiful dream."

With this event, a new era in Native American history begins. Everything can be measured before Wounded Knee and after. Because it is in this moment, with the fingers on the triggers of the Hotchkiss guns, that the members of the U.S. government openly declare their position on Native rights. They are tired of treaties. They are tired of sacred hills. They are tired of ghost dances. And they

What a powerful difference this high-octane gasoline makes!

ADDING INSULT to the historical injuries suffered by Native Americans, who were dispossessed of their lands and resettled on reservations, Madison Avenue in the 1950s and 1960s often exploited and mocked their culture in advertisements. Native Americans remain the only major ethnic group in the United States and Canada whose stereotypes are still used for sports team names, logos, mascots, and chants. Offensive Native American stereotypes can also still be found in movies, children's toys, textbooks, and works of fiction.

are tired of all the inconveniences of the Sioux. So they bring out their cannons. "You want to be an Indian now?" they say, finger on the trigger.

1900: The U.S. Indian population reaches its low point—less than 250,000, compared to an estimated 8 million in 1492.

FAST-FORWARD. 1980: The longest-running court case in U.S. history, the *United States v. Sioux Nation of Indians*, is ruled on by the U.S. Supreme Court. The court determines that, when the Sioux were resettled onto reservations and 7 million acres of their land were opened up to prospectors and homesteaders, the terms of the second Fort Laramie Treaty were violated. The court states that the Black Hills have been taken illegally and that the initial offering price, plus interest, should be paid to the Sioux Nation. As payment for the Black Hills, the court awards only $106 million to the Sioux Nation. The Sioux refuse the money with the rallying cry, "The Black Hills are not for sale!"

2017: Statistics on the Native population today, more than a century after the massacre at Wounded Knee, reveal the legacy of colonization, forced migration, and treaty violations. Unemployment on the Pine Ridge Indian Reservation fluctuates between 85 and 90percent. The housing office is unable to build new structures, and existing structures are falling apart. Many in the community are homeless, and those with homes are packed into rotting buildings with up to five families: 39percent of homes on Pine Ridge have no electricity, and 50percent of the homes on the reservation are infested with black mold. More than 90percent of the population lives below the federal poverty line. The tuberculosis rate on Pine Ridge is approximately eight times higher than the U.S. national average. The infant mortality rate is the highest in North America, and about three times higher than the U.S. national average. Cervical cancer is five times higher than the U.S. national average. The school dropout rate is up to 70 percent. Teacher turnover is eight times higher than the U.S. national average. Frequently, grandparents are raising their grandchildren because parents, due to alcoholism, domestic violence, and general apathy, cannot raise them. Fifty percent of the population over the age of 40 suffers from diabetes. The life expectancy for men is between 46 and 48 years old—roughly the same as in Afghanistan and Somalia.

The last chapter in any successful genocide is the one in which the oppressors can say, "My God, what are these people doing to themselves? They're killing each other. They're killing themselves, while we watch them die."

This is how we came to own these United States. This is the legacy of "manifest destiny." Prisoners are still born into prisoner-of-war camps long after the guards are gone. These are the bones left after the best meat has been taken. A long time ago, a series of events was set in motion by a people who look like me, by *wasi'chu*, eager to take the land and the water and the gold in the hills. Those events led to a domino effect that has yet to end.

Today, as removed as we, the dominant society, may feel from a massacre in

1890, or a series of broken treaties 150 years ago, I have to ask you the question: How do you feel about the statistics of today? What is the connection between these images of suffering and the history that I just related to you? How much of this history do you need to own? Is any of this your responsibility today? I have been told that there must be something we can do, some call to action. For so long I've been standing on the sidelines, content to be a witness, just taking photographs because the solution seems so far in the past.

The suffering of indigenous peoples is not a simple issue to fix. It's not something everyone can get behind, the way they get behind helping Haiti, or ending AIDS, or fighting a famine. The "fix," as it's called, may be much more difficult for the dominant society than, say, a $50 check or a church trip to paint some graffiti-covered houses, or a suburban family donating a box of clothes they don't even want anymore. So where does that leave us? Shrugging our shoulders in the dark?

Fortunately, Native Americans are no longer waiting for the dominant society to fix things, and they are taking things into their own hands. As reported in the *Seattle Post-Intelligencer: In the Pacific Northwest in 1974, Federal District Judge George Boldt dramatically altered the Puget Sound's salmon industry. Boldt ruled that, under the terms of 1854-56 treaties, certain Indian groups had retained title to 50 percent of the western Washington State salmon resource. Hailed at the time as the most significant ruling on Native American treaty law in the twentieth century, Judge George Boldt's ruling held that the United States' mid-1850s treaties with Washington tribes provided that Indians were always entitled to half the salmon and steelhead harvest in their traditional fishing grounds off reservations. Boldt ruled that Washington state had virtually no authority over tribal fishing; in fact, it was the tribes that ceded to non-Indian settlers the rights to fish—not the other way around.*

For tribes whose members battled, demonstrated, got arrested, and were jailed for over more than two decades, during what would become known as the "fish wars," Boldt's ruling was total victory. It had immediate economic and cultural benefits across reservations, restoring pride to struggling tribes that reinvested in fisheries and used money netted from catches to help build tribal governments and enhance reservation infrastructures. In 1994, U.S. District Court Judge Edward Rafeedie reinforced Boldt, stating, "This treaty is not a grant of rights to the Indians, but a grant of rights from them."

But the battle for justice continues today. The Dakota Access pipeline in North Dakota became the focus of heated protests and brought together representatives from more than 300 Native American tribes in 2016, when the Standing Rock Sioux Tribe fought against construction less than a mile from its reservation. The tribe and its allies (including thousands of U.S. veterans) won a temporary victory in the fall of 2016, when the Army Corps of Engineers announced that it would look for alternative routes for the $3.7 billion pipeline. However, within weeks of taking office, President Donald Trump reversed that decision and signed

LONEMAN, SOUTH DAKOTA, 2012. An Oglala Lakota Indian, Mitchell Crow (right), plays with his dog on a mound of used clothes donated to the Pine Ridge Indian Reservation. The reservation is among the poorest in the country, with 80 percent of its estimated 40,000 residents unemployed, nearly all of whom live below the federal poverty line. The average per-capita annual income in the reservation is $4,000. The Native American population suffers from high rates of diabetes, alcoholism, and suicide. In 2007, life expectancy on the reservation was 48 for males and 52 for females. Since then, those estimates have barely improved.
AARON HUEY

an executive memorandum that a few months later that enabled the oil to begin flowing, posing a threat to more than 13 million people living downstream.

The United States continues, on a daily basis, to violate the terms of its treaties with Native Americans. Once again, from Standing Rock to the next pipeline battles in Minnesota and South Dakota, the U.S. government has gone back on its promises.

And so the Indian wars continue. ∎

Aaron Huey is an award-winning *National Geographic* photojournalist and documentary photographer who is most widely known for his walk across the United States in 2002 and his long-term work on the Pine Ridge Indian Reservation. 🐦 *@AaronHuey*

Essay courtesy of TED. Aaron Huey, November 2010. Watch the complete TED Talk on TED.com

seen in a Carlisle class above. But working from a "Kill the Indian: Save the Man" philosophy, these schools left an entire generation traumatized in a cultural no-man's land where they were no longer Native American nor white.

📷 CHARLES CARPENTER, LEFT;
FRANCIS BENJAMIN JOHNSTON, ABOVE

MOUNT RUSHMORE, SOUTH DAKOTA, 1975. Fugitive Native American activist Dennis Banks declares his innocence during a brief appearance at the Mount Rushmore National Memorial (right). At the time, Banks, a Chippewa, and other leaders of the American Indian Movement, or AIM, were being sought by law enforcement in connection with the deaths of two FBI agents during a shootout with members of the group at the nearby Pine Ridge Indian Reservation. Banks was not charged, and two other AIM members were acquitted. But in 1977, AIM activist Leonard Peltier was convicted of the two murders and sentenced to two consecutive life prison terms after a trial that Amnesty International declared unfair. Peltier remains in prison.

📷 RICK SMOLAN

CARLISLE, PENNSYLVANIA, c. 1880. During the Progressive Era, a movement arose to force American Indian children to assimilate. From 1879 to 1918, over 10 thousand Indian children were brought to the Carlisle Indian Industrial School, one of 26 Bureau of Indian Affairs boarding schools, where the pupils were stripped of their tribal identity, forced to adopt Christianity, speak only English, and wear European-style clothes (above). The notion was that this would better prepare them for life outside the reservation, as can be

PINEHILL, NEW MEXICO, DECEMBER 3, 2015. In the 1970s, Ramah Navajo leaders established their own community, called Pinehill, as a satellite of the Navajo Nation reservation and secured a grant from Congress to build an elementary school and a health clinic. In a rare legal victory in 1979, the Ramah Navajo persuaded the U.S. government to return a large swath of ancestral lands, along with all underlying mineral rights. Today, Pine Hill has its own police department, complete with role models like Police Office Deirryck Clichee (above), who dropped by a classroom of young Navajo Head Start students during a regular visit to the Pine Hill Elementary School.
📷 ADRON GARDNER

SINCE 2012, thanks to the tireless work of Elouise Cobell and her descendants, more than 1,700 students have received a Cobell scholarship, including Rene Begay (right), a Navajo who grew up on the Chinle Reservation in Arizona, and who is a modern Indian healer. Unlike traditional medicine men, whose holistic approach to health does not account for the modern science of genetics, Begay has been studying the relationship between DNA and heart health while earning a master's degree in genetics at the University of Colorado. She is now in medical school, specializing in cardiology and genetics, and plans to return to her reservation, where heart disease is endemic, to help her people bridge the divide between traditional healing and science-based medicine.
📷 JAY DICKMAN

FIGHTING THE GOOD FIGHT

KEITH HARPER

Keith Harper, an attorney and diplomat, is the first Native American ever to attain the rank of U.S. ambassador. He is best known as the class counsel for thousands of Native American plaintiffs in *Cobell v. Salazar*, a massive class-action suit against the federal government for its mishandling of Indian trust funds over more than a century. The Obama administration's payment of $3.4 billion to the Indian plaintiffs was the largest class-action award in U.S. history.

JOHN LEWIS was the youngest of the major civil rights leaders. Chairman of the Student Nonviolent Coordinating Committee at just 23, he took part in the Selma marches in 1965 and was severely beaten when police attacked participants at the Edmund Pettus bridge just outside Selma. Over the next decade, Lewis led efforts that registered nearly 4 million black voters across the South, helping transform the nation's political climate. In 1977, President Jimmy Carter placed Lewis in charge of the federal agency that oversees all its volunteer programs, including the Peace Corps and several domestic programs. With the 1980 election of Ronald Reagan, Lewis settled in Atlanta, and in 1981 won election to the Atlanta City Council, where he became an outspoken advocate of government ethics and neighborhood preservation. In 1986, he won a seat in Congress representing Georgia's traditionally African American Fifth District. He has represented the district ever since, making him one of the House's longest-serving members. To honor Lewis' lifetime service to the fight for civil rights, President Barack Obama awarded him the Presidential Medal of Freedom, the nation's highest civilian honor, in 2011. Here he poses with a framed picture of his arrest at the Edmund Pettus Bridge.

DAVID DEAL

AFRICAN AMERICANS

AMERICA'S GRAND DEMOCRATIC EXPERIMENT was paradoxically built upon the economic engine of slavery. Many of the very same Founding Fathers who trumpeted man's God-given right to freedom and equality regarded black people not as human beings but as a commodity, to be bought, sold, and utilized in the "pursuit of happiness," i.e., profit. Ten of the nation's first 16 presidents were slave owners. By 1860, some 4 million enslaved blacks produced more than 60 percent of America's wealth.

Though the Civil War liberated the slaves, for many, their freedom was very short-lived. In the South, white supremacist Jim Crow laws mandated a separate and inferior status for blacks in all walks of life, creating a permanent underclass. In 1896, the U.S. Supreme Court upheld the constitutionality of racial segregation, making it the law of the land for nearly 60 years.

Starting around 1910, millions of Southern blacks began moving to northern cities. But even in the North, racist laws herded African Americans into ghettos, exploited their vulnerabilities, and denied them well-paid jobs, fair mortgages, and decent schools.

The lot of African Americans began to improve only in the 1950s and '60s, with the rise of the civil rights movement. The Supreme Court struck down segregation, and Congress passed historic legislation that opened voting, housing, schools, and workplaces to African Americans. In the ensuing decades, increasing numbers of African American women and men have graduated from universities, and African Americans have risen to positions of leadership in the military, corporate boardrooms, city government, and Congress. In 2008, the country marked a major milestone, electing Barack Obama as its first African American president.

But gaping disparities in income and opportunity remain. Many African American children still grow up poor, in blighted, crime-ridden neighborhoods. Many will spend extended time in prison for minor crimes. And some states continue to use gerrymandering to marginalize the African American vote, and other rules to make it harder for minorities to get to the polls.

So even today, there are echoes of America's original sin, of the time when human bondage was tolerated in a self-proclaimed "land of liberty." ∎

THE AMERICAN INJUSTICE SYSTEM
BY BRYAN STEVENSON

I **GREW UP IN A TRADITIONAL** African American home that was dominated by a matriarch, and that matriarch was my grandmother. She was tough, she was strong, she was powerful. She was the beginning of a lot of arguments in our family, and she was the end of every argument. She was the daughter of parents born into slavery in Virginia in the 1840s. She was born in the 1880s, and the experience of slavery very much shaped the way she saw the world.

My grandmother was tough, but she was also loving. When I was a little boy, she'd come up to me and she'd give me these hugs. And she'd squeeze me so tight I could barely breathe, and then she'd let me go. And an hour or two later, if I saw her, she'd come over to me and she'd say, "Bryan, do you still feel me hugging you?" And if I said, "No," she'd assault me again, and if I said, "Yes," she'd leave me alone. She had this quality that you just always wanted to be near her. The only challenge was that she had 10 children. My mom was the youngest of her 10 kids. And sometimes, when I would go and spend time with her, it would be difficult to get her time and attention, with all my cousins bouncing around her house.

When I was about 8 or 9 years old, I remember waking up one morning, going into the living room, and all of my cousins were running around. My grandmother

DURHAM, NORTH CAROLINA, 2012. Under house arrest for failing to pay back his victims for the articles he stole from them, Rashard Johnson is afraid to set off his monitoring anklet, so he keeps one foot in the house while he smokes a cigarette. At 16, Johnson ran away from home and was arrested and charged as an adult for breaking into houses and possessing stolen goods. North Carolina and New York are the only states that still prosecute 16-year-olds as adults in felony cases and by 18, he had been convicted of numerous nonviolent felonies. Johnson sought to turn his life around, but his felony convictions followed him, making it difficult for him to land a job. After he had served nine months in prison, a judge waived his restitution payment and, thanks to a local law that bans employers from asking if applicants have a criminal record, Johnson has found work with a street ministry to help other at-risk young African American men. 📷 JUSTIN COOK

was sitting across the room staring at me. And at first I thought we were playing a game. I would look at her and I'd smile, but she was very serious. After about 15 or 20 minutes of this, she got up and she came across the room and she took me by the hand and she said, "Come on, Bryan, you and I are going to have a talk." I remember this just like it happened yesterday. I never will forget it.

She took me out back, and she said, "Bryan, I'm going to tell you something, but you don't tell anybody what I tell you." I said, "OK, Mama." She said, "Now you make sure you don't do that." I said, "Sure." Then she sat me down and she looked at me and she said, "I want you to know I've been watching you." She said, "I think you're special." She said, "I think you can do anything you want to do." I will never forget it.

And then she said, "I just need you to promise me three things, Bryan." I said, "OK, Mama." She said, "The first thing I want you to promise me is that you'll always love your mom. That's my baby girl, and you have to promise me now you'll always take care of her." Well, I adored my mom, so I said, "Yes, Mama. I'll do that." Then she said, "The second thing I want you to promise me is that you'll always do the right thing, even when the right thing is the hard thing." And I thought about it and I said, "Yes, Mama. I'll do that." Then finally she said, "The third thing I want you to promise me is that you'll never drink alcohol." Well, I was 9 years old, so I said, "Yes, Mama. I'll do that."

I grew up in the country in the rural South, and I have a brother a year older than me and a sister a year younger. When I was about 14 or 15, one day my

THE IMAGE OF AFRICAN AMERICANS in popular culture has changed dramatically over the past century. During the days of Jim Crow, African Americans were commonly dehumanized and portrayed as comic (left), childlike (middle), or obsequious (above). Such images served to perpetuate the belief in African American inferiority and the "wisdom" of segregation.

A MAJOR SHIFT in the portrayal of African Americans occurred after the civil rights movement in the 1960s, as Hollywood made films that challenged and confronted long-held racist attitudes. The 1967 film *Guess Who's Coming to Dinner* (top, right) was the first to broach the controversial subject of interracial marriage. In 2016, the film *Loving* (right) brought to life the story of Richard and Mildred Loving, an interracial couple who, convicted of violating Virginia's anti-miscegenation laws, appealed their case to the U.S. Supreme Court. There, in a unanimous decision, the court nullified all such laws as "directly subversive of the principle of equality." In 2017, a Pew Research study found that 20 percent of all U.S. marriages were between people of different races or ethnicities.

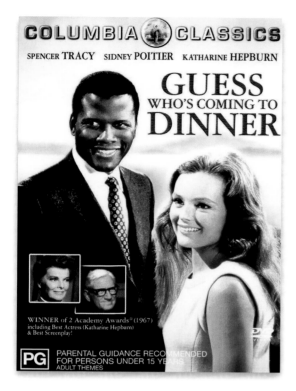

brother came home and he had this six-pack of beer—I don't know where he got it—and he grabbed me and my sister and we went out in the woods. And we were kind of just out there doing the crazy stuff we did. And he had a sip of this beer and he gave some to my sister and she had some, and they offered it to me. I said, "No, no, no. That's OK. You all go ahead. I'm not going to have any beer." My brother said, "Come on. We're doing this today; you always do what we do. I had some, your sister had some. Have some beer." I said, "No, I don't feel right about that. Y'all go ahead. Y'all go ahead."

And then my brother started staring at me. He said, "What's wrong with you? Have some beer." Then he looked at me real hard, and he said, "Oh, I hope you're not still hung up on that conversation Mama had with you." I said, "Well, what are you talking about?" He said, "Oh, Mama tells all the grandkids that they're special." I was devastated.

I'm going to admit something to you. I'm going to tell you something I probably shouldn't. I know this might be read broadly, but I'm 52 years old, and I'm going to admit to you that I've never had a drop of alcohol. I don't say that because I think that's virtuous; I say that because there is power in identity.

When we create the right kind of identity, we can say things to the world around us that they don't actually believe makes sense. We can get them to do things that they don't think they can do. When I thought about my grandmother, of course she would think all her grandkids were special. My grandfather was in prison during Prohibition. My uncles died of alcohol-related diseases. These were the things she thought we needed to commit to not do.

I'm writing today to say something about our criminal justice system. This country is very different today than it was 45 years ago. In 1972, there were 300,000 people in jails and prisons. Today, there are 2.3 million. The United States now has the highest rate of incarceration in the world. We have 7 million people on probation and parole. And mass incarceration, in my judgment, has fundamentally changed our world. In poor communities, in communities of color, there is this despair, there is this hopelessness, that is being shaped by these outcomes. One out of 3 black men between the ages of 18 and 30 is in jail, in prison, on probation, or parole. In urban communities across this country— Los Angeles, Philadelphia, Baltimore, Washington, D.C.—50 to 60 percent of all young men of color are in jail or prison or on probation or parole.

Our system isn't just being shaped in these ways that seem to be distorting around race, they're also distorted by poverty. We have a system of justice in this country that treats you much better if you're rich and guilty than if you're poor and innocent. Wealth, not culpability, shapes outcomes. And yet, we seem to be very comfortable. The politics of fear and anger have made us believe that these are problems that are not our problems. We've been disconnected.

Some of the data coming from our work tell us that in my state of Alabama, like a number of states, if you have a criminal conviction you are permanently

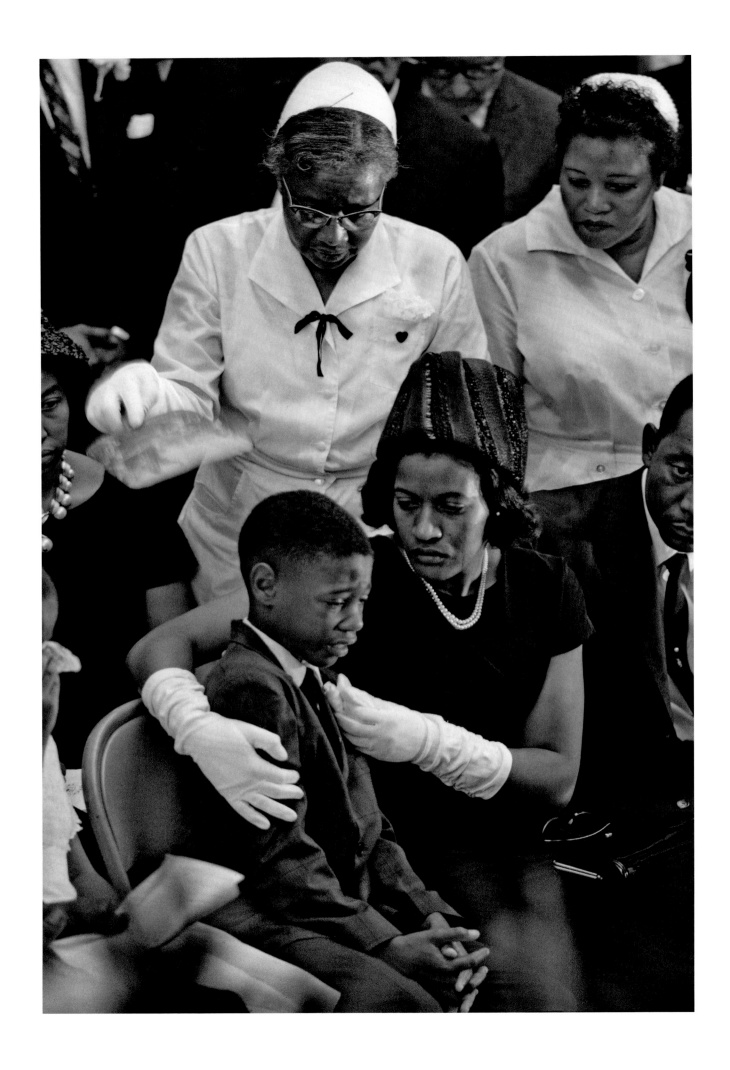

disenfranchised for the rest of your life. Right now in Alabama, 34 percent of the black male population has permanently lost the right to vote. We're actually projecting in another 10 years, the level of disenfranchisement will be as high as it's been since prior to the passage of the Voting Rights Act. Yet in the face of these facts, there is this stunning silence.

The irony, of course, is that there's been a huge decline in crime in the United States over the last three decades. Part of the narrative of that decline is that it's the result of increased incarceration rates.

But one data point that people often forget or ignore in this argument is that in fact, the rate of violent crime has remained relatively stable. The great increase in mass incarceration in this country wasn't really in the violent crime categories. It was the misguided war on drugs. That's where the dramatic increases have come from in our prison population.

We got carried away with the rhetoric of punishment. As a result, we have "three strikes" laws that put people in prison forever for just stealing a bicycle, for low-level property crimes, for using drugs, not crimes against other people. I believe we need to do more to help people who are victimized by crime, not do less. I think our current punishment philosophy does nothing, for no one. And I think that's the orientation that we have to change.

I represent children. A lot of my clients are very young. The United States is the only country in the world where we sentence 13-year-old children to die in prison. We have life imprisonment without parole for kids in this country. Think about it: the only country in the world that locks up children for life.

I sometimes represent people on death row, and we've been taught that the real question is: Do people deserve to die for the crimes they've committed? That's a very sensible question. But there's another way of thinking which is not: Do people deserve to die for the crimes they commit, but: Do we deserve to kill?

The death penalty in America is defined by error. For every nine people who have been executed, we've actually identified one innocent person who's been exonerated and released from death row. It's an astonishing error rate—1 out of 9 people, innocent and yet put to death. Think about that for a moment. In aviation, we would never let people fly on airplanes if for every nine planes that took off one would crash. But somehow we are able to insulate ourselves from this problem if we don't perceive it as our problem. It's not our burden. It's not our struggle.

When I teach my students about African American history, I tell them about slavery. I tell them about terrorism, the era that began at the end of Reconstruction that went on through World War II. For African Americans in this country, that was an era defined by terror. In many communities, black people had to worry about being lynched. They had to worry about being bombed. It was the threat of terror that shaped their lives. And these older people come up to me now, and they say, "Mr. Stevenson, you give talks, you make speeches. You tell people to stop saying we're dealing with terrorism for the first time in our nation's history, after 9/11." They tell me to say, "No, tell them that we grew up with that." That era of terrorism, of course, was followed by segregation and decades of racial subordination and apartheid.

Today in America, we still have a dynamic where we really don't like to talk about our problems. We don't like to talk about our history. And because of that, we really haven't understood what it's meant to do the things we've done historically. We're constantly running into each other. We're constantly creating tensions and conflicts. We have a hard time talking about race, and I believe it's because we are unwilling to commit ourselves to a process of truth and reconciliation. In South Africa, people understood that they couldn't overcome apartheid without a commitment to truth and reconciliation. In Rwanda, even after the genocide, they made a commitment, but in this country, we haven't done that.

Recently, when I was giving a lecture in Germany about the death penalty, one of the scholars stood up after the presentation and said, "It's deeply troubling to hear what you're talking about. We don't have the death penalty in Germany, and we will never have the death penalty in Germany." The room got very quiet, and a woman said, "There's no way, with our history, that we could ever engage in the systematic killing of human beings. It would be unconscionable for us to, in an intentional and deliberate way, to set about executing people."

Yet, in this country, in the United States, in the states of the Old South, where you're 11 times more likely to get the death penalty if the victim is white than if the victim is black, 22 times more likely to get the death penalty if the defendant is black and the victim is white. In the very states where the bodies of people who were lynched are buried in the ground, here we still execute people.

This makes me believe that America's identity is at risk right now. I know we love innovation. We love technology. We love creativity. We love entertainment. But ultimately, those wonders are overshadowed by suffering, abuse, degradation, marginalization.

I believe it's necessary to integrate these two sides of our culture. Ultimately, we need to be more hopeful, more committed, more dedicated to spending time thinking and talking about the poor, the disadvantaged, and thinking about them in a way that is integrated into our own lives.

To be fully human, we must pay full attention not only to the bright and dazzly things, but also to the dark and difficult things, to suffering, to poverty, to exclusion, to unfairness, to injustice.

I had the great privilege, when I was a young lawyer, of meeting Rosa Parks. She used to come back to Montgomery every now and then, to get together with two of her dearest friends, these older women, Johnnie Carr, who was the organizer of the Montgomery bus boycott, an amazing African American woman, and Virginia Foster Durr, a white woman, whose husband, Clifford Durr,

TELEVISION BECAME a powerful vehicle for bringing "the other" into the living rooms and bedrooms of millions of Americans. Norman Lear's groundbreaking 1970s sitcom *All in the Family* used humor to expose the racial, homophobic, and misogynist prejudices of its white blue-collar main character, Archie Bunker. At top, Bunker (Carroll O'Connor), receives an unexpected kiss from "Rat Pack" favorite Sammy Davis Jr. (top).

IN 1966, GENE RODDENBERRY created *Star Trek*, a weekly sci-fi series using the otherworldly adventures of the Starship Enterprise to "make statements about sex, religion, Vietnam, politics, and intercontinental missiles." In 1968, the series featured the first interracial kiss on American television, when evil aliens used mind control to force Captain James Kirk (William Shatner) to lock lips with Lieutenant Uhura (Nichelle Nichols). The kiss (above) was portrayed as involuntary because NBC was concerned it might anger viewers in the Deep South.

THE JEFFERSONS (top), a spin-off of Norman Lear's *All in the Family*, premiered in 1975 and was the first U.S. television series to feature a successful African American family as its main characters. Though their middle-class status placed them squarely in a white world, they spoke candidly about race relations, including African Americans' mistrust of white people. The show's confrontational humor opened a wider debate over race in the United States, which contributed to its enduring legacy.

PREMIERING IN 2015, *Empire* (above) became one of the most popular programs on television, with a distinctly African American approach to the news of the day. One episode opened with Cookie, the show's flamboyant female lead, whipping up an angry crowd following the recent police shootings of unarmed black men. "How much longer are they going to treat us like animals? The American correctional system is built on the backs of our brothers, our fathers, our sons. It is a system that must be dismantled piece by piece... Justice for all, not justice for some." Slate's TV critic Willa Paskin noted that "by opening with a scene of protest, *Empire* [was] both reflecting the culture and declaring its place in it."

represented Martin Luther King Jr. These women would get together and just talk.

Every now and then, Ms. Carr would call me, and she'd say, "Bryan, Ms. Parks is coming to town. We're going to get together and talk. Do you want to come over and listen?" And I'd say, "Yes, ma'am, I do." And she'd say, "Well what are you going to do when you get here?" I said, "I'm going to listen." And I'd go over there, and I would just listen. It would be so energizing and so empowering.

One time I was over there listening to these women talk, and after a couple of hours, Ms. Parks turned to me, and she said, "Now Bryan, tell me what the Equal Justice Initiative is. Tell me what you're trying to do." And I began giving her my rap. I said, "Well, we're trying to challenge injustice. We're trying to help people who have been wrongly convicted. We're trying to confront bias and discrimination in the administration of criminal justice. We're trying to end life without parole sentences for children. We're trying to do something about the death penalty. We're trying to reduce the prison population. We're trying to end mass incarceration."

I gave her my whole rap, and when I finished, she looked at me and she said, "Mmm mmm mmm." She said, "That's going to make you tired, tired, tired." And that's when Ms. Carr leaned forward, she put her finger in my face, she said, "That's why you've got to be brave, brave, brave."

I believe that we, all Americans, every one of us, need to be brave. We need to find ways to embrace these challenges, these problems, this suffering. Because ultimately, our own humanity depends on everyone's humanity. I've learned very simple things doing the work that I do. I've come to understand and to believe that each of us is much more than the worst thing we've ever done, and I believe that is true for every person on the planet. I think if somebody tells a lie, they're not just a liar. I think if somebody takes something that doesn't belong to them, they're not just a thief. I think even if you kill someone, you're not just a killer. And I believe there is a basic human dignity that must be respected by law. I also believe that in many parts of this country, and certainly in many parts of this globe, that the opposite of poverty is not wealth. In too many places, the opposite of poverty is justice.

Finally, despite the fact that it is so dramatic and so beautiful and so inspiring and so stimulating, I believe that, ultimately, we will not be judged by our technology, we won't be judged by our design, we won't be judged by our intellect and reason. Ultimately, the character of a society will be judged not by how it treats the rich and the powerful and the privileged, but by how it treats the poor, the condemned, the incarcerated. Because it's in that nexus that we actually begin to understand who we are as a society.

I sometimes get out of balance. I sometimes push too hard. I get tired, as we all do. Sometimes ideas that come to us in the exhausted dead of night get ahead of our own understanding until later.

I'll end with this story. I've been representing kids who have received very harsh sentences. When I go to the jail and I see my client who's 14, and he's somehow been certified to stand trial as an adult, I start thinking: Well, how did that happen? How can a judge turn you into something that you're not? The judge may have certified him as an adult, but I see a kid.

I was up too late one night, and I starting thinking: Well, gosh, if the judge can turn you into something that you're not, the judge must have magic power. Yeah, Bryan, the judge has some magic power. You should ask for some of that. And because I was up too late, I wasn't thinking real straight, I started working on a motion. I had a client who was 14 years old, a young, poor black kid. I started working on this motion, and the head of the motion was: "Motion to try my

FERGUSON UNIT, TEXAS 1967.
Prisoners (above) work the cotton fields near the correctional facility for young offenders that houses them, depicting a practice dating back to the Jim Crow era, when minor offenses such as "vagrancy" and "mischief" were treated as crimes worthy of prison. The state capitalized on the incarceration of hundreds of thousands of able-bodied black men, leasing their services to the highest bidder, thus supplying cheap labor for farming, logging, roadwork, and mining. As W.E.B. Du Bois wrote, "The slave went free; stood a brief moment

in the sun; then moved back again toward slavery." Teju Cole of *The New York Times* sees the quality of a fable in photographer Danny Lyon's image. The picture is from the 1960s, he wrote, "but...it could have been made a hundred years earlier...Within a single frame, we witness forced labor, the plantation economy, cotton's allure, black subjection, government control, and the facelessness of the impoverished." ◉ DANNY LYON

AVA DUVERNAY'S documentary, *13th*, explores the mass incarceration of millions of African Americans for minor and nonviolent offenses, and their exploitation as virtual slaves for some of America's best-known corporations. The 13th Amendment to the Constitution abolished slavery in 1865—"except as punishment for a crime"—but today, blacks are punished more harshly than whites for the exact same offense. Nearly 900,000 of the 2.3 million people in prison are black and an additional 450,000 are Latino. Prisoners earn as little as 74 cents an hour producing products for U.S. companies including McDonalds and Victoria's Secret. In 2014 thousands of prisoners were freed when laws were changed to reduce many non-violent drug-related sentences. The move made Obama the first president in decades to leave office with a total prison population lower than when he was inaugurated. But the Trump administration began almost immediately to roll back such progress.

poor, 14-year-old black male client like a privileged, white 75-year-old corporate executive."

A couple of months went by, and the day came for me to go to the court knowing I had filed this crazy motion. I was feeling really overwhelmed, and I remember thinking to myself, this kid's life is at stake, it's going to be so difficult, so painful. I sat in the car in front of the courthouse in a mental fog, and when I started walking up to the courthouse, there was an older black man who was the janitor in this courthouse. He came over and he asked, "Who are you?" I said, "I'm a lawyer." He said, "You're a lawyer?" I said, "Yes, sir." He came over, hugged me, and whispered in my ear, "I'm so proud of you." That moment, coming completely out of the blue, was energizing. It connected with something deep within me about identity, about the capacity of every person to contribute to a community, to a perspective of hope.

Well, I went into the courtroom, and as soon as I walked inside, the judge saw me coming in. He said, "Mr. Stevenson, did you write this crazy motion?" I said, "Yes, sir. I did." We started arguing, people started coming in because they were just outraged that I had written these crazy things. Police officers were coming in, and assistant prosecutors and clerk workers. Before I knew it, the courtroom was filled with angry people talking about race, about poverty, about inequality.

Suddenly, in the middle of this holler, out of the corner of my eye, I saw that janitor outside pacing back and forth and looking anxiously through the window. Finally, that older black man, with this very worried look on his face, came into the courtroom and sat down behind me, almost at the counsel table. About 10 minutes later, the judge said we would take a break. At that moment, a deputy sheriff, who was clearly offended that the janitor had come into court, ran over to this older black man and said, "Jimmy, what are you doing in this courtroom?" This man stood up, and he first looked at that deputy, then he looked at me, and he said, "I came into this courtroom to tell this young man: Keep your eyes on the prize. Hold on."

I believe that many of us, like Martin Luther King Jr., believe that the moral arc of the universe is long, but it bends toward justice. That we cannot be fully evolved human beings until we care about human rights and basic dignity. That our survival as individuals is tied to the survival of everyone. That our visions of technology and design and entertainment and creativity have to be married with visions of humanity, compassion, and justice. And above everything else, I am simply here to tell you to keep your eyes on the prize, to hold on. ■

Bryan Stevenson is the founder and executive director of the Equal Justice Initiative (EJI) in Montgomery, Alabama. Under his leadership, EJI has won major legal challenges eliminating excessive and unfair sentencing, exonerating innocent death row prisoners, confronting abuse of the incarcerated and the mentally ill, and aiding children prosecuted as adults. He recently won an historic ruling in the U.S. Supreme Court banning mandatory life-without-parole sentences for all children of 17 or younger. He is a graduate of Harvard Law School and has been awarded 26 honorary doctorate degrees. He is the author of the award-winning *New York Times* best-seller *Just Mercy*. 🐦 *@Eji_Org*

Essay courtesy of TED. Bryan Stevenson, March 2012. Watch the complete TED Talk on TED.com

FORT MEADE, MARYLAND, 1917.
As the United States entered World War I, African Americans enthusiastically joined the war effort as a way to demonstrate their patriotism, with the hope that by sacrificing and supporting the war effort, they would be rewarded on their return with greater civil rights. Here (left), new recruits stand in line to receive Army uniforms before basic training and their deployment to France. Of the 4.7 million American troops who served during World War I, roughly 400,000 were African Americans positioned in segregated units. Most black soldiers continued to experience racism from their white counterparts and were relegated to menial tasks in the rear, but New York's 396th Infantry, a combat regiment known as the "Harlem Hellfighters," distinguished itself in battle. Two soldiers from the unit received the Medal of Honor. Many others were recognized with Distinguished Service Medals and 171 received France's highest

military decoration, the Croix de Guerre. French civilians gave the "Hellfighters" a warm welcome and showed few signs of overt racism. "They treated us with respect," one soldier recalled, "not like the white American soldiers." In cruel proof of how little had changed since they went off to fight, the end of the war in 1918 brought anything but peace as many African American soldiers found themselves targeted in white race riots taking place around the country.

LOUISVILLE, KENTUCKY, 1937.
When the Ohio River flooded in the winter of 1937, it left nearly 400 people dead and more than 1 million homeless along an area that stretched across five states. Already burdened by the Great Depression, the government strained to help victims. African Americans, at the bottom of the economic ladder (above), were often the last to receive assistance. Margaret Bourke-White's memorable picture demonstrated the yawning gap between the country's confident self-image and the misery resulting from both the flood and the broader economic cataclysm.
📷 MARGARET BOURKE-WHITE

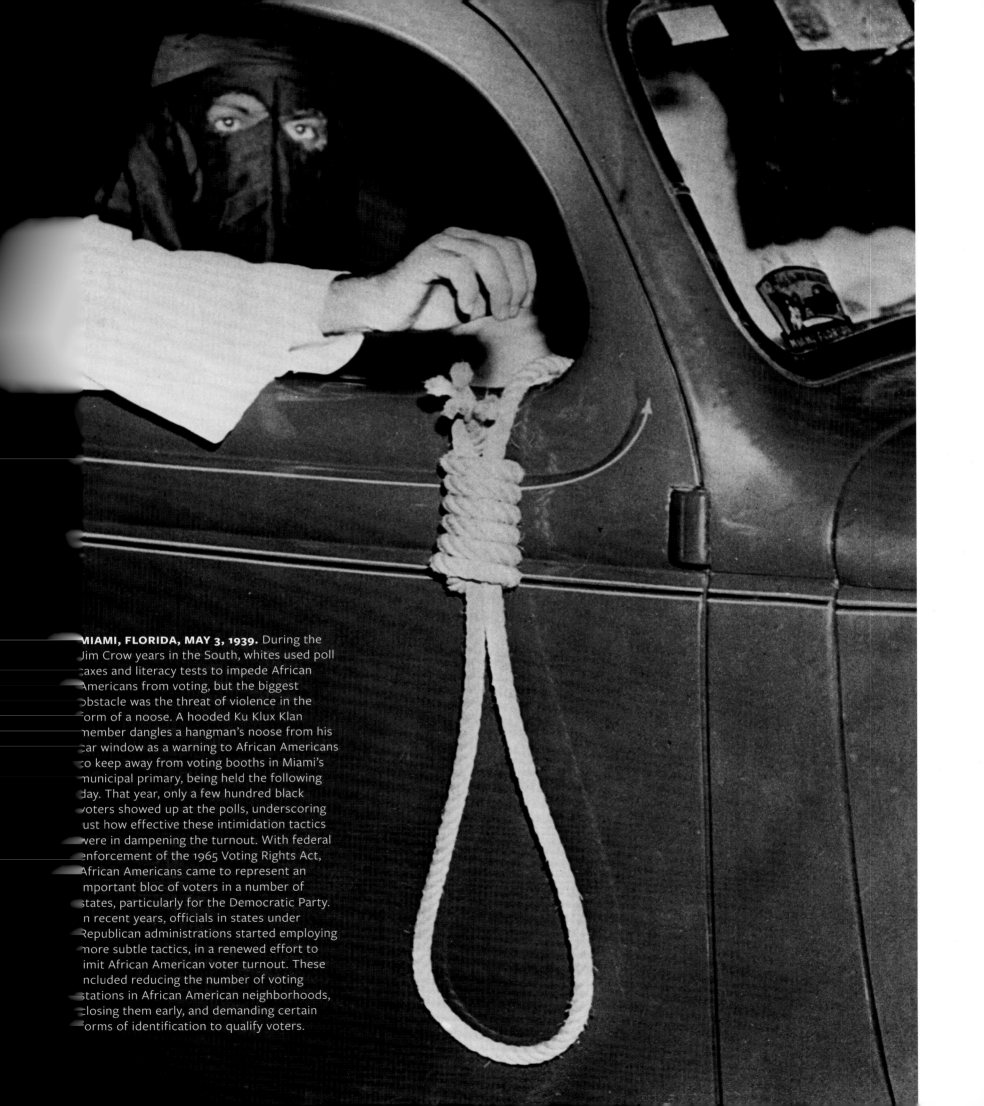

MIAMI, FLORIDA, MAY 3, 1939. During the Jim Crow years in the South, whites used poll taxes and literacy tests to impede African Americans from voting, but the biggest obstacle was the threat of violence in the form of a noose. A hooded Ku Klux Klan member dangles a hangman's noose from his car window as a warning to African Americans to keep away from voting booths in Miami's municipal primary, being held the following day. That year, only a few hundred black voters showed up at the polls, underscoring just how effective these intimidation tactics were in dampening the turnout. With federal enforcement of the 1965 Voting Rights Act, African Americans came to represent an important bloc of voters in a number of states, particularly for the Democratic Party. In recent years, officials in states under Republican administrations started employing more subtle tactics, in a renewed effort to limit African American voter turnout. These included reducing the number of voting stations in African American neighborhoods, closing them early, and demanding certain forms of identification to qualify voters.

WITHOUT SANCTUARY

By JAMES ALLEN

In the United States everything is for sale, even a national shame.

Until I came upon a postcard of a lynching when I was at a flea market, postcards had always seemed trivial to me, the way secondhand, misshapen Rubbermaid products might.

Studying these photos has engendered in me a caution of whites, of the majority, of the young, of religion, of the accepted. Perhaps a certain circumspection concerning these things was already in me, but surely not as actively as after the first sight of a brittle postcard of Leo Frank dead in an oak tree. It wasn't the corpse that bewildered me, as much as the canine-thin faces of the pack, lingering in the woods, circling after the kill.

Hundreds of flea markets later, a trader pulled me aside and in conspiratorial tones, offered me a second card, this one of Laura Nelson (top, right), caught so pitiful and tattered and beyond retrieving—like a child's paper kite snagged on a utility wire. The sight of Laura layered a pall of grief over all my fears.

I believe the photographer was more than simply a spectator at these lynchings. The photographic art played as significant a role in the ritual as torture or the grabbing of these trophy souvenirs—a sort of two-dimensional biblical swine, a receptacle for a collective sinful self. Lust propelled their commercial reproduction and distribution, facilitating the endless replay of anguish.

Even dead, the victims were without sanctuary. ∎

RATHER THAN A STEALTHY ritual held in the dark of night, lynchings were often seen as festive community activities at which attendees posed proudly by the mutilated bodies for postcards later mailed to friends and family. Many saw these ghastly souvenirs not as records of hideous crimes but as the glorification of justice served. Lynch laws at the time allowed for mob killings that circumvented the legal system and constituted a form of terrorism—ritual murders that maintained white supremacy. President Teddy Roosevelt began to denounce lynching in 1903, but only in 1912 did Congress pass legislation banning the mailing of such postcards, making it a federal crime. Shockingly, the first conviction for a lynching didn't happen for another 44 years. More than 4,743 lynchings occurred between 1882 and 1968, according to U.S. newspapers. Yes, you read that correctly: 1968.

STRANGE FRUIT
SUNG BY BILLIE HOLIDAY

Southern trees bear strange fruit
Blood on the leaves and blood at the root
Black bodies swinging in the Southern
  breeze
Strange fruit hanging from the poplar trees

Pastoral scene of the gallant South
The bulging eyes and the twisted mouth
Scent of magnolias, sweet and fresh
Then the sudden smell of burning flesh

Here is fruit for the crows to pluck
For the rain to gather, for the wind to suck
For the sun to rot, for the trees to drop
Here is a strange and bitter crop

MINNEAPOLIS, MINNESOTA, APRIL 28, 1882. Three hours after Frank McManus, an African American, was lynched by a vigilante mob without any trial, his body was still hanging from a lone burr oak tree on the front lawn of Minneapolis Central High School. It drew a crowd of more than a thousand, who cut off pieces of extra rope for souvenirs and posed for pictures with McManus dangling behind them. Spectators who couldn't attend in person could experience the gruesome scene using an 1880s version of virtual reality. The two almost identical photographs (above) are "stereographs," an early form of photography that used a special viewer to make the images appear three-dimensional. As Oliver Wendell Holmes described the experience: "The effect of looking through the stereoscope is a surprise such as no painting ever produced. The mind feels its way into the very depths of the picture. The scraggy branches of a tree in the foreground run out at us as if they would scratch our eyes out." 📷 H.R. FARR

This is the story of how Billie Holiday's "Strange Fruit" became a timeless protest against hatred, bigotry, and oppression. In 1930, Abel Meeropol, a Jewish teacher in New York City, was so haunted by photographs he'd seen of lynchings that he wrote the lyrics to a song, which record producer Ahmet Ertegun later described as "a declaration of war ... the beginning of the civil rights movement." In early 1939, Meeropol persuaded Billie Holiday to add "Strange Fruit" to her act. When she sang it for Milton Gabler, owner of Commodore Records, the song brought tears to his eyes and he immediately offered to record her. But because many people at the time viewed the struggle for racial equality as a left-wing plot, radio stations were reluctant to play the controversial song and Meeropol was accused of being paid by the Communist Party to write it. His response: "I wrote 'Strange Fruit' because I hate lynching, and I hate injustice, and I hate the people who perpetuate it." Jazz composer Marcus Miller, surprised to learn it was "written by a white Jewish guy, says, "'Strange Fruit' took extraordinary courage both for Meeropol to write and for Holiday to sing. The '60s hadn't happened yet. Things like that weren't talked about. They certainly weren't sung about." The song sold over a million copies and in 1999, *Time* magazine named it the "Best Song of the Century." ∎

NEW YORK, 1939. Billie Holiday performs "Strange Fruit" at Café Society, the first integrated nightclub in New York City. To magnify the song's impact, she always made it her closing number and never returned for an encore. 📷 GJON MILI

"Strange Fruit" music and lyrics by Abel Meeropol ©1940 Commodore

MOBILE, ALABAMA, 1956.
In September 1956, a *LIFE* magazine photo essay by celebrated African American photographer Gordon Parks documented the everyday activities and rituals of one African American family living in the rural South under Jim Crow. Though the U.S. Supreme Court in 1896 upheld racial segregation in public places under the doctrine of "separate but equal," the facilities provided to African Americans were rarely equal. One of the essay's most powerful images (left) depicts schoolteacher Joanne Thornton Wilson and her young niece, Shirley Anne Kirksey, in front of the Saenger Theater in Mobile, Alabama. Parks' photographs, seen widely across America, demonstrated that the battle for racial equality was waged not just through epic demonstrations, speeches, and conflagrations, but also through the quiet, but no less effective, actions of private individuals like Wilson. White supremacists in the South were beginning to understand the power of the camera to expose their actions and turn the nation against them. As Parks later recounted, the risk of retaliation for participating in the story published in *LIFE* Magazine was great, both for the photographer and his subjects. But neither Gordon Parks nor Joanne Thornton Wilson would be intimidated.
📷 GORDON PARKS

WILMINGTON, NORTH CAROLINA, 1950. Powerful and haunting imagery such as famed photographer Elliott Erwitt's classic "Segregated Water" (above) shamed the South by depicting the humiliations imposed on African Americans during the civil rights era. If "separating the races" was the goal, then why were the two water fountains so close together? The answer is that physical proximity wasn't the issue, social division was. Segregation was about enforcing a racial hierarchy and ensuring that state and private resources were funneled to whites rather than blacks. As such, it didn't matter if water fountains were right next to each other, as long as whites got to use the better water fountain and blacks were made aware of the fact that theirs was inferior. Segregation of public facilities—including water fountains and restrooms—was officially outlawed by the Civil Rights Act of 1964, signed into law by President Lyndon B. Johnson after a rare cloture vote in the U.S. Senate. (West Virginia Senator Robert F. Byrd, a former Klansman, spoke against the bill on the Senate floor for 14 hours, 13 minutes straight.)
📷 ELLIOTT ERWITT

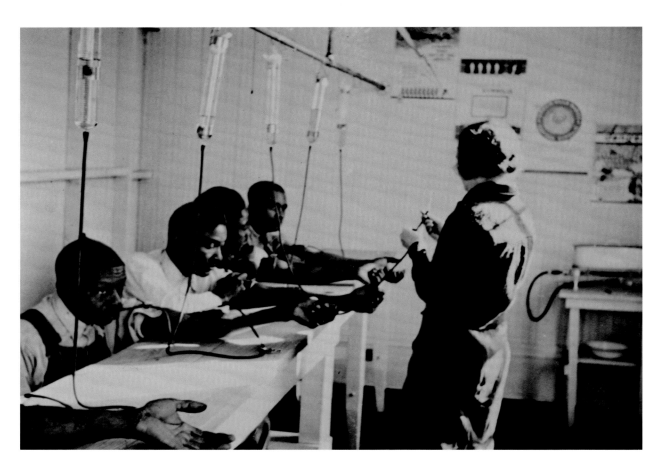

TUSKEGEE, ALABAMA, 1932.
The U.S. government's notorious "Study of Untreated Syphilis in the Negro Male" began in 1932 at Tuskegee University and ran until 1972. Researchers observed nearly 400 poor, ill-educated African American men who were diagnosed with early-stage syphilis but weren't yet showing any symptoms. The researchers hoped to determine, among other things, if syphilis affected African Americans differently from Caucasians. For nearly 40 years, they neither told their subjects they had syphilis nor treated them for it, even after penicillin became the standard cure in 1947. The victims were simply informed that they had "bad blood" and were given placebos along with hot meals and free rides to and from the clinic, inducements to continue their participation. By the time a public outcry ended the study in 1972, only 74 of the original subjects remained alive. The wives of 40 participants had unknowingly contracted syphilis, and 19 children had been born with the disease. It wasn't until 1997 that President Bill Clinton ordered the U.S. government to pay restitution to the survivors of the Tuskegee study, branding its racist exploitation of African American victims as "shameful." ⬚ STANLEY B. BURNS, MD

CHICAGO, SEPTEMBER 6, 1955.
Emmett Till, a 14-year-old African American boy from Chicago, was visiting relatives in Mississippi and stopped at Bryant's Grocery and Meat Market to buy candy. Carolyn Bryant, 21, whose husband ran the store, accused Till of flirting with and whistling at her. Four days later, Bryant's husband and her brother-in-law abducted Till from his relatives' home and then beat him mercilessly, shot him, strung a 75-pound weight around his neck, and dumped him into the Tallahatchie River. Till's body was recovered a few days later. Although Mississippi authorities wanted to bury Till quickly, his mother, Mamie Till Mobley, seen here weeping over her son's battered remains (right), insisted on allowing photographers to capture the ghastly scene and demanded an open casket at the funeral so the world could see what had been done to her child. Tens of thousands of African Americans filed by Till's remains, and images of his battered face, published in *Jet* magazine, incited a generation of young African Americans to join the civil rights movement. The trial of the two killers was a farce, and they were quickly acquitted of both kidnapping and murder by an all-white jury. In 1956, only a year after the trial, they admitted to the murder in a *LOOK* magazine interview, but could not be retried because of double jeopardy. In 2008, 53 years after Till's death, Carolyn Bryant acknowledged in an interview with historian Timothy B. Tyson that the allegations she had made at the trial, accusing Till of being menacing and sexually crude toward her, were false.
⬚ DAVID JACKSON

LITTLE ROCK, ARKANSAS, SEPTEMBER 4, 1957. Elizabeth Eckford, 15, seen here pursued by an angry white mob, was one of nine African American students who tried unsuccessfully that day to attend classes at Little Rock Central High School. Although the school was under federal orders to desegregate, the black students were prevented from entering the school by soldiers of the Arkansas National Guard, under the command of the state's segregationist governor. Three weeks later, after the soldiers prevented their second attempt to attend classes, President Dwight D. Eisenhower put the Arkansas National Guard under federal control and ordered the soldiers to protect the students' safe passage into the school. The Little Rock Nine were the first African Americans to integrate a Little Rock school, a triumph for civil rights. But integration remains a dream unfulfilled. One in 3 African American students now attend majority-African American schools at levels not seen in four decades, tarnishing the achievement of *Brown v. Board of Education.*
📷 WILL COUNTS

**MONTGOMERY, ALABAMA,
SEPTEMBER 3, 1958.** Police officers
push religious and civil rights leader
Martin Luther King Jr. across the
desk at a police station as he is
booked on a charge of "loitering."
King's wife, fellow activist Coretta
Scott King, watches (standing second
from right). During the struggle for
civil rights, police in the South often
filed minor charges such as loitering,
against activists to harass them
and tie them up in court.
📷 CHARLES MOORE

SELMA, ALABAMA, MARCH 10, 1965. Three marches that took place in March 1965 along the 54-mile highway from Selma to Montgomery, Alabama, were decisive in the fight for African American voting rights. Anti-Defamation League National Director Benjamin Epstein and ADL leaders walked alongside Martin Luther King Jr. and other marchers as they set out on March 7, demanding an end to literacy tests and other discriminatory practices that had disenfranchised millions of African Americans across the South. At the Edmund Pettus Bridge just outside Selma, police wielding truncheons and tear gas attacked the unarmed marchers, clubbing many unconscious as TV cameras broadcast the violence nationwide. The second march (above), also led by King (center), took place three days later. This time, marchers reached the bridge without incident, but King led them back to Selma under a federal injunction to await protection for the protest. The third march began on March 21, this time under the watchful eyes of rifle-toting federal troops. Four days later, more than 25,000 marchers descended on Montgomery in a nonviolent show of determination that helped win passage of the 1965 Voting Rights Act. ◎ STEVE SCHAPIRO

SELMA, ALABAMA, MARCH 5, 2015. To mark the 50th anniversary of the first march from Selma to Montgomery, President Barack Obama leads a group of notables (right) across the Edmund Pettus Bridge, the now-notorious span where police attacked and beat marchers in 1965. In a wheelchair, holding Obama's left hand, is Amelia Boynton Robinson, while Representative John Lewis of Georgia holds the president's right hand. Both Robinson and Lewis were clubbed senseless by Alabama state troopers during the original march. ◎ DOUG MILLS

I'M PETRIFIED FOR MY CHILDREN

By MAT JOHNSON

I write novels for a living, and novels are about how characters deal with the intrinsic conflicts that make them who they are—and their efforts to overcome them. Sometimes characters are able to overcome their conflicts and sometimes, in tragedies, they succumb to them, which results in ruin. This is why it troubled me so much to witness recent events unfold like something out of a novel.

Part of the heartbreak of watching the nightmare up the highway from me in Dallas, Texas was seeing, like a story's dramatic conclusion, several of America's greatest inherent conflicts coming together in one moment: fatally disastrous policing; our unresolved racial legacy, dating back to the original sin of slavery and the century of socioeconomic disenfranchisement that followed it; our love of guns, and our recurring shame of the mass murders made possible by them.

I watched that night in Dallas, like everyone else, through the lens of my own backstory: When I saw Philando Castile in Minnesota lying shot in his car, I thought of the time I was pulled over for "speeding" while stopped at a traffic light in East Houston, or when I was pulled over for "making a right-on-red" in Rudolph Giuliani's New York. That time, the cop and I both knew that the light had been green; the stop was just an excuse to run my information through the system because he didn't like the way I looked.

When I saw Castile in Minnesota lying shot in his car, I thought of the times I was pulled over. I thought of what might have happened in those moments if I wasn't privileged enough to pop into my most professorial voice, flash a faculty ID, and access all the adjacent off-white privilege my mixed heritage could provide.

I watched from Dallas, as officers in a police force commended for their de-escalation efforts were murdered in the streets, and thought about teaching at my public university in Texas, where students are able to legally walk through campus strapped with AR-15s on their way to pick up their grades.

And I know others watched the events in Dallas, and watched the unraveling in Baton Rouge, Louisiana, with their own personalized scenes in their head, their

own back stories, their own choice of media-catered facts, their own inherited prejudices, and came to completely different truths about what is going on right now.

When I was growing up, my mother taught me two central things about dealing with the cops while black, the same principles many black parents taught: first, that if you just stay out of trouble and docilely comply with whatever the cops want, you'll be OK; and second, that if the rest of the world saw what was really happening in deadly interactions between black people and the police, they'd see the problem.

At this moment, those ideas seem like wishful self-delusions. I don't know what to tell my kids.

A short while before his life was stolen, slain Baton Rouge Police Officer Montrell Jackson posted a Facebook message that was eerily prescient of the national moment that would soon claim his life. He wrote, "In uniform I get nasty hateful looks and out of uniform some consider me a threat. …These are trying times. Please don't let hate infect your heart." His words, made him exactly the type of officer we need out there. Now he is lost to us.

Right now, in the streets, online, and on TV, we as Americans are fighting over control of the national narrative: Are these acts of violence the fault of the protesters, the police, or a larger criminal justice system that's failing everyone?

I understand why those who feel they aren't directly affected by this issue would be tempted to react to the complexity of what's going on by scapegoating or dismissing recent events as isolated incidents. We all have full, demanding lives. No one wants to add to their daily duties the burden of dramatically changing how our society is functioning.

But I don't have that privilege. What I have is black children. Every time a black person ends up dead after a police interaction, I read the details. I study them. I look for something they did, something they didn't do, something that I can tell my kids to avoid so that if they're ever pulled aside for a minor infraction by the wrong cop, they can come out alive.

But for every single piece of advice I can give them, there is a hashtagged name of someone who did the exact same thing—and died. I'm petrified for my

children. I'm petrified for my friends' children. I'm worried about the good cops out there whose jobs are getting more dangerous because of the injustices perpetrated by others. I'm scared for our country. I fear that if we don't resolve our intrinsic conflicts—our inherent national flaws—that our story will end in ruin. ∎

Mat Johnson is the author of the novels *Loving Day*, *Pym*, *Drop*, and *Hunting in Harlem*, the nonfiction novella *The Great Negro Plot*, and the comic books *Incognegro* and *Dark Rain*. He is a recipient of the United States Artist James Baldwin Fellowship, The Hurston/Wright Legacy Award, a Barnes & Noble Discover Great New Writers selection, and the John Dos Passos Prize for Literature. Mat Johnson is a professor at the University of Houston Creative Writing Program. 🐦 *@Mat_Johnso*

Essay used with permission by the NPR program Fresh Air with Terry Gross/WHYY Philadelphia.

IN THE 1960s, as the civil rights movement tried to end de facto segregation in northern cities like Chicago, many African Americans encountered the same racist hatred they had faced in the South. Those sentiments were on display, from parents and children alike, during a civil rights march through the all-white Chicago suburb of Cicero in 1966 (opposite). African Americans who tried to buy homes in Chicago and its environs were blocked by neighborhood racial covenants and bankers who refused them mortgages. In the places where African Americans were allowed to buy homes, unscrupulous real estate brokers often charged them double and triple what the houses were worth and, if the buyers missed a single payment, brokers could summarily evict them, pocketing any payments already made. African American home buyers received protections in 1968 when Congress passed the Fair Housing Act, which expanded federal prohibitions against discrimination to the private housing market. 📷 BENEDICT J. FERNANDEZ

BALTIMORE, MARYLAND, APRIL 28, 2014. Some police forces that were militarized after 9/11 in order to fight an anticipated threat from terrorism have instead utilized this weaponry on local citizens, as if Ferguson were Fallujah. If patterns of law enforcement established in the past 30 or so years are to continue, a black teenager like 17-year-old Daquan Green, sitting on a curb in Baltimore after the rioting that followed the funeral of Freddie Gray, has a 1-in-3 chance of spending time in jail, likely for one of the nonviolent offenses that are disproportionately enforced in African American communities. The Obama administration relaxed sentencing guidelines for these crimes, reducing the number of African Americans in prison, but under Trump Administration Attorney General Jeff Sessions, the harsher guidelines of the past are being reimposed. 📷 ANDREW BURTON

FERGUSON, MISSOURI, AUGUST 9, 2015. The death of Michael Brown, an unarmed 18-year-old African American shot dead by a white police officer in this middle-class, largely African American suburb of St. Louis, threw fuel on an already-heated national debate over police treatment of young black men. Protesters seized upon the rallying cry of "hands up, don't shoot," believing that "don't shoot" were Brown's last words, but witness accounts did not support that conclusion and a lengthy U.S. Justice Department investigation found that Brown had robbed a convenience store, tried to take the police officer's gun when confronted, fled, and, when found, moved menacingly toward the officer, all of which left little legal room to prosecute. Still, the sense persisted that Brown's death could have been avoided and that American law enforcement demonstrated an indifference to black lives. Here, on the anniversary of Brown's death, young African American men (left) reclaim the "hands up" image as a way of memorializing Brown and the issue that his death brought to national attention. ◎ HUY MACH

WHEN UNARMED TEENAGER MICHAEL BROWN was killed by a police officer in Ferguson, Missouri, on August 9, 2014, activist DeRay Mckesson was working in Minneapolis 550 miles away. Mckesson put his job on hold and headed south to lend his voice and his growing Twitter audience to the protests (above). Since then, he has become a key player in the Black Lives Matter movement and today has a substantial following in both real life and on social media. He also co-created Campaign Zero in partnership with Brittany Packnett (named as one *Time* magazine's 12 New Faces of Black Leadership and who shares the 2015 Peter Jennings Award for Civic Leadership with Mckesson) and Samuel Sinyangwe, an American-policy analyst and racial justice activist. Campaign Zero (see page 99) uses data to report on and help reduce police violence. In early 2017, Mckesson began hosting *Pod Save the People*, a well-regarded podcast launched by Crooked Media, a network founded by former Barack Obama presidential aides Jon Favreau, Jon Lovett, and Tommy Vietor. Guests on the show have included former Obama adviser Valerie Jarrett, fugitive and former National Security Agency contractor Edward Snowden, and Senator Cory Booker.
◎ BRYAN SUTTER

BALTIMORE, MARYLAND, 2015. The front-page headlines of *The Baltimore Sun* (above) trace the story of Freddie Gray, a 25-year-old African American who died in 2015 from a spinal cord injury while in police custody. Six police officers went to trial separately on charges ranging from homicide to false arrest. But the case against one officer ended in a mistrial, and three others were acquitted. Charges were eventually dropped against the remaining two in 2016.

BALTIMORE, MARYLAND, APRIL 28, 2015. African American men (right) weep over the death of Freddie Gray during a protest in Baltimore's predominantly black West Side. The deaths of Gray and other black men from police shootings or mistreatment prompted nationwide protests and soul searching. Americans confronted the fact that, despite evident progress, the path towards racial justice remains slow and disheartening.
📷 YUNGHI KIM

IT WAS A HIGH-STAKES MOVE, in 2016, when San Francisco 49ers quarterback Colin Kaepernick (above, center, with Eli Harold, left, and Eric Reid) refused to follow his team in the tradition of standing for the national anthem. "I'm not going to stand up to show pride in a flag for a country that oppresses black people and people of color," Kaepernick explained. While many criticized him for politicizing professional sports, others called his stance courageous as he risked his reputation to fight for the rights of others. "To me, this is bigger than football, and it would be selfish on my part to look the other way." Eventually, Kaepernick opted to join his fellow players but to kneel instead of stand. This, he said, was his way of supporting veterans while still protesting.
◎ MARCIO JOSE SANCHEZ

ALMOST 40 YEARS EARLIER in 1968, with race riots exploding across the United States, Olympic track stars Tommie Smith and John Carlos decided to use the attention focused on their medal ceremony to protest African American poverty. When the national anthem played, rather than put their hands over their hearts, they gave the black power salute (right). Gestures like these are incredibly risky because—as Kaepernick, Smith, and Carlos all learned—offended fans can transform them from heroes to pariahs in an instant.

BOSTON, MASSACHUSETTS, DECEMBER 10, 2015. Medical students from more than 70 schools across the country, including Harvard, donned their white coats and staged "die-ins" to protest police shootings (far right). Many American doctors argue that the same structural racism that results in police shootings of unarmed blacks is evident in the country's health care system, where studies show that African Americans receive inferior medical care, resulting in poorer health and shorter life expectancies. ◎ DAVID L. RYAN

LOUISVILLE, KENTUCKY, 1963.
Muhammad Ali was perhaps the greatest boxer in the history of the sport. But the inspiration he provided extended far beyond the ring. As a proud African American, he lifted the self-esteem of people whose spirits had been crushed by injustice. People from Kalamazoo to Kinshasa loved his swagger and brash self-confidence. Born as Cassius Clay Jr. and raised a Baptist, Ali converted to Islam, and adopted Muhammad Ali as a replacement for what he called his "slave name" (ironically, though, since he was also named for a Cassius Clay, a renowned nineteenth century Kentucky abolitionist). At the height of his fame, Ali risked career and reputation by refusing to fight in Vietnam, a war he considered unjust. Stripped of his title and banished from boxing for three-and-a-half years, he lost a lengthy period in his athletic prime. But in 1974, at the age of 32, he knocked out a much younger George Foreman and took back his heavyweight crown. Decades later, Ali was brought down by

Parkinson's, but even as his health declined, the champ exhibited an extraordinary gallantry. In one of his last, and least known, acts of goodwill, he tried to leverage his celebrity in the Muslim world to secure the release of Daniel Pearl, a Jewish *Wall Street Journal* reporter abducted—and eventually murdered—by Islamic extremists in Pakistan in 2012. Ali's appeal to Pearl's captors was to "treat him as you would wish all Muslims to be treated by others." University of Southern California professor Sherman Jackson commented on the legacy of Ali to Muslim youth: "A lot of young people in this age of Islamophobia are really almost starved for heroes who can inspire them to straighten their backs and hold up their heads. And nobody really personified that as keenly, as forcefully, as unapologetically, as Muhammad Ali." ◉ STEVE SCHAPIRO

WASHINGTON, D.C., 2009.
The election of Barack Obama to the White House shattered many racial barriers and represented an extraordinary step toward redemption of the country's original sin. At the 2016 Democratic convention, first lady Michelle Obama spoke of "generations of people who felt the lash of bondage, the shame of servitude, the sting of segregation, but who kept on striving and hoping and doing what needed to be done so that today, I wake up every morning in a house that was built by slaves and I watch my daughters—two beautiful, intelligent, black young women— playing with their dogs on the White House lawn." Among Barack Obama's accomplishments was the sense of empowerment he imparted to others. During a visit to the Oval Office, Jacob Philadelphia, 5, wanted to know "if my hair is just like yours," so the president invited him to touch it (above) and see for himself. "So, what do you think?" Obama asked afterward. "Yes, it does feel the same," Jacob said. ◉ PETE SOUZA

SHONDA RHIMES

Prolific showrunner Shonda Rhimes is a force of nature and the first African American woman to create and executive produce a Top 10 network series, *Grey's Anatomy*, which won the coveted Golden Globe for Best Dramatic Television Series. She also created *Private Practice*, *Scandal*, and *How to Get Away With Murder* (for which Viola Davis, as Professor Annalise Keating, won an Emmy as lead actress, the first African American woman to win that award). Rhimes herself has won several GLAAD Media and NAACP Image Awards, as well as received widespread acclaim for the way that her shows openly address race and sexuality. In 2007, *Time* magazine featured Rhimes as one of its "100 People Who Help Shape the World." In 2015, she published a best-selling memoir, *Year of Yes: How to Dance It Out, Stand in the Sun, and Be Your Own Person.*

THE 2016 FILM *MOONLIGHT*, by director Barry Jenkins (left), was nominated for eight Academy Awards and took home three, including Best Movie, Best Actor in a Supporting Role, and Best Adapted Screenplay. *The New York Times* film critic A.O. Scott wrote that "*Moonlight* dwells on the dignity, beauty and terrible vulnerability of black bodies, on the existential and physical matter of black lives." Yet despite such recent recognition, African Americans have barely registered in the history of the Academy Awards. Since 1939, when Hattie McDaniel became the first African American to receive an Oscar for her supporting role in *Gone With the Wind*, only 36 African Americans have won this prestigious Hollywood award. In 2015, when not a single African American was nominated, critics launched the #OscarsSoWhite hashtag, which called out the Academy, while directing attention to the fact that 91 percent of the 6,200 voting members were white. In response, the Academy installed Cheryl Boone Isaacs as its first African American, and third female, president, and among the first items on Boone Isaacs' agenda was to address the film industry's serious issue with diversity. 📷 ART STREIBER

BEFORE SHE WON ELECTION to the U.S. Senate in 2016, Kamala Harris, the daughter of an Indian immigrant mother and a Jamaican American father, was a career prosecutor. While serving as the San Francisco district attorney, Harris created a special hate crimes division, which focused on the bullying of LGBTQ children and teens in the county's schools. As California Attorney General, Harris launched the state's first Bureau of Children's Justice. After the sub-prime mortgage scandal, she helped broker a settlement with California banks that provided $12 billion of debt reduction to the state's homeowners. Throughout her legal career, Harris has also been a strong proponent of gun control, abortion rights, and protections for the elderly. The U.S. Senate may not be the last stop in her public service career. During the second Obama administration, Harris was said to be on the short list for the Supreme Court and in 2016, *Mother Jones* included her among a select group of young Democrats who could one day arrive in the White House. 📷 JOSH EDELSON

WASHINGTON, D.C., JUNE 10, 2009. A police officer examines bullet holes in the glass front of the United States Holocaust Memorial Museum, after James von Brunn, an 89-year-old white supremacist, entered the building and opened fire, killing Special Police Officer Stephen Tyrone Johns. After the shooting, authorities discovered that von Brunn had maintained a website where he posted anti-Semitic essays that praised Adolf Hitler and denied the Nazi extermination of Jews during World War II. Von Brunn died in 2010 awaiting trial for first-degree murder. ⬡ MIKE THEILER

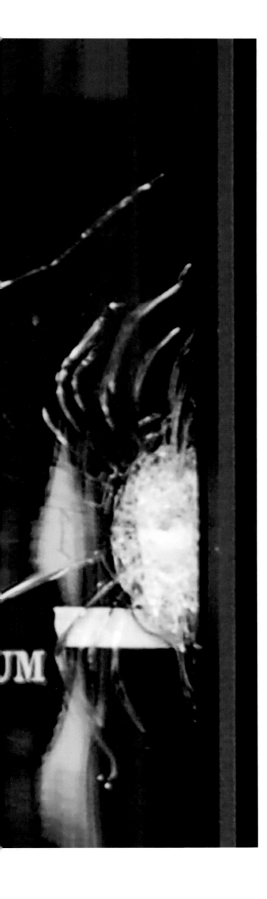

WHERE WERE THE POLICE?
BY CHARLES RAMSEY

EARLY IN MY TENURE as commissioner of the Washington, D.C., Metropolitan Police Department, in 1998, I received an invitation from David Friedman, then director of the Anti-Defamation League's regional office in Washington, to visit the United States Holocaust Memorial Museum. I spent a good part of my tour walking and talking with Irene Weiss, a Holocaust survivor. Many people read about the Holocaust in school and textbooks, but few of us have had the opportunity to hear about it firsthand from someone who actually survived the horror.

I left the museum overwhelmed with emotion. The images were haunting and left me with a strong sense that there were important lessons to be learned, for myself and for every other police officer. I went back a few weeks later, unannounced, and toured the museum again on my own. I found myself drawn back to the pictures of the German police officers, and the more I learned, the more I was disturbed at their involvement in this tragedy.

On the top floor of the exhibition, I saw an image of a police officer and a Nazi militia soldier flanking a snarling, muzzled dog.

A common assumption is that Nazi atrocities were carried out almost exclusively by the military, and by the infamous SA and SS troops. But what I learned that day was that the local police had played an integral role in the atrocities—not just passively permitting them to take place but actively participating in many of them. Over time, the distinctions between local police and the Nazi military became so blurred that the two became synonymous.

As Jews began to be mistreated at the beginning of the Holocaust, Americans asked the question, "Where were the police?" One of the newspaper blowups on display in the museum is from the *The Dallas Morning News* of November 11,

BERLIN, 1933. A police officer (left) from the *Sturmabteilung* (SA), the original paramilitary wing of the Nazi Party, patrols a Berlin street, accompanied by an auxiliary police officer and his muzzled attack dog from the *Schutzstaffel* (SS), whose members swore their allegiance to Hitler. The purpose of these police units was not to protect the German people, but to perpetuate Nazi rule and party ideology. As noted by former Washington, D.C., Police Chief Charles Ramsey: "A common assumption is that that Nazi atrocities were carried out almost exclusively by the military but local police also played an integral role in the atrocities—not just passively permitting them to take place but actively participating in many of them. Over time, the distinctions between local police and the Nazi military became so blurred that the two became synonymous. ... The more I learned, the more I was disturbed at the involvement of the local police in this tragedy. ... American police officers must never become so politicized—as they were in Nazi Germany—that they regard their primary role as carrying out the will of political leaders, or simply looking the other way when political agendas deny fundamental rights."
📷 GEORG PAHL

WASHINGTON, 2014. Philadelphia police recruits tour the United States Holocaust Memorial Museum (right) during a daylong Law Enforcement & Society training program. The tour is part of an initiative designed by the Anti-Defamation League in conjunction with the United States Holocaust Museum to educate federal, state, and local law enforcement about the role of the Nazi police during the Holocaust and to broaden understanding of the role of American police as the protectors of society rather than as an arm of the federal government.

1938. Its banner headline, reporting on the *Kristallnacht* rampage of two days earlier, reads as follows: "Hysterical Nazis Wreck Thousands of Jewish Shops, Burn Synagogues in Wild Orgy of Looting and Terror." What is particularly disturbing is the subheadline: "Policemen Refuse to Halt Organized Riots in Germany."

The newspaper's framing of that question ("Where were the police?") expresses the long-held tradition in our own country that if people are rioting and looting and destroying property, it is the job of the police to intervene. This is fundamental to our view of the police mission: the protection of life and property.

Where were the German police when libraries were being looted and books burned? When Jewish businesses were being illegally targeted? When people were being classified and publicly harassed, and ultimately, imprisoned and slaughtered? Where were the police—and the local politicians, other government officials, civic leaders, and everyday citizens, most of whom stood by silently and watched it all happen?

How then, in Germany in the 1930s, did things get so out of control that Nazis could loot and destroy in an organized and widespread manner without the police even trying to intervene?

In the United States, that kind of complacency on the part of the police seems almost impossible to comprehend, but in our not-so-distant past, Americans have also been forced to ask: Where were the police when people were being lynched because of the color of their skin, and segregation was the law in states across the South?

Whether they pertain to the 1930s or to our times, these are compelling questions; ones I think all police officers should be thinking and talking about.

Could the Holocaust have happened without the active cooperation and participation of the local police in Germany? We may never know the answer to that question. But one thing we do know for certain: Local police forces began to operate in accordance with a set of values totally contrary to their oath of office and totally contrary to the mission of the police in a free, democratic, and pluralistic society.

The Holocaust is probably the most extreme example of just how horrific and far-reaching the consequences can be when police officers violate their oath and fail to protect the basic rights and liberties of citizens. But even small ethical violations on the part of police officers can result in people's rights being denied, their confidence in the police being eroded, and their communities becoming less safe.

Historical explanations of the behavior of the German police point out a trend at the time toward a nationalization and politicization of policing. The stated reasons for the increasingly repressive tactics German police employed then have an all-too-familiar ring to them today.

The police did not call their behavior "zero tolerance" at the time, but the brand of crime control they practiced was "zero tolerance" taken to its most horrific extreme. The concept quickly moved from "zero tolerance" for criminal behavior to "zero tolerance" toward those people blamed as responsible for crime, disorder, and other forms of hardship—in this case, Jews, gays and lesbians, people with mental illness, those with physical and cognitive disabilities, the Roma, and many, many others.

What followed from the "zero tolerance" policies in Nazi Germany was the denial of basic human rights and individual freedoms. Almost from the beginning, local police were intimately involved, and they soon became part and parcel of the Nazi reign of repression and terror.

Of course, the term "zero tolerance" is quite in vogue today. Some people even suggest (quite mistakenly, I would argue) that "zero tolerance" and community policing are one and the same, or at least closely related. What worries me most about this is that the true ideals of democracy are about tolerance—tolerance for different people, different cultures, different viewpoints.

If we are to stand for any type of "zero tolerance," it should be "zero tolerance" for the types of racist attitudes that led to the Holocaust 80 years ago and continue to feed hate crimes in our communities today. That is the type of "zero tolerance" we, as police officers, should be focusing on.

How then should we help the police officers of today understand their role as defenders of the constitutional rights of all people? How do we help them recognize their own biases and prevent prejudice from influencing their decisions?

AMATEUR VIDEO MAR. 3 1991

Los Angeles Times

All 4 in King Beating Acquitted

Violence Follows Verdicts; Guard Called Out

DURING THE FIGHT for civil rights in the 1960s, newspapers and television captured disturbing images of police brutality often aimed at minorities. But in court cases that pitted a police officers's word against that of a poor African American or Latino, judges and juries were more inclined to believe the police officer. Things began to change when video camcorders came along, allowing some victims of police misconduct to show seemingly incontrovertible evidence to support their claims. In 1991, a bystander shot a video of Rodney King being savagely beaten by Los Angeles police and provided the tape to a local television station, leading to charges against the officers. A predominantly white jury chose to focus on a blurry scene at the beginning of the video that showed King lunging at the cops, and acquitted the officers. That verdict led to the 1992 L.A. riots in which more than 50 people died. But the jury in a separate federal trial later convicted two of the officers. In 2015, a smartphone video clearly showed a South Carolina police officer shooting unarmed black motorist Walter Scott in the back while Scott was fleeing from the officer on foot. The video contradicted the cop's claim that he had fired in self-defense, and eventually he pleaded

guilty to federal charges relating to Scott's murder. But not all videos have worked to convince juries of misconduct. In 2016, Philando Castile, a school cafeteria worker in Minnesota, was shot by police officer Jeronimo Yanez during a routine traffic stop. As he lay dying in the car seat next to her, Diamond Reynolds, Castile's girlfriend, streamed the ordeal on Facebook Live. The resulting public outcry made headlines the world over. Announcing that he would bring charges against Yanez, the local county prosecutor, John Choi, contended that "...no reasonable officer knowing, seeing, and hearing what Officer Yanez did at the time would have used deadly force under these circumstances." Yet a jury acquitted the officer of all charges. A few days later, Castile's family was awarded a $3 million settlement that spoke to the city's fears about its chances in civil court.

Unfortunately, the issue of race in our society still divides us. It is difficult to have a discussion on the topic or to get people to see the world through the eyes of someone of another race without a variety of defensive reactions getting in the way. It was my attempt to answer those questions that led me to reflect more carefully on the Holocaust. The events leading up to and including the Holocaust powerfully demonstrate the dangers that can materialize when police offer their allegiance to a person or to a political party rather than holding true to the ethics of their profession.

In response to the impact my visit to the Holocaust museum had on me, I initiated the "Law Enforcement & Society Program." This educational program, created in cooperation with the Anti-Defamation League, has provided more than 130,000 law enforcement officers from a range of federal, state, and local agencies with the opportunity to spend a day at the Holocaust museum and reflect on the role of police in a democratic society.

The day begins with a guided tour of the museum's permanent collection, which traces the history of the Holocaust from the Nazis' rise to power through the end of World War II and its aftermath. The tour is followed by a group discussion among the police officers, museum historians, and educators on the abuse of power under the Nazis and the role of police within the Nazi state. Finally, the session concludes with an interactive conversation between Anti-Defamation League educators and police participants, who are encouraged to discuss their personal reactions and feelings in response to what they have seen. They are prompted to explore in greater depth the role that local police played in the genocide. They discuss how the lessons of the Holocaust can be applied to their own work as police officers today.

In our daily routines as police officers, we spend the vast majority of our time with the most vulnerable in our society—people who are poor and

undereducated; people who may be newly arrived in our country and may speak a different language; people who are afraid and sometimes hopeless; people who may not appreciate, understand, or trust the police. Who but these people have the greatest need of our help?

One of the lessons police recruits pick up from the day they spend at the museum is how to deal with their own personal prejudices while they carry out their very public role as police officers.

Nobody enters this profession without some prejudices. That's just human nature, and police officers are human beings, too. We all come to this job with certain preconceptions about people, certain stereotypes, and even certain prejudices. Exposure to the history of the Holocaust forces our recruits to confront those highly personal feelings in a compelling but supportive way.

The purpose of the training is to remind officers that local police must never become so politicized—as they were in Nazi Germany—that they regard their primary role as carrying out the will of political leaders or simply looking the other way when political agendas deny fundamental rights.

Of course, there are important differences between the two scenarios. In the 1930s and 1940s, local police officers in the Nazi empire not only failed to prevent atrocities from taking place, they also actively participated in many of those atrocities, including the murder of innocent people. That type of blatant criminal behavior is not to be found among the vast majority of our police officers today. But the question—then and now—is still the same: Will police officers have the courage to intervene, to step forward, to challenge their colleagues, to do the right thing?

FERGUSON, MISSOURI, NOVEMBER 24, 2014. Federal law prohibits the use of military force against American citizens. Maintaining security inside the country has always been the job of the police. But the distinction between the two has blurred in recent years, as local police departments—addressing the so-called "war on crime," then the "war on drugs," and finally, the "war on terror"—bulked up with surplus military equipment handed out by the Pentagon. The free military hardware includes helicopters, mine-resistant armored personnel carriers, automatic weapons, night vision scopes, even grenade launchers. When residents of Ferguson, Missouri, took to the streets in August 2014 to protest the police shooting death of unarmed black teenager Michael Brown, heavily armed police exacerbated tensions by moving in armored combat vehicles and firing tear gas and pepper spray. A helmeted SWAT team member (left) threatens a terrified protester on the ground at one such demonstration. Today it is not uncommon for militarized SWAT teams—resembling Navy SEAL teams—to be used for routine drug busts as well. The total value of military equipment acquired by police departments since the late 1990s has reached $4.3 billion. ⓘ LARRY W. SMITH

DALLAS, TEXAS, JULY 8, 2016. When David Brown took over as chief of police in 2010, he transformed the way his officers interacted with Dallas city residents. He radically overhauled use-of-force policies and put all officers through training that motivated them to use all reasonable alternatives before resorting to lethal means. He fired more than 70 cops when they broke the rules. He ordered his officers to facilitate peaceful public demonstrations, not to obstruct or interfere. The resulting trends were impressive: Police shootings declined every year, the murder rate in 2014 hit a 50-year low, and both crime and citizen complaints against the police dropped to their lowest levels in decades. All of which made the events of July 8, 2016 (opposite, left), even more devastating. That afternoon, during a

peaceful downtown protest in support of Black Lives Matter, Micah Johnson, a troubled African American veteran, used a high-powered rifle to shoot white police officers as payback for the recent deaths of unarmed African Americans at the hands of police in other parts of the United States. Johnson, 25, shot and killed 5 Dallas cops and wounded 7 more people before he was killed in a parking garage by a remote-controlled robot carrying an explosive charge. At a memorial service for the slain Dallas officers, President Barack Obama thanked Brown for his service to the Dallas community. The president also took note that under Brown's orders, Dallas police had demonstrated remarkable restraint in neutralizing the shooter. "You evacuated the injured, isolated the shooter, and saved more lives than we'll ever know," Obama said, drawing a standing ovation for Brown, seen here bowing his head at the prayer service (above, right).

SPENCER PLATT

Since 9/11, and again in the wake of the Boston Marathon bombing, we hear police (among others) described as first responders. Everyone was struck by the images in Boston of police officers at the scene of the bombing, rushing in without hesitation to help the wounded with little or no regard for their own safety.

If we really understand our oath—and the role police must play in protecting human rights, civil liberties, and democratic values—then we also have to be the first responders when basic human and civil rights are threatened or denied. Not bystanders. Will we rush in then to intervene, without regard for the personal consequences, just as we do at a bomb scene? Of course, others should follow us and have their role to play, too, but police need to be first, the very first. Our oath as police officers demands that we take this leadership role.

We look at courage in our business as going up against an armed gunman, into a dangerous situation, or facing physical danger. We think less about courage as standing up for what is right. What is more, our systems and organizational cultures often fail to support or reward that kind of courage. When an officer reports misconduct to internal affairs, what kind of reward does he or she get for such courage? Too often, it seems as if the incentives and reward structures are stacked against those who are on the side of right. Too often, those who speak up or say "no" end up ostracized.

Our oath to "serve and protect" means much more than protecting life and property. Our oath also carries with it the unique and awesome responsibility of protecting the constitutional rights of all Americans—of safeguarding the very

freedoms that we cherish and that set us apart from so many other nations on earth.

In recent years, whenever we see the escalation of crime, drug abuse, youth violence, child abuse, security threats, or other serious problems, we hear various calls for the relaxation of the exclusionary rule, the reversal of other Fourth Amendment rights and the overhaul of police Miranda warnings. All of these suggestions have been made in the name of more effective law enforcement and safer communities.

Yes, the police need to work harder and smarter in controlling crime. But in doing so, we must never compromise our staunch defense of the Constitution and the bedrock freedoms it guarantees. We must never buy into the notion— as the police in Nazi Germany did—that taking away individual rights is somehow the way to solve our crime problems and create safer communities.

It's essential that the police are an integral part of the very fabric that holds communities together in a democratic society. Our partnerships and collaborations mean much more when we view ourselves as a part of the fabric rather than as a separate institution trying to engage the public. ◾

Charles H. Ramsey brings over 47 years of law enforcement experience having served in three major city police departments: Chicago, Washington, D.C., and Philadelphia. Ramsey served as president of both the Police Executive Research Forum and Major Cities Chiefs and co-chaired the President's Task Force on 21st Century Policing. He is currently a distinguished visiting fellow of the Lindy Institute at Drexel University and serves as an adviser to the U.S. Conference of Mayors. In December 2015, the City of Philadelphia named the Philadelphia Police Department Training Academy Auditorium the Charles H. Ramsey Training and Education Auditorium. In 2015, a U.S. postage stamp bearing his likeness was approved by the United States Congress and presented in his honor.

BEST POLICING PRACTICES

Campaign Zero has proposed a 10-point package of policy solutions informed by data, research, and human rights principles, with the aim of changing the way police serve communities by protecting and preserving life.

The **proposals** integrate recommendations from communities, research organizations, and the President's Task Force on 21st Century Policing (2015).

1 END BROKEN WINDOWS POLICING
For decades, a focus on minor crimes has led to criminalization of communities of color and excessive force in otherwise harmless situations—such as sleeping in parks, possessing drugs, looking "suspicious," or having a mental health crisis.

2 ESTABLISH CIVILIAN COMMUNITY OVERSIGHT
Usually, police decide what consequences fellow officers should face in cases of police misconduct. Fewer than 1 in 12 complaints results in disciplinary action against the officers responsible.

3 LIMIT USE OF FORCE
In 2014, police killed 253 unarmed people and 91 who were stopped for traffic violations. Police should use deadly force only when there is an imminent threat to an officer's life or to the life of another.

4 INDEPENDENTLY INVESTIGATE AND PROSECUTE
Local prosecutors rely on local police to gather evidence to prosecute criminals, making it hard for them to investigate the same officers in cases of police violence. Such cases should not rely on police to investigate themselves.

5 COMMUNITY REPRESENTATION
White men comprise less than one-third of the U.S. population, but two-thirds of police officers. The force should reflect the cultural, racial, and gender diversity of the communities it serves.

6 BODY CAMS/FILM THE POLICE
Body cameras and cell phone videos have illuminated cases of police violence. Nearly every case where a police officer was charged with killing a civilian relied on video evidence.

7 TRAINING
Police recruits spend 58 hours learning how to shoot firearms and eight hours learning how to de-escalate situations. A training regimen is needed to help police learn the behaviors and skills to interact appropriately with communities.

8 END FOR-PROFIT POLICING
Police should be working to keep people safe, not contributing to a system that profits from stopping, searching, ticketing, arresting, and incarcerating people.

9 DEMILITARIZATION
In 2014, militarized SWAT teams killed 38 people. Police departments should be limited from obtaining or using military weapons on our streets.

10 FAIR POLICE UNION CONTRACTS
Police unions have established unfair protections for police officers, creating one set of rules for police and another for civilians, which in turn makes it difficult for police chiefs or civilian oversight structures to punish police officers who are unfit to serve.

Source: Campaign Zero
For full explanations of the 10 proposals go to www.joincampaignzero.org/solutions

SAN FRANCISCO, APRIL 6, 1942. A Japanese American prepares to board a bus bound for the temporary detention center at the Santa Anita racetrack near Los Angeles. A government report from that year described the man as "labeled, checked against the master list," and "ready to leave." The descriptions were emblematic of the humiliating treatment and the impersonal bureaucracy of the internment procedures. 📷 DOROTHEA LANGE

JAPANESE AMERICANS

IN THE SPRING OF 1942, just a few months after the Japanese attack on Pearl Harbor, the U.S. government ordered nearly 120,000 Japanese Americans to report to assembly points across the West with only the basic necessities they could carry. U.S. soldiers herded these people—two-thirds of them American-born citizens, the others legal immigrants—onto trains that transported them to internment camps stretching from the badlands of several Western states to the swamps of the Deep South. And there, surrounded by barbed wire and armed guards, they languished until 1945.

The internment of these men, women, and children, whose only offense was their Japanese ancestry, was one of the more shameful episodes in U.S. history. The ordeal endured by Japanese Americans serves as a reminder of the harm that can befall defenseless minorities when irrational fears, rank racism, and hatred are allowed to shape official policies.

It is now known that the FBI had already concluded that Japanese Americans posed no internal threat. But the government suppressed that report, bowing to the prevailing political mood, which regarded all Japanese as spies and saboteurs. "The Japanese race is an enemy race," declared Lieutenant General John DeWitt who oversaw the internment operation.

Powerful business interests also had a hand in the wartime internment policy. On the West Coast, where Japanese American-owned farms had produced much of the region's fresh food, white farmers demanded their internment. "If all of the Japs were removed tomorrow, we'd never miss them," the head of a California farmers' association told *The Saturday Evening Post*.

In January 1945, the government finally released the internees, many of whom discovered that their homes, farms, and businesses had been taken over by non-Japanese Americans during their internment, leaving them penniless and with no legal recourse for restitution. It wasn't until 43 years later, in 1988, that Congress officially apologized and provided a mere $20,000 in reparations to each surviving internee. In signing the measure into law, President Ronald Reagan cited "racial prejudice, wartime hysteria, and a lack of political leadership" as the real reasons for the internment—words that bear repeating today. ∎

WHEN BARBED WIRE WAS HOME
BY GEORGE TAKEI

I'M A VETERAN OF THE STARSHIP ENTERPRISE. I soared through the galaxy driving a huge starship with a crew made up of people from all over this world, many different races, many different cultures, many different heritages, all working together. Our mission was to explore strange new worlds, to seek out new life and new civilizations, to boldly go where no one has gone before.

I am the grandson of immigrants from Japan who came to the United States, boldly going to a strange new world, seeking opportunity. My mother was born in Sacramento, California. My father was a San Franciscan. They met and married in Los Angeles, and I was born there.

I was 4 years old when Pearl Harbor was bombed on December 7, 1941, by Japan, and overnight, the world was plunged into a world war. America suddenly was swept up by hysteria. Japanese Americans, American citizens of Japanese ancestry, were looked upon with suspicion and fear and with outright hatred simply because we happened to look like the people who bombed Pearl Harbor. And the hysteria grew and grew until in February 1942, the president of the United States, Franklin Delano Roosevelt, ordered all Japanese Americans on the West Coast to be summarily rounded up with no charges, with no trial, with no due process. Due process, this is a core pillar of our justice system. That all disappeared. We were to be rounded up and imprisoned in 10 barbed-wire prison camps in some of the

SAN FRANCISCO, MAY 2, 1942. Photographer Dorothea Lange, best known for her Depression-era portraits of migrant farmers, captured the plight of Japanese Americans in a series of images that were so disturbing, the government had them impounded and discreetly deposited in the National Archives. Lange was commissioned by the federal government's War Relocation Authority that wanted a documentary record of the camps. Unearthed only in 2006, the photographs show neatly dressed families struggling to retain their dignity in the windowless tar-paper shacks and flimsy wooden barracks where they were forced to live. Accounts by internees told of camps with open sewers, forced labor, and military police who shot anyone who tried to escape. 🖸 DOROTHEA LANGE

most desolate places in the United States: the blistering hot desert of Arizona, the sultry swamps of Arkansas, the wastelands of Wyoming, Idaho, Utah, Colorado, and two of the most desolate places in California.

On April 20, 1942, I celebrated my fifth birthday. A few weeks later, early one morning, my parents woke me, my younger brother, and my baby sister. They dressed us quickly. My brother and I went into the living room and looked out the front window. We saw two soldiers marching up our driveway. They carried bayonets on their rifles. They stomped up the front porch and banged on the door. My father answered it, and the soldiers ordered us out of our home. My father gave us small suitcases to carry, and we walked out and stood on the driveway waiting for our mother to come out, and when my mother finally came out, she had our baby sister in one arm, a huge duffel bag in the other, and tears were streaming down both her cheeks. I will never be able to forget that moment. It is burned into my memory.

We were taken from our home and loaded on to train cars with other Japanese American families. There were guards stationed at both ends of each car, as if we were criminals. We were taken two-thirds of the way across the country, rocking on that train for four days and three nights, to the swamps of Arkansas. I still remember the barbed wire fence that confined me. I remember the tall sentry tower with the machine guns pointed at us. I remember the searchlight that followed me when I made the night runs from my barrack to the latrine. But to 5-year-old me, I thought it was kind of nice that they'd lit the way for me to pee. I was a child, too young to understand the circumstances of my being there.

Children are amazingly adaptable. What would be grotesquely abnormal

The letter reads:

YALE UNIVERSITY
BOARD OF ADMISSIONS
NEW HAVEN · CONNECTICUT

EDWARD S. NOYES, CHAIRMAN
NELLIE P. ELLIOT, EXECUTIVE SECRETARY

MAILING ADDRESS: 1502A YALE STATION

July 14, 1945

Mr. Kinji Imada
10-9-C Rivers, Arizona

Dear Mr. Imada:

This will inform you that your application for admission to the Freshman class in November and the official credentials sumitted in support of it have been carefully considered.

At the time you made your original request for an application for admission to the Freshman class, it was our understanding that the University would be permitted to accept American students of Japanese parentage. We find now that because of the large unit of Navy and Marine Corps students in the University, we are at this time not permitted to accept students of Japanese parentage. We trust that you will be able to continue your education elsewhere.

Very truly yours,

Edward S. Noyes.

AFTER SPENDING the war years in an Idaho internment camp, a Japanese American family returns to its home in Seattle on May 10, 1945, only to find it defaced with racist slogans (far left). Japan's 1941 surprise attack on Pearl Harbor prompted Americans to treat loyal, U.S.-born citizens of Japanese ancestry as if they were the Japanese enemy. On March 23, 1942, military authorities ordered (near left) all Japanese Americans living on the West Coast to report to assembly centers for relocation to internment camps. There, they were issued identity cards like the one pictured above. Some prestigious universities closed their doors to Japanese Americans, boldly citing ancestry as the reason for their exclusion (above, right).
📷 PAUL KITAGAKI JR., ABOVE

became my normality as a prisoner of a war camp. It became routine for me to line up three times a day to eat lousy food in a noisy mess hall. It became normal for me to go with my father to bathe in a mass shower. Being in a barbed-wire camp, a prison, was my normal.

When the war ended, we were released and given a one-way ticket to anywhere in the United States. My parents decided to go back home to Los Angeles, but Los Angeles was not a welcoming place. We were penniless. Everything had been taken from us, and the hostility was intense. Our first home was on Skid Row in the lowest part of our city, living with derelicts, drunkards, and crazy people, the stench of urine all over, on the street, in the alley, in the hallway. It was a horrible experience, and for us kids, it was terrifying. I remember once a drunkard came staggering down, fell down right in front of us, and threw up. My baby sister said, "Mama, let's go back home," because to us, behind barbed wire was home.

My parents worked hard to get back on their feet. We had lost everything. They were in the middle of their lives and starting all over. They worked their fingers to the bone, and they were able to get the capital together to buy a three-bedroom home in a nice neighborhood. As a teenager, I became very curious about my childhood imprisonment. I read civics books that told me about the ideals of American democracy. All men are created equal, we have an inalienable right to life, liberty, and the pursuit of happiness, and I couldn't quite make that fit with what I knew to be my childhood imprisonment. I read history books, and I couldn't find anything about our experience. And so I engaged my father after dinner in long, sometimes heated conversations. We had many,

many conversations, and what I got from them was my father's wisdom. He was the one who had suffered the most under those conditions of imprisonment, and yet he understood American democracy. He told me that our democracy is a people's democracy, and it can be as great as the people can be, but it is also as fallible as people are. He told me that American democracy is vitally dependent on good people who cherish the ideals of our system and actively engage in the process of making democracy work. And he took me to a campaign headquarters—the governor of Illinois was running for the presidency—and introduced me to American electoral politics. And he also told me about young Japanese Americans during World War II.

When Pearl Harbor was bombed, young Japanese Americans, like many young Americans, rushed to their draft board to volunteer to fight for our country. That act of patriotism was answered with a slap in the face. We were denied service and categorized as enemy non-alien. It was outrageous to be called an enemy when you're volunteering to fight for your country, but that was compounded with the word "non-alien," which is a word that means "citizen" in the negative. They even took the word "citizen" away from us and imprisoned us for a whole year.

And then the government realized that there was a wartime manpower shortage, and as suddenly as they'd rounded us up, they opened up the military for service by young Japanese Americans. It was totally illogical, but the amazing thing, the astounding thing, is that thousands of young Japanese American men and women again went from behind those barbed-wire fences, put on the same uniform as that of their guards, leaving their families in imprisonment, to fight for this country.

They said that they were going to fight not only to get their families out from behind those barbed-wire fences, but because they cherished the very ideal of what our government stands for, should stand for, and that was being abrogated by what was being done.

All men are created equal. And they went to fight for this country. They were put into a segregated all-Japanese American unit and sent to the battlefields of Europe, and they threw themselves in. They fought with amazing, incredible courage and valor. They were sent out on the most dangerous missions, and they sustained the highest combat casualty rate of any unit, proportionally.

The 1944 battle for the Gothic Line illustrates what happened. The Germans were embedded in this mountain hillside, rocky hillside, in impregnable caves, and three Allied battalions had been pounding away at it for six months, and they were stalemated. The 442nd was called in to add to the fight, but the men of the 442nd came up with a unique but dangerous idea: the backside of the mountain was a sheer rock cliff. The Germans thought an attack from the backside would be impossible. The men of the 442nd decided to do the impossible. On a dark, moonless night, they began scaling that rock wall, a drop of more than 1,000 feet, in full combat gear. They climbed all night long on that

JUST THE FACTS

DURING WORLD WAR II, MORE THAN

26,000

JAPANESE AMERICAN MEN AND WOMEN FAITHFULLY SERVED IN THE U.S. ARMED FORCES, WHILE MANY OF THE RELATIVES WERE FORCIBLY INTERNED.

—SLATE

ON JANUARY 30, 2017, three days after the Trump White House attempted to institute a travel ban on people attempting to enter the United States from seven Muslim-majority countries, Google Doodle featured Fred Korematsu on its landing page. The son of Japanese immigrants, Korematsu defied the government's 1942 order that sent tens of thousands of Japanese Americans to internment camps during World War II. Arrested and charged with a felony, he challenged the constitutionality of the order in a case that reached the Supreme Court. In a 6-3 decision, the court ruled against him, but Justice Robert Jackson's dissent was particularly eloquent and is remembered to this day. "Korematsu... has been convicted of an act not commonly a crime," he wrote. "It consists merely of being present in the state whereof he is a citizen, near the place where he was born, and where all his life he has lived...[it] did not result from anything he did, said, or thought...but only in that he was born of different racial stock...." and because "...he is the son of parents as to whom he had no choice, and belongs to a race from which there is no way to resign." Forty-one years later, Korematsu's conviction was vacated, but the case was not overturned; that is, the logic the majority used to justify it remains in force, lying in wait, as Jackson predicted it would, "...like a loaded weapon ready for the hand of any authority that can bring forward a plausible claim of urgent need."

sheer cliff. In the darkness, some lost their handhold or their footing and they fell to their deaths in the ravine below. They all fell silently. Not a single one cried out, so as not to give their position away. The men climbed for eight hours straight, and those who made it to the top stayed there until the first break of light, and as soon as light broke, they attacked. The Germans were surprised, and they took the hill and broke the Gothic Line. A six-month stalemate was broken by the 442nd in 32 minutes.

It was an amazing act, and when the war ended, the 442nd returned to the United States as the most decorated unit of World War II. They were greeted on the White House lawn by President Harry S. Truman, who said to them, "You fought not only the enemy but prejudice, and you won."

They are my heroes. They clung to their belief in the shining ideals of this country, and they proved that being an American is not just for some people, that race is not how we define being an American. They expanded what it means to be an American, including Japanese Americans that were feared and suspected and hated. They were change agents, and they left a legacy for me. They are my heroes, and my father is my hero, who understood democracy and guided me through it. They gave me a legacy, and with that legacy comes a responsibility. I am dedicated to making my country an even better America, to making our government an even truer democracy. Because of these heroes and their struggles, I can stand before you as a gay Japanese American, but even more importantly, I can stand before you as a proud American. ∎

With a career of five decades in television and film, **George Takei** is known worldwide for his role in the original three seasons of the television series *Star Trek*, in which he played Hikaru Sulu, helmsman of the Starship Enterprise. He reprised this role in six *Star Trek* movies, and has an extensive résumé in voice-over and documentary narration. A social justice activist who has served as spokesperson for the Human Rights Campaign's "Coming Out Project" and cultural ambassador for Japanese Americans, he is an author and social media megapower, with 2 million followers on Twitter, cited by Mashable.com as the most influential person on Facebook. 🐦 *@GeorgeTakei*

Courtesy of TED. George Takei, July 2014. Watch the complete TED Talk on TED.com

AGAINST THE MAJESTIC backdrop of the Sierra mountains (above), an American flag whips in the wind over the dust-blown Manzanar internment camp in the California desert east of Los Angeles. Photographer Dorothea Lange captured the harsh conditions of daily life in these camps, all of which were located in remote Western deserts or the swamplands of the Deep South. 📷 DOROTHEA LANGE

UNDER THE WATCHFUL EYE of rifle-toting U.S. troops (right), neatly dressed Japanese Americans line up on April 5, 1942, after arriving at a government assembly center at the Santa Anita racetrack outside Los Angeles. Given just one week to settle their affairs, more than 18,000 men, women, and children were crammed into filthy horse stalls and hastily built tar-paper shacks surrounded by barbed wire and armed guards. The Japanese Americans endured communal latrines, open sewers, and sweltering heat until the end of October 1942, when they were relocated to permanent internment camps across the West and Arkansas where they stayed until 1945. 📷 CLEM ALBERS

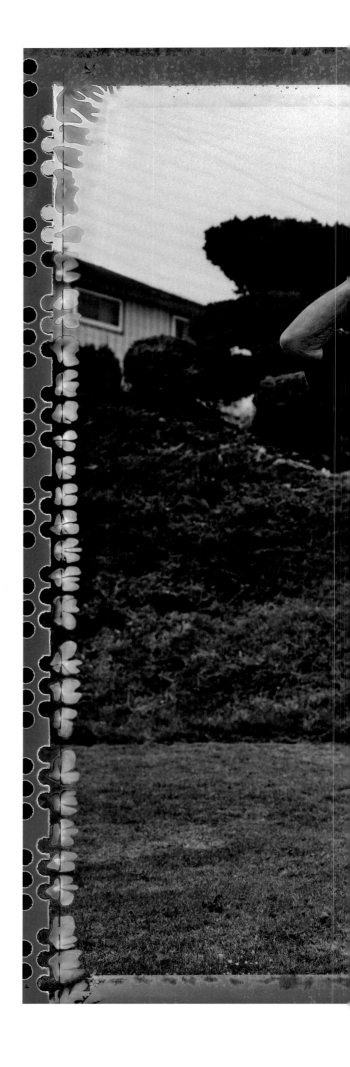

JAPANESE AMERICAN Boy Scouts (above, left to right) Junzo Ohara, 14; Takeshi Motoyasu, 14; and Eddie Tetsuji Kato, 16, all born in Los Angeles, salute the stars and stripes on June 5, 1943, during the morning flag-raising ceremony at the Heart Mountain War Relocation Center in Cody, Wyoming. Despite their internment, Japanese Americans participated in ceremonies like this to demonstrate their loyalty to the United States. "I never thought of myself as a Jap," Kato later told photographer Paul Kitagaki Jr. "I just thought of myself as an American citizen, because that's how I was raised." 📷 PAT COFFEY

THE SAME TRIO, 70 years later (right), stand and salute in Monterey Park, California. This then-and-now photo is part of an historical remembrance project that photographer Paul Kitagaki began after finding pictures of his own family in the National Archive among Dorothea Lange's 1942 photographs of Japanese American internees. "As I examined Lange's work, I realized that every photograph represented an untold story that was quietly buried in the past," Kitagaki says. Since then, he has photographed and recorded the stories of some three dozen of the National Archive's original subjects. 📷 PAUL KITAGAKI JR.

WASHINGTON, D.C., FEBRUARY 24, 2009. Supreme Court Justice Ruth Bader Ginsburg arrives for U.S. President Barack Obama's address to a joint session of Congress.
📷 PABLO MARTINEZ MONSIVAIS

JEWISH AMERICANS

RUTH BADER GINSBURG, born in 1933, is one of only 8 Jews and 4 women to have served on the U.S. Supreme Court and the first Jewish woman justice in the court's history.

Throughout her trailblazing legal career, Ginsburg has felt the sting of both gender discrimination and anti-Semitism. In 1954, she took a job with a Social Security office in Oklahoma, where her husband was working, but when she became pregnant, her boss demoted her and reduced her pay. At Harvard Law School, she had only eight female classmates, who were asked by the dean how they justified taking a spot at the school that otherwise would have gone to a man.

After transferring to Columbia Law School and graduating at the top of her class, Ginsburg had difficulty finding a job at a traditional law firm. "To be a woman, a Jew, and a mother to boot—that combination was a bit too much," she noted later.

In 1971, presenting her first brief before the Supreme Court, against legislation purporting to shield women from the dangerous world outside the family home, Ginsburg commented acidly, "The pedestal upon which women have been placed has all too often, upon closer inspection, been revealed as a cage."

President Bill Clinton, nominating Ginsburg for a Supreme Court seat in 1993, said, "She is to the women's movement what former Supreme Court Justice Thurgood Marshall was to the movement for the rights of African Americans."

Ginsburg has maintained that reputation, supporting abortion rights, defending women in gender discrimination cases, and defending laws that open doors for the nation's minorities. Ginsburg has often used her frail, soft voice to read her dissents aloud—a highly unusual departure from the staid traditions of the Supreme Court—something that *The New York Times* called "the equivalent of shaming your spouse in front of dinner guests." ∎

THE DEVIL THAT NEVER DIES
BY RICHARD BERNSTEIN

THE PICTURES WERE REMINDERS in their way—rows of gravestones at a Jewish cemetery near St. Louis knocked over early in 2017 by some unknown vandals. Published in newspapers around the globe, the images recalled an unavoidable fact of American life, namely that no matter how successful Jews have been in the United States, no matter how assimilated, how accepted, there's always that streak of resentment, the white supremacist impulse to see the Jews as somehow alien, not belonging, a menace to the "purity" of American blood.

Of course, the likelihood is that the toppled gravestones were the work of some otherwise powerless person or persons taking their frustrations out on a group, the Jews, who throughout history have always been available for scapegoating and held responsible for everything from bubonic plague to the Great Depression. There were other incidents as well—the Anti-Defamation League (ADL) reports that in 2016 over 800 Jewish journalists received anti-Semitic tweets with an estimated reach of 45 million; graffiti reading "The Holocaust is fake history" was scrawled on the wall of a synagogue in liberal, tolerant Seattle; so-called "alt-right" white extremists giving each other the Hitler salute at a meeting in Washington, D.C., following the inauguration of

MINNEAPOLIS, MINNESOTA, NOVEMBER 9, 1988. Separated from the original event by 50 years and 5,000 miles, Jewish students and teachers at the University of Minnesota hold a candlelight service commemorating the anniversary of *Kristallnacht*, the "Night of Broken Glass," when laws that should have protected German Jews from violent Nazi anti-Semitism were revealed to be a sham. On the evening of November 9, 1938, Nazi gangs, spurred on by Hitler's propaganda chief, Joseph Goebbels, savagely beat Jewish citizens and destroyed or damaged more than 1,000 synagogues and 7,500 Jewish businesses across Germany. The police, by then acting as an arm of the regime's new racial politics, did nothing to stop the violence. Today, many historians consider *Kristallnacht* to be the night when the Holocaust began. 📷 JOE ROSSI

Donald Trump, whose unexpected election victory was due, at least in part, to his anti-immigration rhetoric. All scary, all worrisome. As the writer Daniel Jonah Goldhagen has noted, hatred of Jews is truly "the devil that never dies," even in America.

Jewish participation in the good fight has been long, difficult, and, for the most part, successful. Jews had to fight hard for acceptance and opportunity in the United States, and their struggle for civil rights and equality began literally the day Jews first set foot in North America.

In 1654, 23 Jews arrived in what was then the Dutch colony of New Amsterdam, now New York City. They were the first Jewish refugees to the North American colonies, having been expelled from Recife in the Portuguese colony in Brazil. Despite the Dutch tradition of tolerance for the Jews, the founder and leader of New Amsterdam, Peter Stuyvesant, saw them as "enemies and blasphemers of Christ" and wanted them expelled. But Stuyvesant did not have his way, which established a pattern that was to repeat itself over the centuries. Back in the Netherlands, Jewish investors in the Dutch West India Company put pressure on the home office to allow the Jews to stay, and they did.

For the next couple of centuries, there wasn't much in the way of blatant persecution of the Jews, in part because there were so few of them—about 15,000 as of 1840, less than 0.1 percent of the total population of 17 million.

Still, the notion that the Jews were a suspect, alien presence never disappeared. In 1862, in a famous incident during the Civil War, Ulysses S. Grant, then commander of the Army of the Tennessee, issued the notorious Order No. 11, which expelled all the estimated 4,000 Jews from his military district, which included Kentucky and Mississippi.

Grant was furious about smuggling across enemy lines, and, indeed, historians agree that some of the smugglers were Jews. Others were not, however, and yet Order No. 11 required only "the Jews as a class" to leave. But in the end, like those 23 Jewish arrivals in New Amsterdam in 1654, none of them were actually forced to go. A Jewish merchant from Paducah, Kentucky, Cesar J. Kaskel, protested the order directly to President Abraham Lincoln, who immediately rescinded it. Grant himself is reported to have regretted issuing it all his life.

Order No. 11 came in the midst of the first great wave of Jewish migration to the United States, consisting mostly of German Jews who arrived in the years just before and just after the Civil War. The Germans were generally well educated, and, whatever anti-Jewish animus they may have encountered, they represented the first great success of Jews in American life. After only a very few years, they formed a sort of Jewish aristocracy—the bankers and philanthropists, the Loebs, the Warburgs, the Guggenheims, and the Schiffs, who became one of the wealthiest communities in American life.

The second wave of immigration was different. It consisted of 2 million poverty-stricken and generally not well-educated Jews from Russia and Eastern

THE BRONX, NEW YORK, 1944.
Even at the height of World War II, anti-Semitism was still rampant in the United States. Vandals scrawled hate messages on a Jewish-owned shop window in the Bronx during the 1944 presidential campaign between the Democratic incumbent, Franklin Delano Roosevelt, and his Republican challenger, Thomas E. Dewey. While Dewey himself was not an anti-Semite, there were concerns among some Jews that the Republican's work as a prosecutor rightfully pursuing, among others, Jewish mobsters may have encouraged the kind of anti-Semitic feelings represented in this defacement.

Europe who arrived between 1880 and 1924. This was the era of the Lower East Side in New York and similar places elsewhere: overcrowded, poverty-stricken, disease-ridden places, the Yiddish-speaking slums that social reformers like Jacob Riis wrote about and photographed.

With more Jews, there was more prejudice. There was the snobbish disdain of men like Henry Adams, the son and grandson of presidents, who complained in 1918 about "a furtive Yacoob or Ysaac still reeking of the Ghetto, snarling a weird Yiddish." Adams' prejudice was matched by a discrimination that echoed the more violent and more systematic hatred of Jews in Europe. Arthur Hertzberg, one of the prime historians of the American Jewish experience, imagines a Jew on his way home from the citizenship ceremony where he has just sworn allegiance to the Constitution, passing "signs in shop windows, advertising for sales help, saying 'No Jews wanted.'"

After World War I, feeling against Jews intensified as anti-immigrant sentiment increased. Wilbur Carr, the head of the United States Consular Service, accused the Jews of being "filthy, un-American, and often dangerous in their habits." The automobile tycoon Henry Ford, who was a kind of anti-Semite-in-chief, financed an explicitly anti-Jewish newspaper, *The Dearborn Independent*, which ran banner headlines like: "The International Jew: The World's Problem."

Richard Snow, in his book "I Invented the Modern Age: The Rise of Henry Ford," reflects on the fact that despite Ford's subsequent claim that he had had a change of heart, "he could not shut down *The International Jew*, a book drawn from the interminable series. It has kept bobbing to the surface in the publishing cloacae of

the world's capitals ever since. By 1933 it had run through 29 editions in Germany alone. Henry Ford is the only American mentioned in *Mein Kampf*. Although the Jews were "increasingly the controlling master" of American labor, wrote Adolf Hitler, "one great man, Ford, to their exasperation still holds out independently."

Sentiments like that helped enact a new law passed by Congress in 1924 that severely cut back the numbers of Jews (and Italians) who could be admitted into the United States, ending the mass migration of Jews from Eastern Europe.

In the 1930s, the Great Depression spurred a revival of the old stereotype, as the historian Irving Howe put it, of "the Jew as a figure of surreptitious accumulation ... performing mysterious rites in the dives of the modern city." Anti-Jewish feeling was fanned most famously by the Catholic priest Charles Coughlin, whose millions of radio listeners heard him spew venom like: "When we get through with the Jews in America, they'll think the treatment they received in Germany was nothing." Adding to anti-Jewish feeling was the America First advocacy of the aviator-hero Charles Lindbergh, who was an unabashed admirer and friend of Hitler and made speeches declaring the Jews to be "not American in interests and viewpoints."

The Jews of course had a collective memory of the pogroms of the Old Country, and they were painfully aware of the vicious persecution of Europe's Jews by the Nazis. For them, it was terrifying to witness this growing crescendo of Jew hatred. It raised the question in many minds: Could "it" happen in America?

But "it" didn't happen. The Jews fought back, creating organizations like the American Jewish Committee to protect their interests. In 1913, the Anti-Defamation League was founded "to put an end forever to unjust and unfair

BUCHENWALD, GERMANY, APRIL 1945. Allied commander General Dwight D. Eisenhower (above, left) surveys the dead bodies of prisoners who had been executed by Nazi guards moments before after U.S. forces liberated the Ohrdruf concentration camp near the German town of Buchenwald. When Eisenhower learned about the horrific scenes of death and mistreatment at the concentration camps, he ordered as many photographs taken as possible to preserve the gruesome record of the brutality. Many of the photos were later used as evidence against Nazi leaders during the 1946 Nuremberg war crimes trials.
◉ WILLIAM NEWHOUSE

USING EMOTIONAL IMAGES such as the one above showing the shadow of a swastika threatening American children, the advertising campaign to persuade Americans to buy war bonds became the most successful in the nation's history. The campaign began on radio, in newspapers, and in magazines and grew to employ Hollywood movie stars, famous entertainers, sport figures, and even familiar comic strip characters. Irving Berlin, the Russian-Jewish immigrant who became the country's best-known composer, discrimination against any sect or body of citizens." The Jews perfected the art of working behind the scenes, making their arguments directly to politicians and officeholders and in books and articles. They also had friends in high places, most notably Franklin D. Roosevelt, who nominated many Jews to high positions, most famously his treasury secretary and close adviser Henry Morgenthau Jr., and was deeply beloved by the Jews as a result.

But most of all, the Jews fought their way into American life by being hard-working, successful, in many instances, by using their wealth to benefit others. A prime example of this was Jacob Schiff, the German-Jewish head of the banking firm Kuhn, Loeb & Co., who donated to causes as diverse as Harvard University and the American Jewish Committee. But, of course, there were successful and rich Jews in Germany, too, and they were helpless in the face of Hitler and German anti-Semitism. People like Schiff were able to exert their influence because the United States was not Poland or Russia or Germany. Many Americans harbored the old dislike of the Jews, but the worst of European anti-Semitism—the violence, the pogroms, the expulsions, the daily insults, and terrors—never happened in America. The Jews weren't loved exactly, but, then again, neither were the Irish or the Italians when they first arrived.

And so, the Jews were able to pull themselves out of the slums of the Lower East Side, and many of them made it big. Yiddish-speaking men like Samuel Goldwyn and the Warner brothers created Hollywood. Jewish-owned stores like Macy's and Bloomingdale's became famous and fashionable. As early as 1909, Jews, who were then roughly 2 to 3 percent of the general population, made up more than 10 percent of the students at Harvard and 25 percent of the students in American medical schools, despite efforts to impose quotas to keep these institutions from becoming "too Jewish." In 1916, Louis Brandeis became the first Jewish American named to the Supreme Court.

From this point on, something unprecedented in Jewish history occurred: The Jewish culture, like the African American culture, became American—or perhaps it was the other way around. The comics who came from the Yiddish theater in New York were the first to cross over—Al Jolson, then Sid Caesar, and then, after him, Woody Allen, Jerry Seinfeld, and Jon Stewart. There were the writers like Saul Bellow, Philip Roth, and Bernard Malamud, who transformed the Jewish experience into American literature. There were Irving Berlin (who wrote "God Bless America"), the Gershwin brothers, and Bob Dylan; scientists like Jonas Salk, who discovered the cure for polio; Hall of Fame baseball legends Hank Greenberg and Sandy Koufax; journalists like Walter Lippmann, Walter Winchell, and David Halberstam. The creators of great American comic book heroes like Superman were Jerry Siegel and Joe Shuster, both Jews; Nat Fleischer invented Betty Boop. A very long list of other cultural icons includes Barbra Streisand, Betty Friedan, Dr. Seuss, Norman Mailer, Estée Lauder, Leonard Bernstein, Steven Spielberg, and many more.

wrote a catchy tune called "Any Bonds Today?" that became the theme song of the government's war bonds program. With this ubiquitous message, war bonds became the principal channel for those at home to show their support for the war effort. More than 85 million Americans—half the nation's population—bought war bonds totaling nearly $186 billion.

JEWISH AMERICANS have figured prominently in fights for the rights and freedoms granted under the U.S. Constitution. Associate Justice Louis Brandeis (above, with his wife, Alice) was a brilliant progressive in his approach to the law and the first Jew ever to serve on the U.S. Supreme Court. Working closely with his Supreme Court colleague, Oliver Wendell Holmes Jr., Brandeis helped to develop the modern, expansive understanding of the limits to "freedom of speech." He was also the first legal thinker to examine the idea of a "right to privacy." Brandeis defended the rights of workers and pushed to curb the power of monopolies, large banks, and corporations. ⌖ HARRIS & EWING

Today, in 2017, three of the United States Supreme Court justices, nine senators, 23 members of the House of Representatives, one state governor (and 23 former governors), plus the mayors of big cities, from Anchorage to Chicago to Tucson, are Jewish. The days of Jewish quotas at places like Harvard and Yale are long gone; one-fifth to one-quarter of the students at those universities are Jews. The ultimate accolade for achievement in science and humanities is the Nobel Prize; 352 American citizens have won it over the years. Nearly a third of them (112) were Jewish. Despite these remarkable achievements across all aspects of American life today, in 2017, the Jews only comprise roughly 2 percent of the American population.

Talent, organization, and hard work produced this remarkable result, but there were also the changes brought about by two world-historical events. One was the Holocaust, the murder of 6 million Jews by the Nazis, which helped to make overt anti-Semitism unacceptable, because it showed so dramatically the horrifying extremes to which bigotry can go. The Holocaust also, weirdly, gave rise to a new strain of anti-Semitism, not widespread but vicious and dangerous, namely Holocaust denial, the slander that the Jews had somehow "invented" the Holocaust in order to gain sympathy and special treatment. But its main effect has been a lesson, seized upon by major figures like Pope John Paul II, who brought into the Catholic Church the idea that anti-Semitism is a sin.

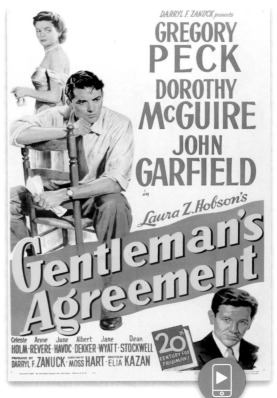

The other event was the creation of Israel and its emergence as a democratic ally of the United States that inspires very favorable feelings among Americans. Polls show that more than 60 percent of Americans side with Israel in the Arab-Israeli conflict and only 15 percent with the Palestinians. Candidates for president vie with each other to show how strong their friendship is with Israel.

Israel has diminished the stereotype of the Jews as weak, parasitical, and preoccupied with money, but its occupation of Palestinian-majority territory has come with a price in deep animosity to Israel, especially on the part of American liberals and leftists, some of whom support a growing boycott, divestment, and sanctions (BDS) movement. ADL believes that while some supporters of BDS may genuinely believe that these efforts will encourage Israel to change policies with which they disagree, the intent and the predominant drive of the BDS campaign is anti-Semitic, since it is fueled by the desire to deny Israel's right to exist.

The struggle, in other words, is not over. Still, as Howe, the great historian of Jewish life in America, wrote, the main Jewish quest in the United States has been for "a normal life." He meant life liberated from the "humiliating passivity," of the "pogroms, upheavals," the constant sense of insecurity and terror that represented the not-so-normal life of the Jews for most of the 2,000 years of the diaspora.

It is fair to say that despite the residue of historic anti-Semitism that remains, despite the occasional spasms of hostility to their very presence on American soil, right now in 2017, more Jews live in conditions of peace and prosperity in

THE 1947 FILM *Gentleman's Agreement* (left, middle) was one of the first Hollywood movies to explore the theme of anti-Semitism. It told the story of a journalist, played by Gregory Peck, who poses as a Jew to research an exposé on anti-Semitism in the polite circles of New York City and Darien, Connecticut, a wealthy New York suburb. The movie was a critical and commercial success, winning three Oscars, including Best Picture and Best Director. Ever since a great wave of Jewish immigrants arrived on American shores in the late nineteenth century, their experiences have provided fodder for a unique school of self-deprecating Jewish humor that has helped define Jewish American stereotypes. The Marx Brothers (left, top) provided what some critics have called "smart slapstick," making movies, such as *Duck Soup* and *A Night at the Opera*, that placed them among the most influential comedians of the twentieth century. Comedian, actor, and filmmaker Woody Allen (above), popularized the character of the neurotic New York Jewish intellectual in such films as *Manhattan* and *Annie Hall*, which set the standard for modern romantic comedy. The self-referential TV series *Seinfeld* (left, bottom), focused on four self-involved singles in New York whose inability to commit to anyone or anything parodied the spirit of the times in the United States. Director and producer Steven Spielberg (with his mother, Leah Adler, above, right) made movies that ranged from *Jaws* and *Raiders of the Lost Ark* to *Schindler's List* and *Lincoln*. He is regarded as one of the most popular filmmakers in history.
📷 STEVE SCHAPIRO, ABOVE;
BRIAN LANKER, ABOVE, RIGHT

the United States than at any other time or place in all of history. They owe it to many things, not least that America, despite its resistance, its waffling, its spasms of the old hatreds, lived up to the principles of religious freedom and toleration. But the Jews also owe their success to their unity in the struggle against bigotry with other persecuted minorities. It's not an accident that two of the young civil rights workers murdered in Mississippi in 1964—in an incident that called global attention to the struggle for racial justice in America—were Jews. Michael Schwerner and Andrew Goodman, cut down along with James Chaney, who was black, were all trying to enable African Americans to register to vote.

Because of their own long experience, the Jews have had a natural sympathy for other victims of hatred and discrimination. That's why Jews have always been overwhelmingly on the liberal side of the political spectrum, large majorities of them in favor of rights for minorities, laws against discrimination, and opposed to restrictions on immigration based on religion or nationality. They have understood that as long as any group is subject to exclusion, all groups are vulnerable, and that to fight for everyone is the only sure way to achieve true equality and respect. There is probably nothing more American than the fact that Jews consider everyone else's struggle their own struggle. ■

Richard Bernstein was born in New York, grew up on a poultry farm in Connecticut, and studied Chinese history at Harvard before becoming one of the first American journalists to be stationed in the People's Republic of China, opening the *Time* bureau in Beijing in 1980. He spent 25 years as a staff correspondent for *The New York Times*, for which he has reported from more than two dozen countries in Asia, Europe, and Africa. His other postings have been as the *Times's* national cultural correspondent and, for five years, daily book critic. He is the author of nine books, most recently, *China 1945: Mao's Revolution and America's Fateful Choice*. 🐦 @R_Bernstein

GOD BLESS AMERICA
BY IRVING BERLIN

While the storm clouds gather far across the sea,
Let us swear allegiance to a land that's free,
Let us all be grateful for a land so fair,
As we raise our voices in a solemn prayer.

God Bless America,
Land that I love.
Stand beside her, and guide her
Thru the night with a light from above.
From the mountains, to the prairies,
To the oceans, white with foam
God bless America, My home sweet home.

When 5-year-old Irving Berlin and his immigrant family reached New York Harbor in 1893, the first thing they saw from the deck of their ship was the Statue of Liberty, her raised arm holding a torch that symbolically lighted the way to their new country. That gesture meant a great deal to Berlin, whose earliest memory was watching his house in Russia burn to the ground in an anti-Jewish pogrom. Berlin grew up to become one of the greatest songwriters in American history, and on the eve of World War II, he wrote "God Bless America" as a love song to the country that had taken him in and given him everything he had. *LIFE* magazine featured him on its cover in 1934 and praised "this itinerant son of a Russian cantor" as "an American institution." "God Bless America" became the unofficial national anthem of the United States in 1938. In a touching tribute at Berlin's 100th birthday, the celebrated journalist Walter Cronkite shared that Berlin "helped write the story of this country, capturing the best of who we are and the dreams that shape our lives." ■

INSPIRED BY "LADY LIBERTY," poet Emma Lazarus, an affluent New Yorker, believed that successful American Jews had a responsibility to welcome less fortunate newcomers of all races and backgrounds. Lazarus wrote "The New Colossus," a poem containing the heralded phrase "Give me your tired, your poor, your huddled masses yearning to breathe free." In 1903, 15 years after Lazarus passed away, the lines of her poem were engraved on a bronze plaque in the pedestal of the Statue of Liberty. ⊙ JAY FINE

THE JEWISH AMERICAN JOURNEY

1903
Oscar Straus is appointed secretary of labor and commerce, the first Jew to hold a Cabinet post.

1903
Emma Lazarus' 1883 sonnet *The New Colossus,* is mounted in the pedestal of the Statue of Liberty. (Today, it's in the Statue of Liberty Museum.) It includes these lines:

"...Give me your tired, your poor, Your huddled masses yearning to breathe free..."

1913 The **Anti-Defamation League** is founded by B'nai B'rith.

1916 Louis Brandeis is first Jew appointed to the Supreme Court.

1917 ADL mounts a campaign to give Americans the facts about Jewish contributions to the war effort.

Between the wars, anti-Semitism reaches a peak following the rise of the Ku Klux Klan, Henry Ford's writings, and Father Charles Coughlin's radio speeches.

By **1932,** the Rosenwald Fund (founded by **Julius Rosenwald** in 1917) has supported the construction of more than 5,000 schools for African American children in the South.

1933 Jerry Siegel and Joe Shuster create the **Superman** character.

1939 Jewish population worldwide reaches a peak of 17 million.

1945 11 million (Today, it's about 13 million worldwide.)

1953 Ethel and Julius Rosenberg are executed for conspiring to sell atomic secrets to the Soviet Union.

1948 The **state of israel** is established as a new nation.

1900 2 million to 3 million Jews in the U.S. (2% of the population)

1900	'10	'20	'30	'40	'50

Between 1880 and 1914, some 2 million Yiddish-speaking Ashkenazi Jews come to the United States from Russia and from the "Pale of Settlement" (what are now Belarus, Lithuania, Poland, Moldova, and Ukraine).

1915 Despite weak evidence, **Leo Frank** is found guilty of the murder of a young girl and while serving a sentence of life in prison is kidnapped and lynched by an anti-Semitic mob that includes elected officials and community leaders.

Frank is posthumously pardoned in 1986.

1921 Fanny Brice introduces her biggest hit song, *My Man,* in **Florenz Ziegfeld**'s *Follies.* Better known today is *Second Hand Rose,* also from the *Follies* of 1921.

1931 George Gershwin's *Of Thee I Sing* is first musical to win a Pulitzer Prize.

1938 Irving Berlin's *God Bless America* becomes America's second National Anthem, after Kate Smith sings it at the 20th anniversary of the end of World War I.

In **World War II,** 500,000 American Jews enlist (half of all Jewish males aged 18–50). Many of them eat "Ham for Uncle Sam" to fit in.

1945 Bess Myerson is the first Jewish Miss America.

1946 Estée Lauder starts her career in cosmetics.

1948 Brandeis University is founded, only Jewish-sponsored college in the U.S.

1955 Jonas Salk's polio vaccine is introduced.

When asked if he owns the patent on it, he says: "There is no patent. Could you patent the sun?" By 2003, polio is eradicated in all but a few countries.

1924
The Johnson-Reed Act severely restricts immigration. 86% of the 165,000 permitted entries are from Northern European countries, effectively diminishing Jewish immigration from Eastern Europe.

1930 Betty Boop, created by Max Fleischer, makes her first appearance.

The movie moguls
Samuel L. Goldwyn (1879–1974)
Louis B. Mayer (1884–1957)
Warner Brothers (Jack 1892–1978, Harry 1881–1958)
David O. Selznick (1902–1965)
They start in cinema's early years and go on to found famous Hollywood studios, where these vaudeville performers, among others, get their start:
Jack Benny, the **Marx Brothers,** and **Molly Picon.**

1927 The **Warner Brothers'** *The Jazz Singer,* starring **Al Jolson** as the son of a cantor, is the first talking picture.

Sources
U.S. Holocaust Memorial Museum; ADL

1969 Golda Meir, whose family came to the United States in 1906, when she was 8, becomes the fourth prime minister of Israel.

1968 Abbie Hoffman and **Jerry Rubin** are arrested for protesting the Vietnam War.

1993 U.S. Holocaust Memorial Museum is opened. The first visitor is the 14th Dalai Lama of Tibet.

In 2002, a federal jury convicts two white supremacists of planning to bomb institutions associated with African American and American Jewish communities, including the Holocaust Museum.

In 2009, James von Brunn, an anti-Semite, shoots and kills Stephen Johns, a museum police officer. (Brunn dies during his trial in 2010.)

1992 Ruth Bader Ginsburg is first Jewish woman appointed to the U.S. Supreme Court.

2016 Presidential election campaign is sullied by **anti-Semitism.**

ADL estimates that there were 2.6 million anti-Semitic tweets over a one-year period leading up to the election.

1957 Leonard Bernstein's *West Side Story,* with book by **Arthur Laurents** and lyrics by **Stephen Sondheim,** opens on Broadway. Based on *Romeo and Juliet,* the show describes a rivalry between two street gangs, one Puerto Rican, the other white.

1978 Isaac Bashevis Singer awarded Nobel Prize for Literature.

1987 250,000 march in Washington, D.C., to protest persecution of Jews in the Soviet Union.

1970 5.4 million Jews in the U.S. (2.6% of the population.)

2000 Joseph Lieberman is first Jewish vice-presidential candidate to be nominated by a major party.

2007 Jewish Theological Seminary accepts gay and lesbian students in rabbinical and cantorial schools.

2010 5.3 million Jews in the U.S. (1.7% of the population.)

'60 **'70** **'80** **'90** **2000** **'10**

1964 *Fiddler on the Roof* opens on Broadway and is the first musical to run for more than 3,000 performances.

1972 Sally Priesand is first female rabbi.

1972 At age 36, **Sandy Koufax** is youngest player ever elected to the Baseball Hall of Fame.

HELLO, NEWMAN!

1994 *Schindler's List,* directed by Steven Spielberg, wins Oscar for best picture.

2001 World Trade Center is attacked.

Conspiracy theorists suggest that Israel orchestrated the attack, and warned Jewish workers. (It is claimed that no Jews died in the towers. In fact, between 270 and 400 did.)

In 2003, ADL publishes a report refuting the idea of a conspiracy, fearing that such a theory would fuel global anti-Semitism.

2017 The Chicago Loop Synagogue is plastered with swastikas and windows are shattered in an apparent hate crime.

Gravestones in Jewish cemeteries in St. Louis and Phildelphia are toppled over.

1963 Betty Friedan publishes *The Feminine Mystique.* In 1996, she establishes the National Organization for Women.

1989 Jerry Seinfeld's long-running TV show starts.

Famous Jewish comedians

Lewis Black	Danny Kaye
Mel Brooks	Jerry Lewis
Lenny Bruce	Gilda Radner
Sid Caesar	Harold Ramis
Billy Crystal	Don Rickles
Rodney Dangerfield	Seth Rogen
Larry David	Garry Shandling
Marty Feldman	Sarah Silverman
Buddy Hackett	Jon Stewart
Andy Kaufman	Gene Wilder

Early 1960s **Freedom Riders** campaign against segregation in the South.

It's estimated that half the white Freedom Riders were Jews, including **Andrew Goodman** (age 21) and **Michael Schwerner** (25) who, with African American **James Chaney** (21), were murdered by the Ku Klux Klan in Mississippi.

The last half of the 20th century sees a flowering of Jewish talent in many areas of the arts.
A partial list includes these famous names...

Woody Allen, filmmaker
Lauren Bacall, actor
Saul Bellow, author
Judy Blume, author
Bob Dylan, musician
Allen Ginsberg, poet
Dustin Hoffman, actor
Donna Karan, couturier
Carole King, musician

Bette Midler, musician
Marilyn Monroe, actor
Cynthia Ozick, author
Itzhak Perlman, musician
Lou Reed, musician
Jerome Robbins, dancer
Paul Simon, musician
Barbra Streisand, musician
Elizabeth Taylor, actor

...these fine artists...

Judy Chicago
Jim Dine
Helen Frankenthaler
Milton Glaser
Philip Guston
Alex Katz
Sol LeWitt
Roy Lichtenstein
Mark Rothko

...and the next generation of actors

Adrien Brody
Jennifer Connelly
Zac Efron
Jesse Eisenberg
James Franco
Jake Gyllenhaal
Jonah Hill
Scarlett Johansson
Natalie Portman

NORMAN LEAR

Director, producer, and writer Norman Lear is one of the most influential people in TV history. In 1971, *All in the Family* inaugurated an era of TV programming that used comedy to confront controversial issues of race, sexuality, and inequality. *Maude* included abortion as a topic of discussion. *The Jeffersons* was the first TV show to feature middle-class African Americans as its main characters. At one point, six of Lear's shows were on TV at the same time—a personal production record that still stands. Lear, now 95, has maintained a busy second career as a political activist, founding People for the American Way, which advocates for First Amendment rights, public education, and campaign finance reform. He also founded the group Declare Yourself to register young voters. Awarding Lear the 1999 National Medal of the Arts, President Bill Clinton said: "Norman Lear has held up a mirror to American society and changed the way we look at it."

NEW YORK, MARCH 9, 2014.
Thousands of ultra-Orthodox Hasidic Jews (left, top) gather in New York on Water Street in Lower Manhattan to pray and to protest against the Israeli government's proposal to draft strictly religious citizens into its army. Hasidic survivors of the Nazi Holocaust began arriving in the United States after World War II. After settling primarily in New York and surrounding regions, it was believed that they would abandon their insular ways and assimilate into the American mainstream. But they have maintained their traditions and grown into the largest Hasidic community outside Israel, where they have long been exempt from military service. Many American Hasidic Jews also maintain Israeli citizenship or have family who live in Israel, a connection that sometimes causes events in Israel, such as the proposed religious draft, to play out in the streets of New York. 📷 CRAIG RUTTLE

PROVIDENCE, RHODE ISLAND, 1989. Toward the end of the twentieth century, American society began a slow move away from homogeneity to allow for more overt displays of racial and religious difference. At Brown University, for instance, sophomore Reuben Beiser (above) found a welcome atmosphere in Hebrew House, a coed wing of one dormitory set aside for Orthodox and Conservative Jewish students who keep kosher and want to maintain their Jewish identity on the secular campus. Here Beiser wears the traditional *talit*, or prayer shawl, around his shoulders and *tfillin*—tiny boxes holding parchment scrolls inscribed messages from the Torah—on his head and left arm as he engages in morning prayers in his dorm room. Thirty years later, colleges and universities are battling a resurgence of anti-Semitism, coming from both the Left and the Right. In 2016, Brown students projecting a pro-Palestinian view prevented a lecture on transgender rights from taking place because the talk was sponsored by the campus chapter of Hillel. Only days later, a Jewish fraternity at Brown was marred by anti-Semitic graffiti that declared "Holocaust 2.0." 📷 BILL BALLENBERG

ST. PAUL, MINNESOTA, JULY 2015.
Amaiya Zafar, a 16-year-old Muslim boxer,
dreams of representing the United States at
the Tokyo Olympics in 2020, but USA Boxing
notified her that she may not compete while
wearing a hijab and modest, long-sleeved
clothing under her jersey and shorts. Many in
the sports world believe that the same
organizations that embraced Muhammad Ali
and Kareem Abdul-Jabbar before 9/11 should
now also embrace young women like Zafar,
who are seek to wear clothing acceptable to
their faith. Another athlete setting the stage
for change is Ibtihaj Muhammad, the first
Muslim American woman to wear a hijab while
competing on the U.S. fencing team at the
2016 Rio Olympics. 📷 AARON LAVINSKY

MUSLIM AMERICANS

IN 1765, **THOMAS JEFFERSON,** then a law student, had a copy of the Quran shipped from England to Williamsburg, Virginia. Jefferson was an avid, curious reader, and a champion of religious liberties. He embraced the religious rights of the people he called the "Mahamdan," enshrining their right to worship in the Declaration of Independence.

In 2007, Keith Ellison of Minnesota placed his hand on Jefferson's Quran and swore his ceremonial oath, becoming the first Muslim in the U.S. Congress.

Current headlines suggest that Islam is hostile to the United States and that Muslims are strangers in this land. In fact, nearly 15 percent of the Africans brought forcibly to this continent were Muslim, like Yarrow Mamout, a slave from Guinea brought to Annapolis, Maryland, in 1752. He gained his freedom and became an entrepreneur and property owner, owning stock in the Columbia Bank of Georgetown.

Muslims' blood, sweat, hopes, and dreams have fertilized American soil for 400 years, with little recognition in our ongoing narrative. From the late nineteenth century to the 1920s, Middle Eastern immigrants, in particular from Syria and Lebanon, settled in the Midwest. Now, nearly 4 million Muslims call America home, and halal shawarmas, hummus, and falafel are as American as apple pie.

The oldest standing mosque in the United States was built as far back as 1934, in Cedar Rapids, Iowa. Despite the anti-Muslim protests today, more than 2,000 mosques are found from the Bay Area to New Mexico, North Dakota to Texas, from the Boston suburbs to the tip of Florida.

The Immigration and Nationality Act of 1965 relaxed restrictive quotas, bringing in skilled professionals who became entrepreneurs, doctors, engineers, and blue-collar workers. They included the parents of the comedians Aziz Ansari and Hasan Minhaj. In 2017, Minhaj celebrated the First Amendment at the White House Correspondents' Dinner, roasting President Donald Trump's anti-Muslim policies.

Islam is both us and them, West and East. It cannot be contained in tweets or bans or stereotypes. It's rooted in the soil, bearing fruit that will continue to make America great. ■

I AM THE SON OF A TERRORIST: HERE IS HOW I CHOSE PEACE
BY ZAK EBRAHIM

ON NOVEMBER 5, 1990, A MAN named El-Sayyid Nosair walked into a hotel in Manhattan and assassinated Rabbi Meir Kahane, the leader of the Jewish Defense League. Nosair was initially found not guilty of the murder, but while serving time on lesser charges, he and other men began planning attacks on a dozen New York City landmarks, including tunnels, synagogues, and the United Nations' headquarters. Thankfully, those plans were foiled by an FBI informant. Sadly, the 1993 bombing of the World Trade Center was not. Nosair would eventually be convicted for his involvement in the plot. El-Sayyid Nosair is my father.

I was born in Pittsburgh, Pennsylvania, in 1983, to him, an Egyptian engineer, and a loving American mother and grade school teacher, who together tried their best to create a happy childhood for me. It wasn't until I was 7 years old that our family dynamic started to change. My father exposed me to a side of Islam that few people, including the majority of Muslims, get to see. It's been my experience that when people take the time to interact with one another, it doesn't take long to realize that for the most part, we all want the same things out of life. However, in every religion, in every population, you'll find a small

NEW YORK, FEBRUARY 20, 2017. One of President Donald Trump's first executive orders was a sweeping ban preventing entry into the United States by people from seven Muslim-majority countries. The order prompted protest demonstrations across the country. At one such demonstration in front of New York's City Hall, Muslim American women wearing head scarves conduct evening prayers. Federal courts blocked implementation of the ban, declaring it unconstitutional. Chief Justice Roger Gregory of the U.S. Court of Appeals for the Fourth Circuit described the executive order as using "vague words of national security, but in context, drips with religious intolerance, animus, and discrimination." ◎ JUSTIN LANE

percentage of people who hold so fervently to their beliefs that they feel they must use any means necessary to make others live as they do.

A few months prior to his arrest, my father sat me down and explained that for the past few weekends, he and some friends had been going to a shooting range on Long Island for target practice. He told me I'd be going with him the next morning. We arrived at Calverton Shooting Range, which, unbeknownst to our group, was being watched by the FBI. When it was my turn to shoot, my father helped me hold the rifle to my shoulder and explained how to aim at the target about 30 yards away. That day, the last bullet I shot hit the small orange light that sat on top of the target, and to everyone's surprise, especially mine, the entire target burst into flames. My uncle turned to the other men and, in Arabic, said, "*Ibn abuh*." Like father, like son. They all seemed to get a really big laugh out of that comment, but it wasn't until a few years later that I fully understood what they thought was so funny. They thought they saw in me the same destruction my father was capable of. Those men would eventually be convicted of placing a van filled with 1,500 pounds of explosives into the sublevel parking lot of the World Trade Center's North Tower, causing an explosion that killed 6 people and injured over 1,000 others. These were the men I looked up to. These were the men I called *ammu*, which means uncle.

By the time I turned 19, I had already moved 20 times in my life, and that instability during my childhood didn't really provide an opportunity to make many friends. Each time I would begin to feel comfortable around someone, it was time to pack up and move to the next town. Being the perpetual new face in class, I was frequently the target of bullies. I kept my identity a secret from my classmates to avoid being targeted, but as it turned out, being the quiet, chubby new kid in class was more than enough ammunition. So for the most part, I spent my time at home reading books and watching TV or playing video games. For those reasons, my social skills were lacking, to say the least, and growing up in a bigoted household, I wasn't prepared for the real world. I'd been raised to judge people based on arbitrary measurements, like a person's race or religion.

So what opened my eyes? One of my first experiences that challenged this way of thinking was during the 2000 presidential elections. Through a college prep program, I was able to take part in the National Youth Convention in Philadelphia. My particular group's focus was on youth violence, and having been the victim of bullying for most of my life, this was a subject about which I felt particularly passionate. The members of our group came from many different walks of life. One day toward the end of the convention, I found out that one of the kids I had befriended was Jewish. Now it had taken several days for this detail to come to light, and I realized that there was no natural animosity between the two of us. I had never had a Jewish friend before, and frankly, I felt a sense of pride in having been able to overcome a barrier that for most of my life I had been led to believe was insurmountable. Another

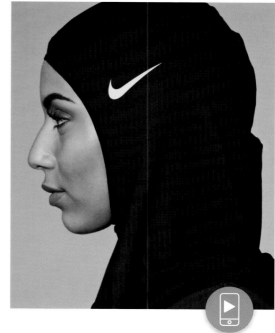

AMERICANS WHO VALUE TOLERANCE and justice have been challenged by those who would feed the flames of Islamophobia. A cover story in *Time* (opposite), addressed the issue head on, describing the hostility that met efforts to open mosques in New York and rural Wisconsin; Quran burnings in Florida on the anniversary of the 9/11 attacks; and the persistent demonization of Islam on extremist news outlets. At the 2017 Academy Awards ceremony, audiences saw Islam in a different light when Mahershala Ali (above), won as Best Supporting Actor for his performance in *Moonlight*, the first Muslim to take home an Oscar. Nike has helped normalize the hijab head scarf worn by observant Muslim women by marketing a lightweight, pull-on version with the company's distinctive Swoosh (above, right).
📷 MARK RALSTON

major turning point came when I found a summer job at Busch Gardens, an amusement park. There, I was exposed to people from all sorts of faiths and cultures, and that experience proved to be fundamental to the development of my character. Most of my life, I'd been taught that homosexuality was a sin, and by extension, that all gay people were a negative influence. As chance would have it, I had the opportunity to work with some of the gay performers at a show there, and soon found that many were the kindest, least judgmental people I had ever met. Being bullied as a kid created a sense of empathy in me toward the suffering of others, and it does not come naturally to me to treat people who are kind in any way other than the way I would want to be treated myself. Thanks to that feeling, I was able to contrast the stereotypes I'd been taught as a child with real-life experience and interactions. I don't know what it's like to be gay, but I'm well acquainted with being judged for something that's beyond my control.

Then there was *The Daily Show*. On a nightly basis, Jon Stewart forced me to be intellectually honest with myself about my own bigotry and helped me to realize that a person's race, religion, or sexual orientation had nothing to do with the quality of one's character. He was in many ways a father figure to me when I was in desperate need of one. Inspiration can often come from an unexpected place, and the fact that a Jewish comedian has done more to positively influence my worldview than my own extremist father is not lost on me.

One day, I had a conversation with my mother about how my worldview was starting to change, and she said something to me that I will hold dear to my heart for as long as I live. She looked at me with the weary eyes of someone who had experienced enough dogmatism to last a lifetime, and said, "I'm tired of hating people." In that instant, I realized how much negative energy it takes to hold that hatred inside of you.

Zak Ebrahim is not my real name. I changed it when my family decided to end our connection with my father and start a new life. So why would I out myself now and potentially put myself in danger? Well, that's simple. I do it in the hopes that perhaps someone, some day, who is compelled to use violence, may hear my story and realize that there is a better way: That although I had been subjected to this violent, intolerant ideology, I did not become fanaticized. Instead, I choose to use my experience to fight back against terrorism, against the bigotry. I do it for the victims of terrorism and their loved ones, for the terrible pain and loss that terrorism has forced upon their lives. For the victims of terrorism, I will speak out against these senseless acts and condemn my father's actions. And with that simple fact, I stand here as proof that violence isn't inherent in one's religion or race, and the son does not have to follow the ways of his father. I am not my father.

One of the reasons I decided to share my story publicly was because I knew that my experience was unique among Muslims. I wanted to show people that although I had been exposed to an interpretation of Islam that many people are afraid of, I did not become radicalized. And if someone like me, who was exposed to an ideology that preached hatred of anyone who didn't fit into a very narrow and arbitrary idea of what it means to be good, could promote peace, then what does that say about the vast majority of Muslims in the world who are never exposed to the same sort of indoctrination?

As we have seen a concerted effort to attack Western citizens by groups like ISIS, the so-called Islamic State, we have also seen a rise in nationalist ideologies both in the United States and Europe. I believe these two trends are inextricably linked. Groups like ISIS do not pose an existential threat to the West, and yet they, as well as their white supremacist counterparts in Europe and the United States, attempt to frame this as a battle between Islam and Western civilization. This plays directly into the hands of groups like ISIS, who wish to sow fear in the citizenry. Isolating fearful communities along ethnic, nationalist, or religious lines has been a goal of supremacists of all kinds, for all time.

I can tell you firsthand that fear and isolation are two of the most important ingredients in radicalizing someone. You separate those you hope to indoctrinate from those you wish to teach them to fear. It was exposure to those who I was taught to hate that made me reject my father's beliefs. If my father had not gone to prison and had been able to continue to isolate me, I don't know what path I might have ended up on.

This is why I find a great deal of hope in the interactions between Muslim and Jewish communities. Leading up to the election of Donald Trump as president of the United States, we have witnessed a dramatic rise in hate crimes targeting minority religious groups, particularly Jews and Muslims, and their places of worship. Although it is easy to become disillusioned by this trend, it has also

RALEIGH, NORTH CAROLINA, FEBRUARY 12, 2015. The FBI reports skyrocketing attacks on Muslims, hundreds of cases of vandalism and that a dozen mosques have been burned after the inflammatory of rhetoric during the 2016 presidential campaign. When three Muslim students, Deah Barakat, 23; his wife, Yusor, 21; and her sister, Razan, 19, were killed at the University of North Carolina in Chapel Hill, it appeared to be another gruesome episode of anti-Muslim violence. Stephen Hicks, a 46-year-old neighbor, admitted that he shot all three in the head, telling police that the killings were the outcome of a dispute over a parking space in their apartment complex in Raleigh. But there is reason to believe that Hicks' disdain for all religions and religious people—Christians, Muslims, Jews—may have excited his hatred. "When it comes to insults, your religion started this, not me," Hicks wrote on Facebook in an attack on all faiths. "If your religion kept its big mouth shut, so would I." The victims' families maintain he singled out the three students because they were Muslim. Both women wore a hijab. "Two years ago, we had to convince people Muslims felt threatened," said Farris Barakat, Deah's brother. "Today, if you don't know that Islamophobia is a real thing, you're not following the news." Hicks was charged with three counts of first-degree murder. Thousands of mourners attended the funeral for the three students, held on the soccer field at North Carolina State University, and a rabbi in Raleigh presented the families with a book containing thousands of letters of condolences. 📷 SAMUEL CORUM

created example after example in which Muslim and Jewish communities, as well as others, have come together in support of one another. This lays waste to the fiction that I was raised to believe, and that supremacists place at the foundation of their beliefs, that things do not or should not change. ∎

Zak Ebrahim was born in Pittsburgh, Pennsylvania, the son of an Egyptian industrial engineer and an American school teacher. When Ebrahim was 7, his father shot and killed the founder of the Jewish Defense League, Rabbi Meir Kahane. From behind bars, his father, El-Sayyid Nosair, co-masterminded the 1993 bombing of the World Trade Center. Ebrahim spent the rest of his childhood moving from city to city, hiding his identity from those who knew of his father. He now dedicates his life to speaking out against terrorism and spreading his message of peace and nonviolence. 🐦 *@ZakEbrahim*

Courtesy of TED. Zak Ebrahim, September 2014. Watch the complete TED Talk on TED.com.

FIGHTING THE GOOD FIGHT

RABIA CHAUDRY

Attorney Rabia Chaudry fights for the civil rights of American Muslims. As founder of the Safe Nation Collaborative, which provides education on the Islamic faith, she fosters dialogue between Muslim communities and law enforcement. *Serial*, the most listened-to podcast in history, was made after Chaudry approached *This American Life* about the story of Adnan Syed, a Muslim American high school student serving life imprisonment after being convicted for murdering his former girlfriend. Chaudry had evidence that she believed proved Syed's innocence. Following *Serial*, which has been downloaded more than 100 million times, Syed's conviction was overturned, and he is now awaiting a new trial. Chaudry's 2017 book, *Adnan's Story: The Search for Truth and Justice After* Serial, details the role that anti-Muslim bias played in Syed's wrongful conviction.

AUSTIN, TEXAS, JANUARY 29, 2015. For nearly a decade, Austin has attracted thousands of participants to a peaceful gathering called "Texas Muslim Capital Day," where Muslims from around the United States visit the State Capitol building, meet with lawmakers, and spend time with friends and family. But in 2015, attendees were met by anti-Muslim protests (above, left). Demonstrators alleged that Muslims were working to replace the U.S. legal system with Islam's Sharia religious legal code. Shouting over their placards, the protesters also accused local Muslims of financing terrorism and demanded that they "go home"—despite the fact that many were U.S.-born American citizens. Anti-Muslim bigotry, fueled by right-wing media and think tanks, has only intensified since, rising to a crescendo with the 2016 election campaign.
◎ NINA BERMAN

BOSTON, FEBRUARY 2017. The Muslim American community was thrown into disarray when President Donald Trump issued his first executive order banning travel to the United States by people from seven predominantly Muslim countries. The ban, announced on January 27, 2017, with no warning, caused chaos at airports around the world. If put into effect, this ban would have blocked entry to relatives, friends, and business associates from those countries for three months (even those with green cards or who were enrolled in universities) and could have been renewed indefinitely. In response, Muslim Americans and sympathetic non-Muslim supporters rallied across the country in protests, like this one (above) in Boston. A federal court blocked the order, as well as a subsequent second, more limited travel ban issued as a replacement, on First Amendment grounds because both appeared to be targeting people on the basis of their religious faith. In June, a scaled-down version of the ban on the nationals of 6 countries was put into effect provisionally ◎ KEIKO HIROMI

CHINO, CALIFORNIA, JULY 6, 2016. Roughly 3.3 million Muslims live in the United States. They are one of the most racially diverse religious groups in the country, and represent about 1 percent of the total population. One of the greatest challenges facing this minority today is how to raise Muslim children according to their faith and how to help them protect their religious identity in an increasingly hostile environment. Here, at a mosque in Chino, California, fathers and sons pray together to mark Eid al-Fitr, the end of daily fasting during the monthlong Ramadan. 📷 FREDERIC J BROWN

RAISING AMERICAN MUSLIM KIDS
BY WAJAHAT ALI

I'M UP AT 3 A.M., BURPING my new baby girl, Nusayba, smelling her fresh, new baby skin and rubbing her soft, bald head.

Like most parents with young kids, I think about their future: What will my daughter's first word be? Will she like spicy South Asian food, or will I have to shame myself by ordering "mild"? Will my American Muslim daughter be allowed to leave the Trump detention camps if she grows up to be a "10"? Would that make her eligible for a Trump beauty pageant?

I often muse about a potential dystopic future when I see the orange, thin-skinned Republican president speaking. He has already recommended "extreme vetting" of Muslims and once said he'd "absolutely" require Muslims to register in a special database. He retaliated against Khizr and Ghazala Khan, the Gold Star parents of an American Muslim soldier. His words unleash casual anti-Muslim bigotry: A poll found that 50 percent of people surveyed supported his proposal to bar Muslims from entering the country.

This is the America we're raising our two Muslim kids in. My wife's friend Khadeeja Abdullah, the mother of a 1-year-old, said she had recently seen a viral video of a young Muslim boy asking if he would be kicked out of the country if Donald Trump became president. "My heart shattered into pieces. Our children should not live in fear," she said.

I didn't live in fear growing up in Fremont, California, in the 1980s and 1990s. Like the Khans, my parents are Muslim immigrants originally from Pakistan. My parents didn't keep their own copy of the Constitution in their pockets, but they were known to bust out Mervyn's coupons and exquisite dal recipes on command. Islam was a vibrant reality for us, comfortably

embedded within memories of watching *ThunderCats* cartoons on Saturdays, listening to Dad's Jimi Hendrix CDs, and seeing my mother's sari collection.

I have now been transformed into a professional adult in his 30s, just like my parents were when they had me. Their generation was forged from immigrant steel and clarified butter. They built mosques out of abandoned shops, drove two states away to find halal meat, started American Muslim institutions, worked full-time, raised kids, taught us the Quran, and found time to make lamb biryani for an extended family of 12 living in a two-bedroom apartment.

I am not doing that. I can barely catch up on my Netflix shows. But I still want my children to know the rich cultural and religious traditions given to me—traditions that I took for granted.

In recent conversations with about a dozen other American Muslim friends and parents, I found a lot of agreement on the challenge we're facing: Our kids will know a kind of anti-Muslim bigotry that we never did. At the

**MINNEAPOLIS, MINNESOTA,
NOVEMBER 8, 2016.** America is a
land of contrasts. Even as the nation
was in the grip of a presidential
election campaign punctuated by
harsh anti-Muslim rhetoric, there
were signs of remarkable
achievement toward the dream of
equality and tolerance. On November
8, 2016, Ilhan Omar, a former child
refugee from war-torn Somalia, won
a seat in the Minnesota state
Legislature, the first Somali-born
Muslim lawmaker elected in the
United States. Omar learned to speak
English less than three months after
she arrived here. She later graduated
from North Dakota State University
with a degree in political science and
international studies. After returning
to her adopted home state of
Minnesota, she became a political
organizer. On the evening of her
victory, she proudly wore native
Somali attire. ◻ RICHARD MARSHALL

same time, there's also a healthy debate on how to raise practicing Muslim children here.

Hina Khan-Mukhtar, a mother of three in the San Francisco Bay Area, said the only way is for us to transform into "Super-Muslims," minus the cape. "In America, you can't be a mediocre Muslim," she said. "You have to be the best of the best, and you have to show your kids that you have a 'superior product' that you are offering them. There are so many '-isms' calling for their attention and for their loyalty—individualism, atheism, materialism, extremism. Islam needs to trump them all."

Unfortunately for my children, I excel in mediocrity. This Ramadan, I opened my fasts at home with a date and some takeout food. I usually prayed Maghrib, the evening prayer, by myself in the family room. My wife, a full-time doctor and supermom, pregnant with our second child at the time, did her best to join me, but her schedule left her exhausted.

I felt guilty that my son, who is about to turn 2, was experiencing the most broke Ramadan ever. I wanted to give him the 2016 version of what I had growing up when my mother, grandmother, cousins, and I would assemble in the kitchen and prepare the pakoras, samosas, and fruit *chaat* of the Ramadan *iftar* meal. My father would come home and lead us in prayer. On the weekends, we'd host *Milad* parties with people reciting poetry in praise of the Prophet Muhammad.

One potential route for producing "superior Muslims" is to follow the model of Orthodox Jewish Americans and invest tremendous time and

resources to create enclosed schools or home schooling co-ops for our communities.

This environment might protect kids from bullying—and also from the task of becoming a professional Muslim. I went to an all-boys Catholic high school, and I was often asked to be the cultural ambassador of 1.6 billion people, to explain head scarves and fasting. Even though I had to be a walking Wikipedia, it encouraged me to become bolder with my Muslim identity.

Army Major Jason Moy, my old law school roommate, is skeptical of Muslim-only environments. "Complete isolation is never a winning strategy," he told me. "I am a firm believer in allowing our children to be completely

TEQUESTA, FLORIDA, 2003.
First-generation Pakistani Americans Asma and Sarah Azimi celebrate their college graduations. Asma, 22, received her degree in education from the University of Michigan, and Sarah, 26, graduated from Eastern Michigan University with a B.A. in communications. The sisters said they would honor the Muslim tradition of arranged marriages, but would be the first women in their family to pursue careers outside the home. 📷 JACEK GANCARZ

involved in American culture, holidays, and food."

Thankfully, American Muslim kids can find halal hot dogs at their local mosques, which have doubled in number since the attacks of Sept. 11, 2001, a sign that despite the rising bigotry, Muslim communities are able to thrive in the United States.

I have never been culturally, spiritually, or intellectually fulfilled by most of my neighborhood mosques, especially as many still relegate women to side entrances. They tried their best and have evolved considerably, but the hodgepodge of Salafism, Deobandi Islam, and traces of watered-down Sufism that I usually encountered didn't move my soul.

For this reason, my family and I are spiritual nomads, not tied to any particular institution.

Razi Hashmi, a State Department employee and the parent of two young children, is also part of the "unmosqued" community. He is investing in a new project called "Make Space" in Virginia, a spiritual home for young Muslim parents, couples, and millennials seeking a haven to practice their Islam and raise their children.

We live not too far away, and we took my son, Ibrahim, there for *Eid* prayers recently. He wore his *kurta* and ran around the hall as the young imam preached about tolerance and requested donations so that the worshipers could purchase their own space and finally leave the rented space in an Afghan restaurant.

We're trying to retain so much of the good we inherited from our parents, throw away the rotten parts and improvise along the way. "We're going to have to start from scratch," said Willow Wilson, who writes the *Ms. Marvel* comic book series, which stars a teenage Muslim superhero. "In my local community, we've been actively discussing creating a kind of 'Saturday school' curriculum, so that kids get religious instruction in a community setting, but from sources we trust and in which we can actively participate." The sources we don't trust: shady, unqualified imams and right-wing religious material published overseas.

Instead, we're turning to our peers and our collective best judgment, as well as centuries-old traditions.

At home, my wife and I now deliberately pray in front of the kids. I prostrate toward Mecca and recite the Arabic verses out loud.

Two weeks ago, during my night prayers, my son came up next to me, bowed and turned his head, and smiled. There is no compulsion in religion, nor should there be. It's up to him and Nusayba to embrace or reject the faith and our traditions. My job is only to plant the seeds with care. ∎

Wajahat Ali is the author of the play *The Domestic Crusaders* and creative director of Affinis Labs, a hub for social entrepreneurship and innovation. 🐦 *@WajahatAli*

ASTRONAUT IN TRAINING
José M. Hernández does his best Superman impersonation aboard NASA's McDonnell Douglas C-9B (dubbed the "vomit comet") in April 2005. These zero gravity flights simulate the weightlessness that astronauts will experience in space. Fortunately, for first-time Zero-G trainees, the interior of the plane is padded in all directions.

LATINO AMERICANS

JOSÉ HERNÁNDEZ (left) had to travel much farther to reach outer space than his fellow astronauts.

The son of poor Mexican migrant farmworkers, Hernández spent his childhood summers picking fruits and vegetables in California's sunbaked Central Valley while his non-migrant classmates spent their summers playing. Tired, sweaty, and splattered with mud at the end of every day, Hernández's father warned him, "This is your future if you don't study in school."

Hernández first dreamed of becoming an astronaut in 1969, when he was only 7, as he sat with his family watching a tiny black-and-white TV in cramped migrant quarters as Neil Armstrong walked on the moon.

But the odds against the aspiring spacefarer were enormous. As his family moved north with the changing crops, his education was intermittent, forcing him to constantly switch schools.

Once in school full-time, he never looked back. Gifted in math and science, Hernández earned a B.S. in electrical engineering, soon followed by a master's degree in advanced electrical and computer engineering.

Hernández went to work at the Lawrence Livermore National Laboratory, where he and a colleague developed the first full-field digital mammogram to aid in the early detection of breast cancer. In 2001, he joined NASA as a technician on the space shuttle program, but his application for astronaut training was rejected 11 times. Unwilling to give up, he applied one more time and was finally accepted in 2004.

On August 28, 2009, after supporting five space shuttle operations on the ground, it was Hernández's turn to soar. The migrant farmworker's son, now a mission specialist aboard the Space Shuttle *Discovery*, traveled to the orbiting International Space Station. Two hundred and fifty miles above the Earth, he became the first person to tweet in Spanish from space. *"Espero la cosecha de mi sueno sirva como inspiración a todos!"* he tweeted triumphantly. "I hope the harvest of my dream serves as inspiration to all!"

Today, Hernández heads a successful space consultancy, as well as a foundation that provides college scholarships for other Latino Americans. ∎

A PEOPLE ON THE VERGE
BY RAY SUAREZ

AS THEY DO EVERY SPRING, proud parents and happy graduates gathered for commencement exercises for McKinney Boyd High School in McKinney, Texas, in the far corner of the Dallas-Fort Worth Metroplex.

The valedictorian was the kind of young woman who would make everyone in the Texas city proud, especially in the growing Mexican American population. Larissa Martinez lived in a one-bedroom apartment with her mother and sister. She had been admitted to Yale University, got a coveted full ride, and said she wanted to prepare for medical school. A lot of people connected to McKinney Boyd High knew those things about Larissa, but as she walked to the lectern in cap and gown to deliver her valedictory speech, wearing her National Honor Society stole, she knew there was one thing many in the audience did not know: Larissa had entered the United States illegally in 2010, and on the day of her greatest triumph, was still not a citizen, or a legal resident.

"I am one of the 11 million undocumented immigrants living in the shadows of the United States," she said. Her reason for using her valedictory address to reveal her status, Martinez said, was simple. "The most important part of the debate, and the part most often overlooked, is the fact that immigrants, undocumented or otherwise, are people too."

In just six years, she had succeeded in her new home. She raced ahead of many of her native-born classmates. Her English bore only a slight trace of a

NEW YORK, MARCH 3, 2017. Between 2001 and 2009, authorities found the bodies of some 2,500 migrants who died in the Sonoran Desert from heatstroke, dehydration, and attacks by bandits and border patrols. Thousands of backpacks (right), abandoned by immigrants desperately crossing Arizona's treacherous Sonoran Desert, underscore the hazards that migrants face as they venture north to escape poverty, political repression, or to join family members already in the United States. This photograph was taken at *State of Exception,* an art installation at New York City's Parsons School of Design. RICHARD BARNES

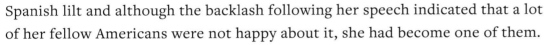

Spanish lilt and although the backlash following her speech indicated that a lot of her fellow Americans were not happy about it, she had become one of them.

The high-schooler's story is an old one. She is part of a steady march of people from the rest of the hemisphere to a country that wanted their strong backs, but did not always want them. A century ago, there were 48 stars on the flag. Woodrow Wilson was in the White House and was leading his country into war in Europe. There was no Taco Bell, JLo, Ricky Ricardo, Selena, Big Papi, nor U.S. Surgeon General Antonia Coello Novello.

If you wanted to find America's Latinos in the second decade of the twentieth century, where would you have looked? You could have headed for mines in Arizona, cigar factories in Florida, farms in California and Texas, and the teeming, polyglot streets of New York.

There were old, established barrios in San Antonio, Tucson, and Los Angeles, a new Mexican community on the far South Side of Chicago, and an old Cuban one in Tampa. It is safe to say that back then, the vast majority of Americans had never met a fellow American who spoke Spanish.

Today, a hundred years later, it is estimated that more than 57 million Latinos live in the United States, and the Census Bureau projects that by the early 2050s, when the country tips into minority/majority status, there will be close to 140 million. The United States will be almost one-third Latino, tracing their ancestry to a vast range of places, from neighborhoods huddled right up against the fence that marks the Mexico-U.S. border, clear down to the Beagle Channel at the southern tip of South America. They are Fortune 500 CEOs, busboys, landscapers, state governors, Cabinet secretaries, drywallers, nannies, and Major League Baseball stars.

MCKINNEY, TEXAS, JUNE 3, 2016. Speaking at her high school graduation ceremony, valedictorian Larissa Martinez (above) reveals she is one of the country's 11 million undocumented immigrants. Martinez, who was accepted to Yale University on a full scholarship, defended immigrants like herself as "people who have become part of American society and way of life, and who yearn to help make America great again without the construction of a wall built on hatred and prejudice." While her speech drew praise in many quarters, others called for her immediate arrest and deportation.

COTULLA, TEXAS, 1928. Lyndon Baines Johnson, then a young teacher at a segregated school for poor Mexican children, sits with his students for their class picture (above, left). As president, Johnson attributed his successful campaign to win passage of the 1964 Civil Rights Bill (and his Voting Rights Act the following year) to the discrimination he had witnessed as a teacher against Mexican Americans. He went on to appoint more Mexican Americans to positions in the federal government than any previous president.

Significantly, they...we...are native born, immigrants, and from families who have lived on what is now U.S. soil since long before there was a United States.

It has been a century of breathtaking change, heartbreaking challenge, and steady, if insufficient, progress. Over the last hundred years, migration from the Spanish-speaking countries in the rest of the hemisphere started small, and steadily picked up steam. In the early 1900s, the population of the United States was 103 million people, about 14 million of whom had been born somewhere else on the planet. Of that number, just a little over half a million were born in Latin America.

It has been a century of struggle as well as growth. Nineteenth-century attitudes carried over by the country's Anglo majority from its earliest encounters with Spanish speakers persisted well into the twentieth century. It would take resistance, boycotts, strikes, court cases, and decades of insistent demand to instill the notion that this country's Latino citizens were not just an army of strong backs and weak minds, exploitable, deportable, and extended full legal rights only as an option.

It's important to remember that we're here because Uncle Sam was over there. Although the ancestors of millions who make up today's Latino communities across the country were still back in the Old Country, the United States had been branching out for decades, investing heavily in Latin America, and exerting its influence on politics, especially in the Caribbean and Central America. Shipping lines, railroads, bananas, coffee, and most of all, sugar, sent generations of American businesspeople south, looking to make a buck while satisfying the appetites of their countrymen.

The resistance to Spanish rule that had created Cuban exile communities in the United States was over. The American victory in the 1898 Spanish-American War gave Cubans what many had wanted for decades: their own country, even if it was now dominated by the United States instead of faraway Spain. It would be more than 40 years before the United States would stop selling arms to a corrupt Cuban president and watch him lose a civil war to a communist insurgency led by Fidel Castro. The human tide of Cubans that would transform Florida after the revolution was unimaginable a century ago. Today, it is hard to imagine Florida without the Cuban American community, now more than a million strong.

In the nineteenth century, the United States had occupied, then purchased, vast areas of northern Mexico, suddenly bringing centuries-old Spanish-speaking communitiies under U.S. control. As President Woodrow Wilson contemplated entering World War I, the Rio Grande Valley of Texas, the Sangre de Cristo Mountains of New Mexico, and the old Californian mission towns of San Diego, San Francisco, and Santa Barbara were the homes of a new American people rooted in Latin American culture but growing under the Stars and Stripes.

The nineteenth century had been a violent one around the world. In the

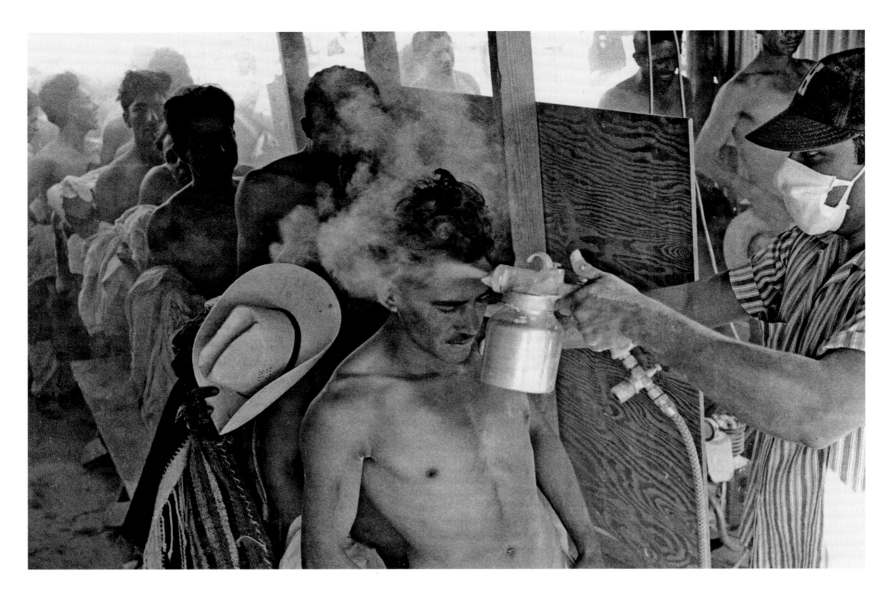

United States it was no different, as wars were fought by empires squabbling over the natural riches of North America. The people who would become the Latinos of the United States watched their homes become battlefields in wars between native people and Europeans, Americans, and Mexicans, and Americans and Spaniards. That century of violence roughed out the borders between the modern nations of the hemisphere, and by 1900, the front lines moved from battlefields to courtrooms and legislatures.

In 1917, Puerto Ricans had just been made American citizens by an Act of Congress. The United States had invaded and occupied the Caribbean island in 1898 in the war with Spain, and in the following two decades, *puertorriqueños* had lingered as a people of ambiguous status, no longer citizens of Spain, not yet citizens of the United States, but citizens of an island administered by a governor appointed in Washington. In 19 years of occupation, federal courts were called upon again and again to define the status of merchandise from Puerto Rico. American business leaders really wanted sacks of coffee, sugar products, and bananas defined in law. Eventually, the courts got around to the people who began to arrive on the same boats as the bananas.

HIDALGO, TEXAS, 1956. The first stop for Mexican laborers brought to work in the United States under the Bracero Program was this fumigation station near the border, where they were frisked for contraband, then herded past health officials who sprayed them with DDT. The program began during World War II, when Mexicans were needed to make up for American manpower shortages. Although originally intended as a temporary measure, the Braceros became the country's largest guest-worker program and a fixture in American agriculture until it was ended in 1964. Through it, more than 4.5 million Mexicans crossed the border to work on American farms. Many were mistreated, but others were grateful for the opportunity to provide for their families. Either way, the Bracero Program profoundly affected the country's demographics, with many Latino American families tracing their roots in the United States back to ancestors who first came as *braceros*. 📷 LEONARD NADEL

SACRAMENTO, CALIFORNIA, MARCH 2, 1969. Labor leader Dolores Huerta rallies Latino farm workers during their strike against California's grape growers. Huerta, a skilled organizer and tough negotiator, partnered with Cesar Chávez to form the United Farm Workers, which overcame enormous odds to improve working conditions and the civil rights of thousands of Latino laborers. The recipient of numerous awards, including the Presidential Medal of Freedom, Huerta is one of the nation's most admired Latina role models.
📷 ALBERT HARLINGUE

The lives of my grandparents, children at the time, were transformed along with the lives of millions of Puerto Ricans yet unborn with the passage of the Jones-Shafroth Act. Even though they were now American citizens, most people in Puerto Rico continued to live as they had for generations, in small towns and on farms.

In El Paso, Texas, thousands of miles to the west, families fleeing the tumult of the Mexican Revolution poured across the southwestern border into California, Texas, Arizona, and Colorado. Mexico was struggling to emerge from more than 30 years of authoritarian rule, which had stunted the growth of Mexican democracy. After the era called the *Porfiriato*, new political rivalries blossomed into open conflict, coups, and assassinations.

The fight for control of Mexico's resources and politics plunged the country into a vicious and sustained war that ended up killing an estimated 1 out of every 10 Mexicans, and sending hundreds of thousands into exile. The war made national heroes of Emiliano Zapata and Pancho Villa, a president out of Venustiano Carranza, and refugees out of men, women, and children whose towns and farms were repeatedly overrun in years of bloody fighting. Desperate people headed north on the railroads, originally built by Mexican presidents to send exports north.

American employers were hungry for labor, and many prized what they believed were the traits of the Mexican worker: docility, physical strength, and the ability to work in dangerous and unhealthy environments. As European immigration shifted from the countries of the north and west to the south and east, Mexicans began to be prized because, it was believed that, unlike European immigrants, they would eventually be going home.

Among the thousands who crossed the border in 1917 were José and Faustina García. They were schoolteachers, but their educational credentials were not recognized in Texas, so José became a dry goods merchant in Mercedes, right near the border in the Rio Grande Valley. Six of the García children would eventually become medical doctors, an amazing feat in a world of segregated schools and deep structural prejudice.

One of them, Héctor, crossed the border in 1917 as a 3-year-old. He would grow up to defy the stereotypes and contempt of his Anglo neighbors in South Texas and become a medical graduate of the University of Texas system, a major in the U.S. Army, and after the war, a founder of the American GI Forum, a civil rights and political organization. The group became a defender of the rights of Latino veterans to collect their service-related benefits, helped to defeat the poll taxes that kept many Latinos from voting in the Southwest, and later became a potent and influential political organization wooed by politicians like the Texas senator, and later President, Lyndon Baines Johnson.

History can present any people with tough and persistent ironies. In the nineteenth century, Latin American independence leaders headed to battle to evict Spanish colonial masters from their lands, thrilled by the words of Jefferson, Washington, and Paine. Now living in the land of the Founders and the Framers in the twentieth century, they often found that the promise of being "created equal" and endowed with "inalienable rights" was not necessarily recognized, in law or in custom, by their American neighbors.

In the 1960s and 1970s, the labor organizers Cesar Chávez and Dolores Huerta persuaded the poorly paid, poorly housed, and poorly fed workers in the California fields that the only way they could stand up to the growers was to form a union. On the ground in the state's productive farming regions, and in the produce sections of the country's supermarkets, Chávez and Huerta played a tough, smart, and strategic game. They encouraged the workers to join multiethnic alliances between Mexican and East Asian field workers, and harnessed the buying power of middle-class shoppers across the country who showed their solidarity by boycotting California grapes and lettuce.

The unionizing workers were locked out of the fields. They were attacked by growers and local law enforcement, and in turn fought against strike-breakers bused into the fields from south of the border. Huerta was educated, the daughter of politically active parents, and had taught school before she became a community organizer. Chávez's family lost their property and business in Arizona during the Great Depression, and headed to California to become migrant workers. Chávez's formal education ended in the seventh grade. He and Huerta pooled their formidable skills to leverage the concerns of the poorest American workers in a way that touched, engaged, and mobilized forces far beyond the California fields.

The Mexican barrios of the American Southwest, like the black towns and neighborhoods of the Jim Crow South, were created by a social and legal web of forces designed to keep people apart. In the 1900s, in the same municipality, Mexican and Anglo American residential and commercial areas would be separated by a rail line or a county road. On the Anglo side, even in poor towns, there were street lights, sewers, and paved streets. On the Mexican side, there were open sewers, communal water spigots, and dirt streets that became nearly impassable after a heavy rain.

Today when Americans hear the word "segregation" in discussing schools, they are likely to recall a social policy intended to separate blacks and whites. But a hundred years ago, if you said the phrase "Mexican School" to Americans in the Southwest, they knew you were talking about the separate, and decidedly unequal, school buildings and shoddy educational materials begrudgingly provided to Mexican and Mexican American kids. The landmark U.S. Supreme Court case that ended school segregation once and for all, *Brown v. the Board of Education of Topeka, Kansas*, had an important predecessor. *Mendes v. Westminster School District of Orange County* focused on the unconstitutionality of Mexican schools in California and became the impetus forcing the Southwestern states to desegregate.

LOS ANGELES, NOVEMBER 8, 1994. When California's Republican Governor Pete Wilson (celebrating, above) came from behind to defeat his Democratic opponent in 1994, it was largely because of his strong support for Proposition 187. The controversial anti-immigrant ballot initiative, which won with nearly 60 percent of the vote, asserted that the people of California were "suffering economic hardship caused by the presence of illegal immigrants" and "personal injury and damage caused by the criminal conduct of illegal immigrants..." In response, 187 would prevent undocumented immigrants from using non-emergency public health care, public education, and other state-run social services. It would also require that children and their parents or legal guardians prove their legal status in the country. But soon after its passage, the law was challenged in federal court, where it was found unconstitutional on the basis that it usurped the federal government's authority over immigration. 📷 KEVORK DJANSEZIAN

HUNTINGTON PARK, CALIFORNIA, JANUARY 16, 1996. After a federal judge imposed an injunction on Proposition 187, demonstrators voiced their support for his move (above). They saw the law as discriminating against ethnic minorities, especially Latinos. A permanent injunction from the federal court followed. Governor Pete Wilson appealed that ruling, but Wilson's Democratic successor, Gray Davis, withdrew the appeal in 1999, effectively killing the law. Looking back, Proposition 187 appears to have been the first sign of an impending storm, with passions over immigration soon becoming even more contentious, and engulfing the nation. 📷 NICK UT

For all the exclusion, lack of opportunity, and unequal treatment of the barrio of a century ago, it played an important role. For families who had lived in the country for centuries and for the greenest of greenhorns, it offered a foothold, and a source of stability, as they began their journey up the American ladder. The neighborhoods provided employment, a spiritual and cultural home, and Latino space. Away from the daily indignities of the Anglo city, police power, and a political system that offered virtually no representation of their interests, it was something that belonged to them. Whether they were from Havana, Cuba, San Juan, Puerto Rico, Monterrey, Mexico, or from right there in Texas, that meant a lot.

After World War II, the map of the world, and the U.S. laws governing immigration, both got a lot more complicated in ways that spurred new decades of growth in the Latino population. Proxy wars fueled by the superpower rivalry between Washington and Moscow pitted Soviet-sponsored against American-backed political movements throughout the hemisphere.

There were left-right standoffs in Guatemala, Venezuela, the Dominican Republic, El Salvador, Nicaragua, and elsewhere. Violence, economic calamity,

and political unrest set hundreds of thousands of families in motion, creating big new Central and South American communities in Queens, N.Y., Washington, D.C., Houston, and Los Angeles.

The United States turned away from its European-centered immigration laws in 1965, toward formulas that opened the country to immigrants from the rest of the world. New rules made it possible for a single family member to stake a claim on American soil and eventually bring in other family members.

If you look at the migration patterns of just about every other big group that has come to the United States, especially from Europe, there has been a repeated pattern: a run-up, a spike, and then a falling off of the numbers in a compact number of decades. Latinos in the United States have a story that is completely different. They have been here since before there was a United States, and their numbers increased during the seizure and annexation of the places where they were already living. This was followed by a run-up, a spike, and then a steady, continuous influx of new Spanish-speaking people from beyond the borders, as conditions changed in various countries at various times.

Geography is part of the explanation. A nineteenth-century immigrant could not easily make the trip to the United States, or return to Dublin, Naples, or Minsk. Proximity and modern communication may help explain the persistent family ties and obligations between the United States and the rest of the hemisphere. In 2016 alone, it was estimated that more than $70 billion in remittances was sent to Latin America and the Caribbean. Through good and bad times, Latinos in the United States remain connected—and generous—to families "back home." Towns across Latin America boast buildings, schools,

THROUGH TELEVISION, movies, and Broadway plays, the stories of Latino Americans became part of the nation's diverse cultural mix. *I Love Lucy*, one of the most popular TV sitcoms during the 1950s, starred Cuban American Desi Arnaz as the band leader husband of American actress Lucille Ball, and introduced one of the first ethnically mixed couples on TV (opposite). The 1957 Broadway play *West Side Story* was one of the first productions to deal with the prejudice Latino immigrants faced in the United States. Puerto Rican actress Rita Moreno (above, left), won an Oscar in the 1961 movie version. *Zorro*, produced by Walt Disney, was another popular TV drama in which the masked hero (above) fights for justice in California of the 1820s, when it was ruled by Mexico.
📷 HERBERT DORFMAN, ABOVE, LEFT

stores, and homes built with money produced by their toil in *el Norte*, even as cousins, parents, brothers, and sisters become more settled in their new homes.

Although Latino Americans have been part of the story of the land that became the United States for more than 500 years, there are many Americans who treat us as perpetual foreigners, never quite full members of the club. When young Sebastien de la Cruz sang "The Star-Spangled Banner" at half-court in 2013, to open yet another championship run for the Spurs in San Antonio, tweeters around the country saw the boy resplendent in his mariachi costume in the silver and black theme colors and took to social media to complain. One asked, "Why couldn't they get an American to sing the National Anthem?"

The young Texan didn't sing Francis Scott Key's words with an accent. He was standing on a basketball court in a city founded in 1691 by Spanish priests and soldiers near an Indian settlement. A rebel army of American migrants and native Spanish speakers broke the land away from Texas more than 180 years ago. The Stars and Stripes have flown over San Antonio since 1846. Yet all that thousands of his fellow Americans could see was a foreigner, a Mexican.

If getting to safety, getting food on the table, and securing their rights was the challenge of the twentieth century, then gaining recognition as full members of the American people may be the challenge for Latino Americans in the twenty-first century. Just as the people themselves are a work in progress, so is the task of getting the rest of America to see what we see down at half-court, singing out "… and the home of the brave!" In other words, a countryman.

When Aroldis Chapman fires a sizzling strike toward home plate at more than 100 miles per hour…

When Catherine Cortez Masto or Marco Rubio rise to speak in pitched legislative battle in the U.S. Senate…

When Junot Díaz accepts the Pulitzer Prize in Literature…

When Ellen Ochoa and Franklin Chang-Díaz head into space aboard a NASA rocket…

Or Justice Sonia Sotomayor grills a lawyer making arguments before the highest court in the country…

… it is the culmination of a deep, complicated, and long history of encounter, exclusion, struggle, acceptance, and finally, getting ahead in a country where a vast community's best days are hopefully still ahead, in a more perfect union. ∎

JUST THE FACTS

IN 2016 ALONE, MILLIONS OF LATINO IMMIGRANTS SENT OVER

$70 BILLION

OF THEIR HARD-EARNED, MINIMUM-WAGE DOLLARS BACK TO SUPPORT THEIR FAMILIES IN LATIN AMERICAN AND THE CARIBBEAN.

—THE WORLD BANK

Veteran journalist **Ray Suarez** is currently the John McCloy Visiting Professor of American Studies at Amherst College. He was the host of *Inside Story* on Al Jazeera America, chief national correspondent for the *PBS NewsHour*, and host of NPR's *Talk of the Nation*. He is the author of three books, most recently *Latino Americans: The 500-Year Legacy That Shaped a Nation* (Penguin, 2013). He has been honored with the Public Policy Leadership Award from UCLA, and the Ruben Salazar Award from the National Council of La Raza. He is a member of the Hall of Fame of the National Association of Hispanic Journalists.
🐦 @RaySuarezNews

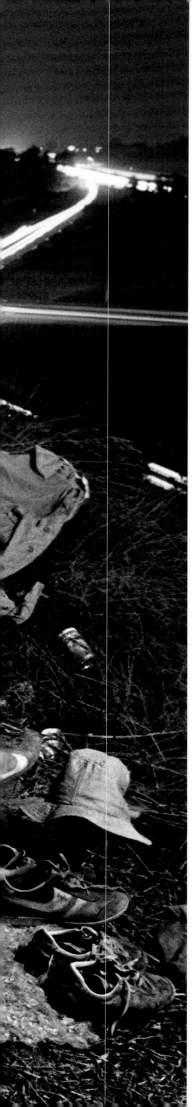

ENCINITAS, CALIFORNIA, JULY 25, 1989. Three brothers and two friends (left), all from Guatemala, bed down for the night on a hillside overlooking Interstate Highway 5 near San Diego. According to *Los Angeles Times* photographer Don Bartletti, who won a Pulitzer Prize for his photos of Latino migrants, these young men, who had only recently crossed the border from Mexico illegally, chose this perch to be close by the strip mall below, where they waited each day for drive-by offers of work from building contractors and homeowners. "We're living like animals here," one of the men told Bartletti. "We don't live like this back home. We have houses and beds. But we don't have work. We don't have money. We only have dreams."
📷 DON BARTLETTI

MCALLEN, TEXAS, MAY 28, 2010. U.S. Border Patrol agents stand guard (top, right) over two dozen undocumented migrants caught shortly after they crossed the nearby Rio Grande River, which forms part of the U.S.-Mexico border. From 1980 to 2008, Border Patrol guarding the southern border apprehended a little more than 1 million immigrants annually. But in succeeding years, the number steadily dropped, and only 400,000 were apprehended in 2016. Officials attribute the shift to better border security, fewer opportunities for immigrants in the changing U.S. economy, and, after the 2016 election campaign, an enhanced perception among immigrants that they will not be welcomed here. Still, Border Patrol says that for every undocumented migrant who is caught, another evades arrest.
📷 SCOTT OLSON

SAN ANTONIO, TEXAS, 2014. Immigrants make up the fastest-growing group of people incarcerated in the United States. From the mid 1990s to the mid 2010s, the average daily number of immigrant detainees has more than quadrupled, from roughly 8,000 to 34,000. The increase may be due to a little-known Congressional directive sometimes referred to as the "bed mandate." Inserted into the Department of Homeland Security's appropriations bill, where it was passed with overwhelming support

from both Republicans and Democrats, it required DHS to maintain a certain number of beds—today, 34,000—for detention of unlawful immigrants. There has always been debate as to whether those beds only needed to be "available" or whether they needed to be filled, but the practical result is that as the number of beds maintained by DHS has risen, so has the number of detainees. Under pressure to fill such a quota, officials have been sweeping up not only people crossing illegally from Mexico to work in the United States, but also legal immigrants convicted of minor infractions and women and children seeking asylum. Once they've been detained, immigrants can be held indefinitely in a legal limbo, with little

to no due process or representation. Some of the detention centers are run by private, for-profit corporations, and charges of abuse and neglect have been rampant. Still, immigration judges eventually allow some detainees, like Mirza Dalila, 21, and her daughter, Valery (above), to remain in the United States. Mirza and Valery left their native Honduras, where gang violence threatened them. They were apprehended on the border and sent to an immigration detention center in Dilley, Texas, the largest in the country. They spent a month in Dilley before being taken in by the Mennonite House in San Antonio, a church-run shelter that provides refuge for asylum-seeking families. 📷 CHRISTOPHER GREGORY

DEPORTEE
BY WOODY GUTHRIE

The crops are all in
And the peaches are rotting
The oranges piled up
In their creosote dumps
You're flying 'em back
To the Mexican border
To spend all their money
To wade back again

Some of us are illegal
And others not wanted
Our work contract's up
And we have to move on
Six hundred miles to that Mexican
    border
They chase us like outlaws
Like rustlers, like thieves

The skyplane caught fire
Over Los Gatos Canyon
A fireball of lightning
Shook all our hills
Who are all these friends
Who are scattered like dried leaves
The radio said
They were just "deportees"

Good bye to my Juan
Goodbye Rosalita
Adios mis amigos Jesus why Maria
You won't have a name
When you ride the big airplane
All they will call you
Will be "deportees"

On January 28, 1948, a U.S. government plane deporting 28 Mexican migrant workers crashed in Los Gatos Canyon, California, killing everyone on board. The victims had been brought temporarily into the United States through the Bracero Program, an immigration policy enacted in 1942 that imported workers from south of the border to make up for labor shortages during World War II. During harvest season, American farmers routinely exploited the migrants. Working conditions were so hazardous and the workers were treated so badly a Department of Labor official in charge of the program described the Bracero Program as "legalized slavery." Folk singer Woody Guthrie, known for his songs about the disadvantaged, read about the crash in *The New York Times* and was outraged that authorities couldn't even be bothered to name the dead, referring to them as anonymous "deportees." To memorialize their deaths, Guthrie wrote "Deportee (Plane Wreck at Los Gatos)" to remind listeners that these were human beings whose lives had been forgotten. *Time* magazine columnist Joe Klein described Guthrie's composition as "the last great song he would write." In 2013, when New Yorkers Delila Paz and Edgey Pires of the *The Last Internationale* recorded their own version of Guthrie's song, they discovered that the local community was creating headstones to name every single individual who died on the flight. ∎

NUEVO LEÓN, MEXICO, 1956. Prospective workers (right) line up at the Monterrey Processing Center in Mexico before their admission into the United States under the Bracero Program. The initiative brought cheap Mexican labor to American farms. ⒸⓄ LEONARD NADEL

EUGENE, OREGON, 2003. Latino Americans are the fastest-growing minority segment of the U.S. population, and by by 2050 demographers predict that more than a quarter of all Americans will have Latino roots Here, wearing traditional Mexican dresses, sisters Irene and Araceli Guzmán and Claudia Pelayo practice for an upcoming dance performance, while their little brother, Fernando Pelayo, dressed in his traditional *charro* suit (used by mariachis), looks on. Their father, Fernando Guzmán, came to the United States in 1995 as a construction worker. Now a contractor, he built the home behind them.
📷 BRIAN LANKER

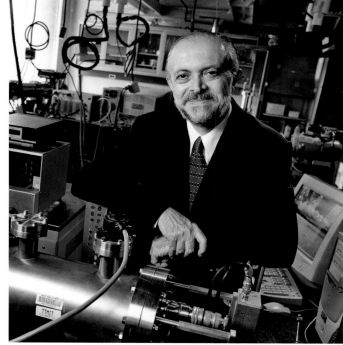

BEFORE SONIA SOTOMAYOR (left) was nominated by President George H. W. Bush to serve as a judge on the federal district court for the Southern District of New York, minorities accounted for only around 10 percent of federal judges. As the first Latina U.S. Supreme Court justice, Sotomayor famously commented that when deciding cases related to racial inequity, "I would hope that a wise Latina woman, with the richness of her experiences, would more often than not reach a better conclusion than a white male who hasn't lived that life." Born in the same year that *Brown v. Board of Education* was decided, Sotomayor once described herself as "the perfect affirmative action baby" and during her tenure in the Supreme Court, she has made it abundantly clear that she sees the Court's role as one of protecting the civil rights of "historically marginalized" groups. Reading the eight dissents Sotomayor wrote for the Court's 2015-2016 term, Adam Liptak, Supreme Court correspondent for *The New York Times*, found "a remarkable body of work from an increasingly skeptical student of the criminal justice system, one who has concluded that it is clouded by arrogance and machismo and warped by bad faith and racism." 📷 RYAN KELLY

JENNIFER LOPEZ (above, left) achieved worldwide fame as a singer, dancer, and actor. Breaking through industry barriers that held back women of color, she became the first Latina to earn $1 million per film. Lopez has enlisted her fame to advance numerous humanitarian causes, including her Lopez Family Foundation, that provides quality health care and education to disadvantaged Latino women and children. Since 2015, Lopez has served as the first-ever global advocate for girls and women at the United Nations Foundation and as a spokesperson for the U.N. Secretary-General's "Every Woman, Every Child" initiative, which runs maternal health, education, and gender-based anti-violence programs.

MEXICAN-BORN CHEMIST Mario Molina (above) won the Nobel Prize for Chemistry in 1995 for his discovery that escaping Freon gas in refrigerators and air conditioners was thinning out the protective ozone layer of the Earth's atmosphere. The world's scientific community rallied around his discovery, halted the use of Freon for the good of the planet, and made Molina an environmental hero. Sadly, such common purpose seems all but impossible today, when the science on man-made climate change and global warming has become a political football. 📷 JIM HARRISON

FIGHTING THE GOOD FIGHT

AMERICA FERRERA

Playing the lead role of Betty Suarez in the TV series *Ugly Betty*, America Ferrera won critical acclaim as Best Actress in 2007 at the Golden Globe Awards, the Screen Actors Guild Awards, and the Primetime Emmy Awards, the first for a Latina. Born in Los Angeles to Honduran parents, Ferrera's professional success has made her a role model for young Latinas. She is also active politically, using her celebrity to encourage Latino Americans to vote. Ferrera was the opening speaker for the Women's March on Washington on January 21, 2017.

NEW YORK, JANUARY 21, 2017. The day after Donald Trump was sworn in as president, almost 5 million men, women and children in more than 30 other countries (including 400,000 in New York City, above) marched in protest. As reported on CNN: "The election of a president whom detractors view as misogynistic and backward-thinking has done nothing less than spark a wholesale resurgence of feminism. ... His incendiary comments about women and his divisive policies on reproductive rights and other issues lit a fire under a movement that had failed to excite younger generations of women who benefited from the battles of the last century and saw no need to keep fighting. They do now. And so do their mothers and grandmothers." © RICK SMOLAN

AMERICAN WOMEN

IN THE NOT SO DISTANT PAST, American women weren't allowed to vote, own property, go to college, or work at most professions. Indeed, as recently as 1973, banks wouldn't issue a woman a credit card in her own name or provide her with a loan without a male co-signer.

The majority of changes that lifted restrictions on women's rights have come about only in the last hundred years. These rights were not granted out of the kindness of men's hearts; women had to fight hard for them.

It wasn't until 1920 that women finally won the right to vote. In the ensuing decades, activists like Alice Paul called for the adoption of an Equal Rights Amendment, while Margaret Sanger, a public health nurse, pushed for the legalization of birth control. Only in 1936 did the Supreme Court rule that birth control information itself was no longer obscene. A woman's right to have an abortion wasn't secured until 1973.

The Feminine Mystique by Betty Friedan in 1963 launched a second wave of feminism. Documenting the unhappiness of her Smith College classmates who had become frustrated housewives, the book inspired new generations of women to seek fulfillment beyond homemaking.

Today, women outnumber men on many American college campuses and represent half the country's workforce. They serve in Congress, play professional sports, and serve in military combat roles—all roles once reserved only for men.

Yet 95 years after it was proposed, there is still no Equal Rights Amendment, and women still earn less than men doing the exact same job. Abortion rights are under attack. And unlike many other Western democracies, the United States has still never had a female president.

Women's rights have come a long way over the past century. But there is still a long way to go before women can say they're truly equal citizens. ■

STRIVING FOR A 50/50 WORLD
BY TIFFANY SHLAIN

RECENTLY, IT'S BEEN EASY TO FEEL there are forces conspiring to drag the women's movement backward. In moments like these, backward is a good place to look to gain some perspective on how far we've come. We need to see where we really are on the arc of history, feel the momentum of that past, and then swiftly turn our gaze to the future, so we never stop envisioning the world we want to see and what it's going to take to get there. The world I want to see is 50/50—with equal opportunities for women and men or however you identify.

I know I felt the full force of women's strength as I stood with my husband and two daughters, crammed tightly in the Women's March on Washington, on January 21, 2017. The power of women is immense and greater than we even realize.

I have to admit, I really understood the true depth and history of this power only recently, even though I've always thought of myself as a feminist. It's in my DNA. My great-grandmother marched, my mother marched, I've marched. While I was growing up, my mom, Carole Lewis, was writing her PhD thesis on the importance of mentors and mothers on successful women. And my dad wrote books about women and power.

But a couple of years ago, I learned a new fact that completely blew my mind.

SAN FRANCISCO, 1969. In the 1960s, the Women's Liberation movement targeted bras as symbols of female servitude and male oppression. But contrary to popular lore, few women actually burned their bras as a public protest. That legend stemmed from a feminist protest at the 1969 Miss America beauty pageant in Atlantic City, New Jersey, where women threw their bras, along with mops, pots, and feminine products, into a "freedom trash can" in defiance of traditional female roles. A female reporter at the demonstration drew an analogy between the feminist protesters and opponents of the Vietnam War, many of whom had burned their draft cards. As a result, the bra-burning trope erroneously became a catchphrase of the feminist era, particularly among male detractors, who used it to ridicule the women's movement.

At an event, I met a woman named Laura Liswood, who has convened elected female presidents and prime ministers for the United Nations for the past 20 years.

I asked her how many female heads of state there had been when she began her gatherings. And she said, "15." I was shocked the number was so high. "Well, how many are there now?" I asked, again thinking it couldn't have increased that much. And then she again threw out a number that almost knocked me down: "Oh, around 50."

Fifty?

How did I not know that there were around 50 elected female presidents and prime ministers? And that made me think: I have been telling a story of scarcity for so long, maybe it's time to tell a new story about abundance.

Not knowing something so important about women and power also made me think: what else didn't I know?

Let me start with the stark reality that, despite the progress women have made over the past 100 years, we still have a long way to go. For example, even though women make up half of the world's population in 2017:

For every $1 men earn in the United States, women earn 77 cents. Women of color, even less.

Of 870 Nobel Prize winners, 48 have been women. That's 5 percent.

IN THE 1950s and 1960s, it was common for advertisers to portray women as childlike, as subservient to men, and as sexual objects (above). But in the decades that followed, TV shows and movies increasingly reflected feminist themes. The award-winning 1970s sitcom *The Mary Tyler Moore Show* (opposite), was the first to dramatize the challenges facing a single woman in the workplace. In another first, the show garnered critical acclaim for raising issues such as equal pay for women, premarital sex, and divorce.

Of 116 current elected heads of state, 21 are women. That's 18 percent. That's the bad news. The good news:

Women now outnumber men in college, and more women graduate than men.

Twenty years ago, there were no women CEOs of Fortune 500 companies. Now there are 26.

In 1970, less than 10 percent of medical students were female. Now, it's over 50 percent.

Eighteen percent of American cities are headed by female mayors.

And that astounding total of 50 heads of state I couldn't believe when I met Laura Liswood in 2015? It's now grown to 62. Unfortunately, not in our own country.

These and other eye-opening statistics set me off on a journey to examine where we are today on the greater arc of history of women and power. It also focused me on what it's going to take to get to a 50/50 world. I'm not talking just politics and boardrooms. I'm talking across all parts of society, truly shifting the gender balance to benefit everyone.

To help me figure out where things stand today, where we are on this arc, I looked at the history of humanity. I had to look hard, since most of history as we know it was written by men, and women have been left out. I wanted the rest of the story.

It turns out, way back in the Neolithic Age, it's believed that things were pretty egalitarian between the sexes. Women and men had equal social status, and the earliest written laws reflected this. Women could choose to marry and divorce. Women were healers, shamans, religious leaders, warriors, and lawmakers. All genders were respected. This was what it was like 10,000 years ago! Just let that sink in for a minute.

But then, like many times on our journey, the story takes a dark turn as the balance shifted. My father, Dr. Leonard Shlain, wrote a book called *The Alphabet Versus the Goddess* that attributed this shift to literacy rewiring our brains. Some people pin the change on the rise of agriculture, which favored physical strength and the conquest of land. Others point to the development of military and political power. Whatever the reasons, over the centuries, in most parts of the world, the voices of women became increasingly silent.

In 2350 B.C., in ancient Mesopotamia, one of the earliest laws was, "If a woman speaks to a man out of turn, her teeth will be smashed in by a burnt brick."

Those centuries of imbalance were big mountains to climb. Many of the wise, independent, rebellious women of their day had to pay a price. Between 1500 and 1800, an estimated 50,000 women in Europe and the Americas were labeled witches and put on trial, then executed by being burned alive. A lot of powerful women were lost from our narrative.

That imbalance became embedded in political structures. Even our own country, which I do love, was established with the line "All men are created equal." This was during a time of slavery. Clearly, they didn't mean "*All* men." And clearly, they didn't mean women. Women couldn't own property. We had the same legal status as children. We couldn't vote. We were considered property. We could be used and abused with no recourse.

But no mountain was going to truly hold our power back. Women were rising in art, science, and culture. And pioneers were gathering, coming together to fight for more rights. Momentum was building in Europe, the United States, and dots around the globe, for what we now call "the first wave of feminism."

In 1848, 300 women—and some men—convened in Seneca Falls, New York, and declared, "All men and women are created equal." The suffragist fight was under way, and it was not pretty. Women were thrown in jail, beaten, and force fed. And yet, they persisted.

Seventy years after Seneca Falls, women in the United States won the right to vote. On August 26, 1920, the Nineteenth Amendment to the Constitution was finally ratified, enfranchising all American women and declaring for the first time that they, like men, deserve all the rights and responsibilities of citizenship.

But the battle wasn't over yet. Only three years later, emboldened by the constitutional amendment victory in 1923, the National Women's Party proposed an amendment to the Constitution, the Equal Rights Amendment (E.R.A.), that prohibited all discrimination on the basis of sex. That was over 90 years ago. It was reintroduced in the 1970s and every year since—and to this day, it still has not been ratified, though soon, it may be. In March 2017, Nevada voted for ratification. If a few more states follow—and Congress repeals the original 1979 ratification deadline (later extended to 1982)—it could go through.

As I absorbed examples from the past about how long real social change takes, it struck me over and over again that we can't become complacent, we can't take any of these hard-fought rights for granted. And if we want our daughters and sons to experience a more equal world, we have to accelerate the pace of change.

Ironically, while all the strides and struggles were happening in the United States—women gathering, creating support groups, fighting for more rights—there were also a lot of exciting things happening on an international scale. By 1970, three countries had elected women as heads of state and we start to see other action around the globe. One of my favorites: in 1975, 90 percent of women in Iceland went on strike. Banks, businesses, and factories had to close, while men scrambled to care for their children and keep things running. The country screeched to a standstill, and Iceland has been better ever since. Women proved how important they were and began earning more seats in parliament and positions in the workforce. Iceland voted in the first democratically elected female president, Vigdís Finnbogadóttir, in 1980, and she served for 16 years. (Today, Iceland ranks first in gender equality in the World Economic Forum's Global Gender Gap Index and is the first country to make equal pay required by law).

JUST THE FACTS

IN 2016,

2/3

OF AMERICAN WOMEN WERE EITHER THE PRIMARY OR CO-BREADWINNER OF THEIR FAMILIES.

—CENTER FOR AMERICAN PROGRESS

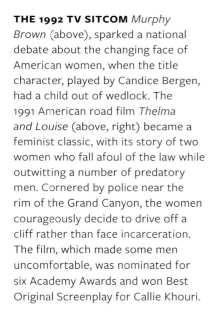

THE 1992 TV SITCOM *Murphy Brown* (above), sparked a national debate about the changing face of American women, when the title character, played by Candice Bergen, had a child out of wedlock. The 1991 American road film *Thelma and Louise* (above, right) became a feminist classic, with its story of two women who fall afoul of the law while outwitting a number of predatory men. Cornered by police near the rim of the Grand Canyon, the women courageously decide to drive off a cliff rather than face incarceration. The film, which made some men uncomfortable, was nominated for six Academy Awards and won Best Original Screenplay for Callie Khouri.

The year of the strike in Iceland, the United Nations brought together the first international women's conference. Over 6,000 delegates from 133 countries traveled to Mexico City, and gathered in person for two weeks to discuss the status of equal rights for women on a global scale. They made a collective plan: they'd convene again in Copenhagen in 1980, in Nairobi in 1985, and Beijing in 1995.

It was there that Hillary Clinton famously declared, "Human rights are women's rights, and women's rights are human rights, once and for all."

It was also in the mid 1990s that my new friend Laura Liswood started assembling her council of women leaders. It's good to remember this was the 1970s, '80s, and '90s. All the connecting was done with faxes, long-distance phone calls, letters, and long plane rides, just to have face-to-face conversations.

Today, it's a whole different world. The Internet has accelerated the pace of change in so many ways. We can connect across continents, bringing power and opportunity to far more voices. In addition to that transparency and responsibility, today's world also gives us more ways to learn from each other—person to person, and country to country. There are over 400 studies showing that making changes that foster gender equality—from all levels, business, politics, and culture—makes life better for everyone—not just women. Everyone.

Over half of the countries that rank highest in gender equality across different sectors also rank highest on the global happiness index. A lot of these countries pay for early child care and high-quality education. They have national parental

leave—for both men and women. Instead of this idea of "Stay at home, mom," they're supporting parents. Period.

Because dads are being deprived of their power, too. The power of nurturing and raising the next generation. A recent study in the United States showed that 50 percent of men who are offered paid paternity leave feel they can't take it. Men have their own entire history of stereotypes and expectations to wrestle with, too.

Those men who are equal parents may be the next chapter, paving the way to something better: 50/50 isn't just about women getting more power, it's about everyone getting more power. It's about opening up the whole idea of what power is. Moving beyond the binaries of men and women. When we have more diverse leadership, we have more diverse character strengths, like empathy, bravery, social intelligence, social responsibility, and humility. And that makes us *all* stronger.

So, how do we really get there, to the world we want to see?

I turned to the person who blew my mind and set me down this path in the first place. I asked Laura Liswood: "How do we get to 50/50?"

Here's what she said:

"Change itself goes from the unthinkable to the impossible to the inevitable. I often liken it to a standing ovation. First people jump up, and say this is the best thing they've ever seen. Then another larger group stands up, and says,

FEMINISM'S GROWING PAINS have played out on the covers of the nation's most widely read magazines. In 1998, *Time* magazine generated a groundbreaking debate (above, left), between iconic feminist figures like Gloria Steinem and Betty Friedan, who advanced the struggle for equal pay and reproductive rights, and the so-called third wave of feminists, whose focus extended to issues of diversity, poverty, the environment, and marriage equality. *New York* magazine's February 2016 provocative cover story (above, center), declared that the rise of the independent, single professional woman represented a radical upheaval in American life, with profound social and political implications. For the first time, the article asserted, the country has "an entirely new population of adult women who are no longer

economically, socially, sexually, or reproductively dependent on or defined by the men they marry." The exemplar of the new American woman, Oprah Winfrey, was the subject of a September 30, 2010, cover story in that venerable chronicler of American business, *Fortune* magazine (opposite, right). Winfrey, a media mogul and philanthropist, is the nation's first and only African American multibillionaire. Facebook CEO Sheryl Sandberg, profiled in *Time* magazine in March 2013 (above), encouraged women to rigorously pursue their careers and seize both the opportunities and challenges of becoming a boss.

'Yes, yes, this was excellent.' Then the larger group gets up and says, 'Yeah, yeah, this was OK.' And then finally the last group gets up because they can't see the stage. Change can be very disruptive and unsettling for people. And often, there's some group of people who want to revert to the 'good old days,' which were often not actually very good for most people. But the rest of us—we need to stand up and keep clapping."

On January 21, 2017, we did just that. Nearly 5 million people participated in women's marches held in almost more than 600 cities all over the world. We filled the streets with our bodies, the air with our words. Together, we marched toward the summit.

It is easy, sometimes, to get discouraged, when we think the fight for equality might be moving backward. But when we actually look back, we can see how far we've come in the past 100, 40, 20 years. We can vote, hold office. Laws now give women control of their own bodies and their own lives. That just wasn't true before. We're raising our girls (and boys) to know they'll be able to do anything—because they will.

And it's not just the girls who'll build a more equitable world. We won't get to 50/50 unless the other 50 percent helps. We need more men to want this, too. Because we're building a better life for them, and their sons and daughters, too. For all genders. Research shows that a gender-balanced world makes life better for everyone.

And yes, there's a lot more work to do. But today, we have more knowledge, and more tools, than any generation before us. The Internet has made it possible for almost everyone on the planet to connect. The path to 50/50 will be built alongside all the real-world big and small actions that need to happen to get us there. Online, we can share our challenges, ideas, and opportunities. We can organize. And we can do it faster than ever before. We saw that after the election, when a whole new movement sprung up overnight.

We have a fight ahead of us. We have to keep on pushing for equal representation in history, in government, in compensation, in the home, in the office, in the school, on the field, in film, and in all other aspects of society. The great American struggle for equal opportunities for women continues. But our willingness to struggle is what *makes* America great, and that justice we're searching for, we'll find. I truly believe that striving for 50/50 equality is the right vision to help us get there. ∎

Tiffany Shlain is an Emmy-nominated filmmaker, founder of The Webby Awards and co-founder of 50/50 Day (50-50Day.org), an annual event with thousands of screenings and discussions around the globe exploring what it's going to take to get to a more gender balanced world. Her films and work have received over 80 awards and distinctions including premieres at The Sundance Film Festival, a Disruptive Innovation Award from Tribeca Film Festival, inclusion in NPR's list of best commencement speeches. The U.S. State Department sends Schlain and her films to represent America at embassies around the world to foster dialogue. She runs the Let it Ripple Film studio in San Francisco and is a Henry Crown Fellow of The Aspen Institute. ▼ *@tiffanyshlain, tiffanyshlain.com*

Essay adapted from the film script 50/50 by Tiffany Shlain, Sawyer Steele and Julie Hermelin.

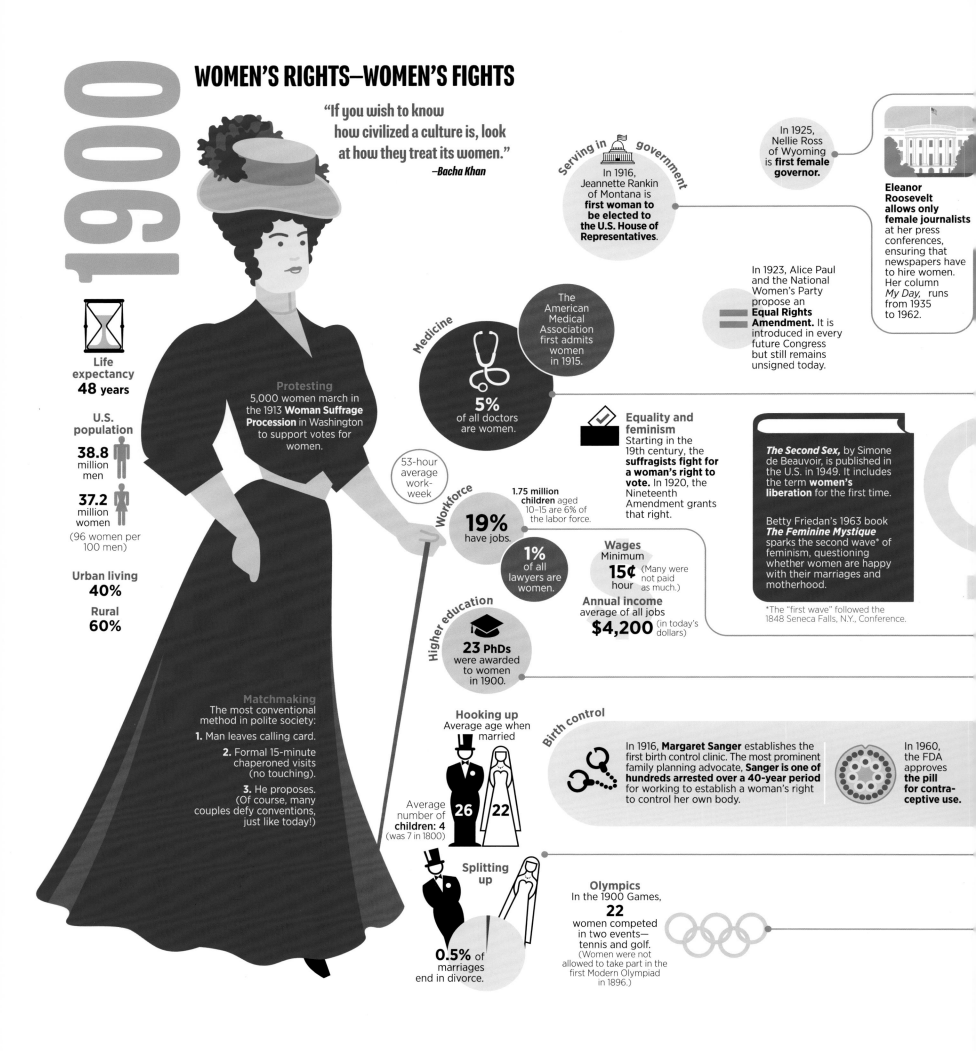

WOMEN'S RIGHTS—WOMEN'S FIGHTS

1900

"If you wish to know how civilized a culture is, look at how they treat its women."
—*Bacha Khan*

Serving in government
In 1916, Jeannette Rankin of Montana is **first woman to be elected to the U.S. House of Representatives**.

In 1925, Nellie Ross of Wyoming is **first female governor.**

Eleanor Roosevelt allows only female journalists at her press conferences, ensuring that newspapers have to hire women. Her column *My Day,* runs from 1935 to 1962.

In 1923, Alice Paul and the National Women's Party propose an **Equal Rights Amendment.** It is introduced in every future Congress but still remains unsigned today.

Medicine
The American Medical Association first admits women in 1915.

5% of all doctors are women.

Life expectancy 48 years

U.S. population
38.8 million men
37.2 million women
(96 women per 100 men)

Urban living 40%
Rural 60%

Protesting
5,000 women march in the 1913 **Woman Suffrage Procession** in Washington to support votes for women.

53-hour average work-week

Workforce
19% have jobs.

1.75 million **children** aged 10–15 are 6% of the labor force.

1% of all lawyers are women.

Equality and feminism
Starting in the 19th century, the **suffragists fight for a woman's right to vote.** In 1920, the Nineteenth Amendment grants that right.

Wages
Minimum **15¢ hour** (Many were not paid as much.)

Annual income average of all jobs **$4,200** (in today's dollars)

The Second Sex, by Simone de Beauvoir, is published in the U.S. in 1949. It includes the term **women's liberation** for the first time.

Betty Friedan's 1963 book *The Feminine Mystique* sparks the second wave* of feminism, questioning whether women are happy with their marriages and motherhood.

*The "first wave" followed the 1848 Seneca Falls, N.Y., Conference.

Higher education
23 PhDs were awarded to women in 1900.

Matchmaking
The most conventional method in polite society:
1. Man leaves calling card.
2. Formal 15-minute chaperoned visits (no touching).
3. He proposes. (Of course, many couples defy conventions, just like today!)

Hooking up
Average age when married
26 **22**
Average number of **children: 4** (was 7 in 1800)

Birth control
In 1916, **Margaret Sanger** establishes the first birth control clinic. The most prominent family planning advocate, **Sanger is one of hundreds arrested over a 40-year period** for working to establish a woman's right to control her own body.

In 1960, the FDA approves **the pill for contraceptive use.**

Splitting up
0.5% of marriages end in divorce.

Olympics
In the 1900 Games, **22** women competed in two events— tennis and golf. (Women were not allowed to take part in the first Modern Olympiad in 1896.)

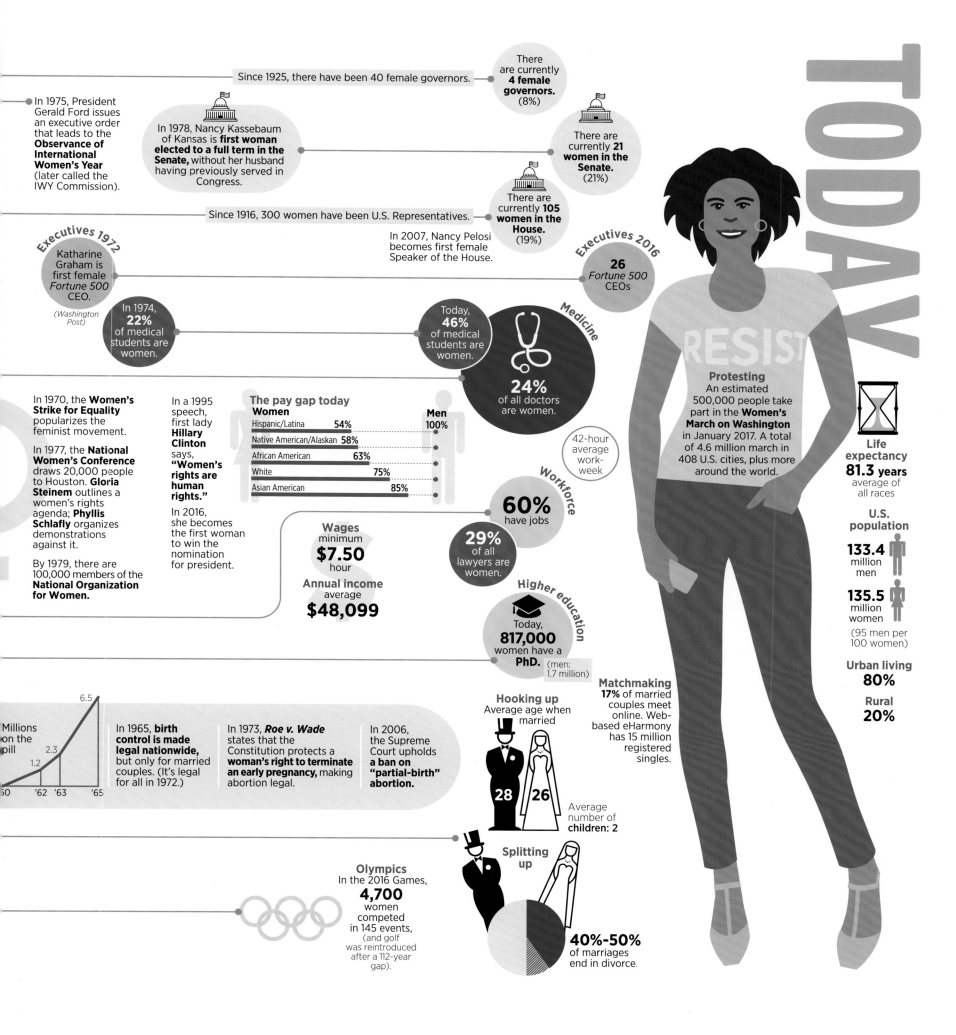

TODAY

Since 1925, there have been 40 female governors.

There are currently **4 female governors.** (8%)

In 1975, President Gerald Ford issues an executive order that leads to the **Observance of International Women's Year** (later called the IWY Commission).

In 1978, Nancy Kassebaum of Kansas is **first woman elected to a full term in the Senate,** without her husband having previously served in Congress.

There are currently **21 women in the Senate.** (21%)

Since 1916, 300 women have been U.S. Representatives.

There are currently **105 women in the House.** (19%)

In 2007, Nancy Pelosi becomes first female Speaker of the House.

Executives 1972
Katharine Graham is first female *Fortune 500* CEO.
(*Washington Post*)

Executives 2016
26 *Fortune 500* CEOs

In 1974, **22%** of medical students are women.

Today, **46%** of medical students are women.

Medicine
24% of all doctors are women.

Protesting
An estimated 500,000 people take part in the **Women's March on Washington** in January 2017. A total of 4.6 million march in 408 U.S. cities, plus more around the world.

Life expectancy
81.3 years average of all races

In 1970, the **Women's Strike for Equality** popularizes the feminist movement.

In 1977, the **National Women's Conference** draws 20,000 people to Houston. **Gloria Steinem** outlines a women's rights agenda; **Phyllis Schlafly** organizes demonstrations against it.

By 1979, there are 100,000 members of the **National Organization for Women.**

In a 1995 speech, first lady **Hillary Clinton** says, **"Women's rights are human rights."**

In 2016, she becomes the first woman to win the nomination for president.

The pay gap today

Women		Men 100%
Hispanic/Latina	54%	
Native American/Alaskan	58%	
African American	63%	
White	75%	
Asian American	85%	

42-hour average work-week

Workforce
60% have jobs

29% of all lawyers are women.

Wages
minimum **$7.50** hour
Annual income average **$48,099**

Higher education
Today, **817,000** women have a PhD. (men: 1.7 million)

U.S. population
133.4 million men
135.5 million women
(95 men per 100 women)

Urban living 80%
Rural 20%

Millions on the pill
6.5 / 2.3 / 1.2
'60 '62 '63 '65

In 1965, **birth control is made legal nationwide,** but only for married couples. (It's legal for all in 1972.)

In 1973, *Roe v. Wade* states that the Constitution protects a **woman's right to terminate an early pregnancy,** making abortion legal.

In 2006, the Supreme Court upholds **a ban on "partial-birth" abortion.**

Matchmaking
17% of married couples meet online. Web-based eHarmony has 15 million registered singles.

Hooking up
Average age when married
28 / 26
Average number of **children: 2**

Splitting up
40%-50% of marriages end in divorce.

Olympics
In the 2016 Games, **4,700** women competed in 145 events, (and golf was reintroduced after a 112-year gap).

175

NEW YORK, JANUARY 8, 1917. Margaret Sanger, a public health nurse (far left), talks with supporters outside a Brooklyn courthouse, where she and several other suffragists are on trial for opening the first birth-control clinic in the United States. Sanger demanded that women should have the right to control their own bodies. Nearly 60 years would pass before the U.S. Supreme Court guaranteed a woman's right to have an abortion.

NEW YORK, AUGUST 1913. Militant suffragists Elizabeth Freeman and Elsie MacKenzie traveled slowly from New York to Boston in a horse-drawn "suffrage caravan" to campaign for women's voting rights. During their two-month journey they stopped to give lectures on women's suffrage. The activists paid their way by selling copies of *The Boston Women's Journal* and, as reported in *The New York Times*, "by enchanting their audiences with a hurdy-gurdy which can play a variety of tunes." Carrier pigeons were used to keep the women in touch with Boston. In Hartford, Connecticut, just as they were beginning a talk, a police officer placed them under arrest for breaking a city law that prohibited vehicles adorned with advertising to pass through the city. The officer instructed the suffragists to drive behind him to the station, but when he turned around, they had driven off at a gallop in another direction. After being apprehended, Freeman and MacKenzie engaged a lawyer who negotiated on their behalf with the chief of police, and it was agreed that charges would be dismissed if they kept covered their signs throughout the remainder of their time in Hartford. According to police records, the suffragists' horse "was a steed of artistic temperament" named Lausanne, who had cost the women $59.98.

DURING WORLD WAR II, a shortage of manpower to build aircraft, tanks, and guns opened the door for women to work at jobs previously held only by men. At the Douglas Aircraft Company in Long Beach, California, female workers (left) installed fixtures in the tail section of a B-17 bomber. The women who worked at the factories that supported the war effort became popularly known as "Rosie the Riveter," after Norman Rockwell's iconic portrait, which appeared on the cover of the *Saturday Evening Post* on May 29, 1943.
ALFRED T. PALMER

JUST THE FACTS

IN 2016, FEMALE

CEOs

HAVE OUT-EARNED AND OUTPERFORMED THEIR MALE COUNTERPARTS.

—*BLOOMBERG*

YOU DON'T OWN ME
SUNG BY LESLEY GORE

You don't own me
I'm not just one of your many toys
You don't own me
Don't say I can't go with other boys

And don't tell me what to do
Don't tell me what to say
And please, when I go out with you
Don't put me on display 'cause

You don't own me
Don't try to change me in any way
You don't own me
Don't tie me down 'cause I'd never stay

I don't tell you what to say
I don't tell you what to do
So just let me be myself
That's all I ask of you

I'm young and I love to be young
I'm free and I love to be free
To live my life the way I want
To say and do whatever I please

GLORIA STEINEM
ON HOW
WOMEN VOTE

NEW FEMINIST:
SIMONE
DE BEAUVOIR

MONEY FOR
HOUSEWORK

BODY HAIR: THE
LAST FRONTIER

Ms.

WONDER WOMAN FOR PRESIDENT

PEACE AND JUSTICE '72

Lesley Gore was only 17 years old when she recorded "You Don't Own Me," a song whose themes of defiance, independence, and self-respect sent it to the top of the charts in 1963 and later turned it into a feminist anthem for younger generations. The song unapologetically declares that a woman is not a man's possession, to be controlled or treated as a toy or sexual plaything. Women, the song asserts, control their own destiny. Although it was written by two men, the song's powerful message of female empowerment, delivered in Gore's passionate vocals, emboldened many young women to stand up for themselves for the first time. Some even say the song helped spur the second wave of feminist activism that began in the 1970s. The song reached No. 2 on the *Billboard Hot 100*, surpassed only by the Beatles' smash "I Want to Hold Your Hand." The song resurfaced in 2012 as a feminist video urging women to vote in the presidential election. The video opens with Gore herself announcing, "I'm Lesley Gore, and I approve this message." Gore died in 2015 of lung cancer at the age of 68, leaving behind Lois Sasson, her partner of 33 years. Her obituary in *The New York Times* stated that Gore, born into a Jewish family in Brooklyn, New York, had made herself "the voice of teenage girls aggrieved by fickle boyfriends, moving quickly from tearful self-pity to fierce self-assertion." On November 27, 2016, "You Don't Own Me" was inducted into the Grammy Hall of Fame. ∎

WHEN *MS.* MAGAZINE LAUNCHED in 1972 (left), it reflected a new era of female empowerment. Created by Gloria Steinem (right) and Patricia Carbin, *Ms.* focused on issues of women's rights, sexual harassment, and domestic violence. From its first issue, the magazine refused to run advertisements for any products considered to be harmful to women's health or self-image.
YALE JOEL, RIGHT

BOSTON, APRIL 19, 1967. A Boston Marathon official (above, in street clothes) tries to pull Kathrine Switzer, No. 261, out of the race, furious that a woman has dared to enter the all-male competition. It took a body block by a supportive male runner to clear the way for Switzer, who became the first woman to complete the difficult 26.2-mile course as an official entrant. Switzer had obscured her gender by registering as "K.V. Switzer." Her determination to compete opened the way for millions of women to participate in the sport. Today, half the nation's marathon runners are women. In 2017, Switzer, 70, returned to Boston to run again in the marathon. Her time: 4 hours and 31 minutes—just a little slower than her historic 4 hour and 20 minute run 50 years earlier.

MARIN COUNTY, CALIFORNIA, SEPTEMBER 30, 1969. A woman blissfully breastfeeds her baby (right) at a picnic at Mount Tamalpais, just north of San Francisco. One of the most visible aspects of the women's liberation and hippie movements of the 1960s and 1970s was the increasing comfort that many women began to feel with their bodies. Among more educated and affluent women, breastfeeding was also an act of defiance against the baby formula industry, which promoted the idea that breastfeeding was old fashioned, lower class and, to some, repulsive. 📷 ROBERT ALTMAN

WASHINGTON, D.C., JANUARY 24, 2011. Anti-abortion activists and pro-choice demonstrators challenge each other with signs in front of the U.S. Supreme Court during the annual March for Life protest. The march, organized by abortion opponents, has been held every year since 1974, when the high court's ruling in the landmark case of *Roe v. Wade* guaranteed a woman's right to have an abortion. In recent years, anti-abortion advocates have been successful in limiting the availability of abortions in several Southern states. 📷 CHIP SOMODEVILLA

AN EPIDEMIC OF SUICIDES among teenagers in recent years has made it very clear that sticks and stones are not the only way adolescents inflict long-lasting damage on each other. Recent studies show that the most frequent targets of bullying in the United States are middle-school students, gay and transgender people, immigrants, and Muslims. While bullying isn't new, online bullying has taken the problem to a new level, making it possible for targets to be shamed, libeled, or attacked by anonymous and untraceable accusers. As a result, more than 160,000 American children miss school every day out of fear of being bullied. Approximately 50 percent of all teenagers have been the victims of cyberbullying, and girls are somewhat more likely than boys to engage in gang stalking (where a group of kids target one kid for coordinated and persistent abuse).

Many institutions, including the Centers for Disease Control and Prevention, the U.S. Department of Education, and the Anti-Defamation League, have launched initiatives to teach parents, teachers, students, and the general public about the damage that bullying causes. So has Cynthia Germanotta, the mother of singer Lady Gaga, who heads the Born This Way foundation. Joining them in their efforts is 18-year-old photographer Mary Anne Marcondes, who produced the image (above) with her friends after being bullied herself in high school.
🄯 MARY ANNE MARCONDES

IN 1999, THE R&B GIRL BAND Destiny's Child (right) gave voice to young women who suddenly had to navigate a threatening new online cyberscape of revenge porn and cyberstalking. *The Writing's on the Wall*, the group's second album, became one of the largest-selling R&B albums of all time and transformed the trio into superstars. "Independent Women," featured in the film *Charlie's Angels*, still holds up as an anthem to female strength, assertiveness, and to closing the wage gap between men and women. Commenting in *The Guardian* in 2007, writer Laura Barton observed the song explains that "a woman should not require a man to buy her shoes, house, automobile, or the rocks she is rockin', but should instead head out to find gainful employment and, therefore, financial liberation." 🄯 GILLIAN LAUB

BENTONVILLE, ARKANSAS, 2012.
On a visit to the Crystal Bridges Museum of American Art, a young girl (left) gazes up at the original painting of Norman Rockwell's iconic "Rosie the Riveter," which appeared on the cover of the *Saturday Evening Post* on May 29, 1943. Rockwell's historic World War II image presented a powerful woman with a rivet gun on her lap and a copy of Hitler's *Mein Kampf* beneath her shoes. Since so many able-bodied men were fighting abroad, women became a crucial addition to the workforce in American shipyards and factories, producing war supplies and munitions. The experience was liberating, as women proved to the world (and to themselves) that they were easily capable of doing "a man's job." An unexpected side benefit was that white women ended up working side-by-side with African American women, breaking down long-held social barriers. Mary Doyle, the 19-year-old who posed for Rockwell's painting, was paid $10 for her modeling work (equivalent to $140 in 2017). When the painting was sold at Sotheby's in 2012 for nearly $5 million, Mary, 89, was there in the audience.
📷 RUSSELL COTHREN

INTERNATIONAL SPACE STATION, 2010. The first woman in space was Soviet Russian cosmonaut Valentina Tereshkova, completing 48 orbits of Earth in 1963. Since then, 58 of the 556 members of our species who have ventured into space have been women. NASA's current class of 112 astronauts includes 16 women, among them mission specialists Dorothy Metcalf-Lindenburger (above left), Stephanie Wilson (front) and flight engineer Tracy Caldwell Dyson (above right). Together with Japanese astronaut Naoko Yamazaki, they pause from their duties aboard the International Space Station to pose for a group photo. Their mission marked the first time that four women were in space at the same time.

INSPIRING THE NEXT generation of explorers, *Hidden Figures* (right), the movie that outsold *Rogue One: A Star Wars Story* on the weekend it premiered, is the true story of three forgotten African American women who played a critical role at NASA in the early years of the U.S. Space Program. The real figures were Dorothy Vaughan, Katherine Johnson, and Mary Jackson, all brilliant mathematicians. A second generation of African American women, the actresses (from left) Janelle Monáe, Taraji P. Henson, and Octavia Spencer, portrayed them in the 2016 film *Hidden Figures*. And in February 2017, in honor of Black History Month, Milwaukee elementary school students (from left) Ambrielle Baker-Rogers, Morgan Coleman, and Miah Bell-Olson posed as NASA mathematicians for their own version of the film's powerful poster. When actress Henson saw the image, she shared it with her 9.8 million Instagram followers, which turned it into a national sensation. "Hidden figures no more!" wrote one of her fans.
📷 AMANDA EVANS

WOMEN FROM MINORITY backgrounds have risen to top leadership positions at some of the biggest U.S. corporations. Ursula Burns, chairwoman and CEO at Xerox (above, left), is the first African American woman CEO to head a Fortune 500 company. In 2014, Forbes rated her the 22nd most powerful woman in the world. Pepsico Chairwoman and CEO Indra K. Nooyi, (above, right) was born and raised in India. Today, as head of the world's second-largest food and beverage business, Nooyi has been ranked 13th on the *Forbes* list.

***TIME* MAGAZINE HAS DESCRIBED HER** as "The Most Powerful Woman on the Internet." Susan Wojcicki (right) was Google's 16th employee and is today YouTube's CEO. As a mother of five, Wojcicki believes that having children makes her even more effective as a leader at work. She has helped to encourage a parent-friendly culture at Google. Under her leadership, expectant moms are allocated special parking places; new mothers are offered 18 weeks of paid parental leave

and new fathers are given 12 weeks of parental leave. Wojcicki is the daughter of a Polish American father, and her grandfather was a member of the Polish Peasant Party, serving in that country's parliament until the communist takeover in 1947. Her mother, Esther is an American journalist, educator, and vice chair of the Creative Commons board of directors.

📷 ALEX WONG, ABOVE, LEFT; BAUER-GRIFFON, ABOVE, RIGHT; NORMAN JEAN ROY, RIGHT

FIGHTING THE GOOD FIGHT

MEGAN SMITH

Megan Smith was the first woman to serve as the chief technology officer of the United States, a position created by President Barack Obama to help harness the power of data and technological innovation for the good of the nation. Educated at the Massachusetts Institute of Technology, Smith has contributed to numerous engineering projects, ranging from the construction of a space station to solar cookstoves. She held several senior positions

at Google, was the former CEO of Planet Out, and now serves on the boards of Vital Voices, a nonprofit nongovernmental organization that works to advance women's empowerment and political participation. Smith also co-founded the Malala Fund, which raises money so that Malala Yousafzai, the Pakistani activist for female education and the youngest-ever Nobel Peace Prize laureate, can pursue her efforts for girls' empowerment.

NEW YORK, JUNE 29, 2014. It took several decades of legal challenges, funding boycotts, and demonstrations before the Boy Scouts of America lifted its ban on gay scout leaders in 2015. A year earlier, members of the Brooklyn Scouts for Equality, a Boy Scout troop that supported the move, marched in New York's annual Gay Pride Parade. In a sign of how much more open the organization has become on the issue of gender equality, it only took a few weeks of deliberation for it to admit transgender males. Joe Maldonado became the first openly transgender boy to join the Scouts, on February 7, 2017.
📷 JAMES ESTRIN

LGBTQ AMERICANS

THE LGBTQ MOVEMENT FOR EQUALITY dates back to the years after World War II—when contemporary homophobia also really began. Homosexuality was medicalized and pathologized; electroshock therapy and other treatments promised to "cure" it. During the McCarthy era, fears about sexual deviance often intertwined with anti-Communism.

At the same time, gay consciousness was starting to arise. In the 1950s and early 1960s, pioneering organizations like the Mattachine Society and the Daughters of Bilitis held the first official gay protests. On June 27, 1969, the night gay icon Judy Garland died at age 67, a handful of police officers raided the Stonewall Bar in New York's Greenwich Village. They had done so countless times before, but this night was different. The crowd fought back, rioted, and barricaded the cops inside the bar.

Stonewall was a catalyst. Within months, organizations like the Gay Activists Alliance emerged, demanding equal rights for gays and lesbians. Gay liberation joined the ranks of women's liberation, the civil rights movement, and the antiwar movement.

Attitudes shifted after the trauma of AIDS in the 1980s and 1990s. Ellen DeGeneres came out on her sitcom in 1997; in 1998, *Will and Grace* featured a gay leading man; *Brokeback Mountain*, about two closeted gay cowboys, was an Oscar contender and winner in 2005. By 2015, transgender characters populated TV series like *Transparent* and *Orange Is the New Black*.

In 1996, the movement won its first Supreme Court victory, as the justices threw out a Colorado ban against LGBTQ nondiscrimination laws. Seven years later, Texas sodomy laws were ruled unconstitutional. It would take nearly 20 years for same-sex marriage to become a constitutional right, but the logic of that decision was implicit in the earlier ones: if gay people are people, when gay people get married, it's marriage. And that is a fundamental right.

None of this was as inevitable as it may seem in retrospect. Governments can change laws, but society progresses because of people. Today, the vast majority of Americans under the age of 30 support full legal and social equality for LGBTQ people. ■

MY LIFE IN THE MOVEMENT
BY CLEVE JONES

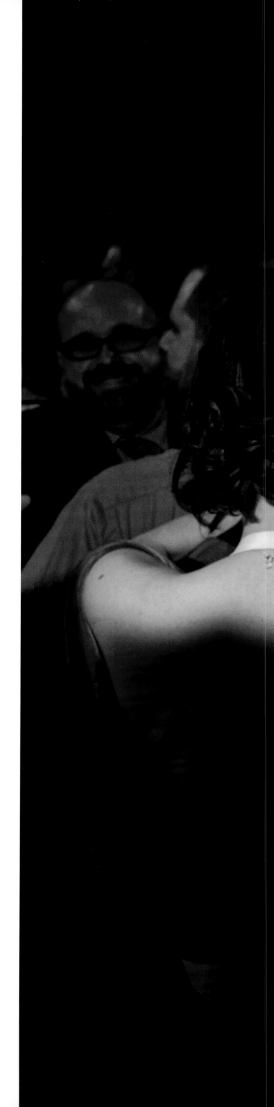

I KNEW I WAS GAY from my earliest memories, but for a good part of my adolescence, I thought I was the only person on the planet who felt this way. I was teased and slang words were tossed my way. I had already experienced quite a bit of bullying, and I was terrified that I was going to get found out. Only misery lay ahead.

My father was a psychologist, so I went to his library. It was horrifying for a 14-year-old kid to suddenly discover that his feelings were not only deemed criminal but were also considered a psychological illness. For gay men and women who grew up in the 1960s, that was our reality. It was frightening and lonely, and I thought I would spend my entire life as an outsider. I felt that my life was over before it had really even begun, because it just seemed then that there was no way to have a decent life and to be gay. I often felt so lost I even considered suicide. I actually stockpiled pills to kill myself. That was my solution. I wish I could say that was just a thing of my own past. But it's not. Even today, every year, we lose an awful lot of young people, teenagers, who take their own lives because they're gay or transgender.

My turning point came one day in 1971, when I stumbled upon an issue of *LIFE* magazine with an astonishing cover story headlined "Homosexuals in Revolt." That's where I learned about Stonewall, the rebellion in New York's Greenwich Village that had happened two years earlier. I was a not very macho, 17-year-old kid living in Phoenix, Arizona, and in a matter of minutes, those

SEATTLE, WASHINGTON, DECEMBER 9, 2012. Hundreds of same-sex couples (right) attend a group wedding reception at a downtown Seattle theater on the day that Washington state declared gay marriage legal. During the first dance, Terry Gilbert blissfully rests his head on the chest of his new husband, Paul Beppler. 📷 DAVID RYDER

NEW YORK, NEW YORK
APRIL 21, 1966. Just as African Americans once staged sit-ins at segregated lunch counters in the South, the Mattachine Society, an early gay rights group, used staged "sip-ins" to challenge New York State liquor regulations, which enabled bars to refuse to serve gay customers on the theory that gays were "disorderly." Targeting a bar where they knew they would be denied service, Matachine members alerted the news media ahead of their visit and invited them to document the event. In this encounter (left), a bartender at Julius' Bar refuses to serve three members of the group after they announced, "We are homosexuals, we are orderly, we intend to remain orderly, and we are asking for service."
📷 FRED W. MCDARRAH

nine pages of text and photographs revealed to me that there were other people like me; that there were a lot of us; that we were organizing; that there was a community; and that there were places where we could live safely. One of these places was San Francisco.

I went there as soon as I could, skipped college, got a phone-sales job, followed gay liberation politics, and eventually met and worked for a gay activist named Harvey Milk. In 1977, Harvey was elected as the first openly gay member of San Francisco's Board of Supervisors. He's often described as the first openly gay person to be elected to public office, but that's inaccurate, and in my book *When We Rise,* I credit the half-dozen or so individuals who came before him. Harvey's historical significance was that he became the gay community's first shared martyr, after his assassination in 1978 by an aggrieved straight politician named Dan White.

Word of Harvey's killing spread far and wide, and even though gay people had lost many people to violence, to suicide, to drugs and alcohol, here was this symbolic figure who struck a chord with people. For those of us in San Francisco, it was inspiring to see this guy, who was really just one of our local neighborhood characters, assume worldwide significance.

Eighteen months before Harvey was shot and killed, a minor celebrity actress named Anita Bryant led a campaign to overturn a gay rights ordinance in Miami-Dade County, Florida. After winning the vote by a wide margin, she vowed to take her campaign nationwide. The gay community in San Francisco realized that this woman posed a big threat to everything we had accomplished, so Harvey channeled the anger into a march. He didn't want violence, so we

IN 1971, TWO YEARS after a violent police raid at the Stonewall Inn in New York, *LIFE* magazine ran a major story on the gay struggle for civil rights (opposite top, middle). It was called "the most shocking and, to most Americans, the most surprising liberation movement yet," as homosexuals were "proudly confessing what they had long hidden." The article spoke of the "savage discrimination" against gays, their newfound pride in their sexual identity, and their readiness for "direct confrontation with conventional society." Negative reader response to the issue reflected the discomfort of a country not yet prepared to embrace gay rights.

AS AIDS CUT its deadly swath across the United States, *Newsweek* ran a cover story in 1987 (opposite bottom) that put a human face on the epidemic. AIDS was still seen as a disease that afflicted only gay men and as "AIDS hysteria" swept the nation, it was not uncommon to hear people say that those with AIDS deserved their fate. Compassion, and concerted efforts to find a cure, would not come until years later—after the disease had spread to heterosexuals. According to a poll in the early 1980s conducted by the *Los Angeles Times*, 50 percent of respondents felt that AIDS patients should be forcibly quarantined.

In an April 1986 editorial for the *Chicago Tribune*, one expert on AIDS, Professor John Phair of Northwestern University, likened the paranoia to the anti-communist backlash in the 1950s and the internment of Japanese Americans in World War II. "With the AIDS crisis, public hysteria has surfaced again, stimulating irrational, insensitive, and sometimes illegal responses. Such actions threaten to tarnish our history again, and could be as paralyzing as the disease itself."

created a march route that went for miles and miles, up and down some of the steepest hills in San Francisco. The reason we did this was first, of course, to show our anger and our determination throughout the city. But Harvey knew that violence would work against us, so he made sure that by the end of it, everyone who marched would be just too worn out and exhausted to break windows or fight the police.

I was working for Harvey at City Hall. At that time, there were only a few local jurisdictions in the country that had passed any kind of legal protections for the people we now call LGBTQ, but the backlash to repeal these protections was gaining speed. We had a loss in Dade County, and defeats in the cities of Wichita, Kansas, St. Paul, Minnesota, and Eugene, Oregon. In San Francisco, protest marches followed every loss.

Then California State Senator John Briggs, a Republican, put Proposition 6 on the state ballot for November 1978. If approved by voters, Prop. 6, also known as the Briggs Initiative, would have banned gay people from working in any capacity in California public schools. We saw it as a direct attack on gay people, on workers, on teachers. We thought we were going to lose, but we took it on.

Harvey thought it was essential that the young people who were joining gay liberation in droves at the time needed to be organized in an effective way. My first responsibility in the campaign was to head out and visit all the campuses, and pull together the usually very small gay student organizations that existed at that time to build a coalition. Our main message to the community was that we had to come out in force. During the campaign, we saw literally tens of thousands of ordinary people knocking on doors and saying, "Please, I'm your neighbor. I live down the street. I'm gay. If this passes, it will hurt me. It will harm my family."

We all had to take many risks—there were potential repercussions that could have been very serious. Harvey never diminished that. But everyone had a responsibility to themselves, he said, to their families, to their community, and to the movement, to come out of the closet.

Contrary to all predictions, we won that election by a million votes. It would be decades before we won another statewide election like that. I enjoy reminding people, especially young people, about that campaign, because we've all been through so much. But it has been largely forgotten—that back then, in that early period in the movement, we were actually able to win.

A few weeks after our victory, my friend, my boss, Harvey Milk, was assassinated at City Hall, along with San Francisco Mayor George Moscone, by a former supervisor, Dan White.

On that morning, I was scheduled to work in Harvey's office at City Hall and was out doing an errand. When I returned, there were police everywhere. I came around the corner and saw Harvey's feet sticking out in the hallway—I recognized the secondhand wingtip shoes he'd bought at a thrift store. We couldn't leave the scene while the police were doing their thing, so a few of us staffers played the tape that he'd left for us in case of his death, because he had predicted his assassination.

I used to tease him for it, telling him he wasn't important enough to get shot, so it was pretty eerie and very horrible. I was sitting in his office listening to his voice predicting his death, while his body was there in the hallway. Harvey Milk's death was the single most important moment of my life. Meeting Harvey, seeing his death, it fixed my course.

Once the shock wore off, I got a staff job with the Democratic Party in the California State Assembly in Sacramento, working on gay rights and monitoring the Assembly's health committee. Part of my job was to scan the federal Centers for Disease Control's weekly newsletter, the *Morbidity and Mortality Weekly Report*.

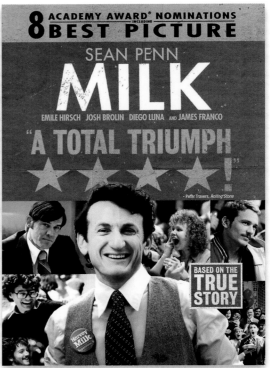

In June 1981, I read an article about several cases of pneumocystis pneumonia and Kaposi's sarcoma, a cancer, among young, previously healthy homosexual men. I remember being very puzzled and alarmed. I cut it out and put it on the bulletin board in my office. About a month later, *The New York Times* did its first story about it. I cut that out, too. I got a call from Dr. Marcus Conant, who at the time was a dermatologist at the University of California at San Francisco (UCSF). Because of my connections in Sacramento, he wanted to talk with me. He took me to dinner at the Zuni Café in San Francisco and told me that he thought there was a new virus, sexually transmitted, maybe dormant for many, many years, and that it attacked the immune system in some way that he couldn't understand. "It is fatal," he said.

There was something about the way the doctor delivered this information that went right to my heart. I said to him, "Well, then we're all dead." And he said, "You know, maybe."

The doctor took me to meet a young man who was dying at the UCSF hospital, in an isolation ward. And it was pretty horrifying to see close up what the disease had done to him. That was in the summer of 1981. By the fall of 1985, almost everyone I knew was dead or dying, or caring for someone who was dying.

I tested positive myself for HIV in roughly 1985—it's all a bit of a blur, those days. I didn't get seriously ill for several years after my diagnosis—long, nightmarish years of death and misery all around me; but then I got very sick. My immune system collapsed; I was allergic to many of the drugs used to treat

NEWSWEEK'S COVER story on gay rights in June 1977 (left, top), illustrated how a former beauty queen was mobilizing evangelical Christians to fight gay activists. The 2008 film *Milk* examined the life and untimely death of pioneering activist Harvey Milk (left, middle). As the first openly gay man voted into office in California, Milk paved the way for other gay politicians. Comedian Ellen DeGeneres was a major movie and TV star when she decided to come out in 1997 (left, bottom) the first gay lead character on American network TV. Many critics predicted that the public would turn against her, but DeGeneres' popularity only grew. *Will & Grace* (top) followed in DeGeneres' footsteps and throughout its eight-year run, earned 16 Emmy Awards and 83 nominations for what the Smithsonian Institution called its "daring use of comedy." In 2014, the Smithsonian added items from the show as part of its collection documenting the history of gay, lesbian, bisexual, and transgender individuals. In 2015 Amazon Studio's *Transparent* (above) became the first family sitcom with a transgender main character. The series won Golden Globe and Peabody awards for its sensitive exploration of gender-identity issues.

opportunistic infections, particularly pneumocystis pneumonia. So I moved to a little cabin in a redwood forest 90 minutes north of San Francisco, thinking that would be as good a place as any to finish up.

But, as it happened, in late 1994, Dr. Conant got me into one of the first trial studies for what we now call the "AIDS cocktail," a combination treatment consisting of three separate drugs. I responded almost immediately. It saved my life. I ran into a friend at the grocery store. He too had been in the same study, and he too was responding well to the meds. And he said, "Well, I guess we're not going to die." And I said, "No, I guess we're not going to die." And then he said, "But we'll never be happy again." And I thought, that's true. We'll never be happy again. But, you know, I'm 62 now. I'm healthy. I'm happy and very grateful to be alive.

One day, back in late November 1985, while I was organizing the seventh anniversary Memorial Candlelight Virgil and March to remember Harvey Milk and Mayor Moscone, I came up with the idea for the AIDS Memorial Quilt.

I was digesting news that the death toll from AIDS in San Francisco had already reached a thousand, most of them gay men, and it struck me, as I was standing on the corner of Castro and Market streets in the heart of San Francisco's gay Castro neighborhood, with its beautiful Victorian homes and cafés and restaurants and clubs, that there was nothing that let the world know that this was the epicenter of an ongoing horror.

If this had been a meadow with a thousand corpses rotting in the sun, then people would look at it, and maybe they'd be compelled to respond. But no one was noticing. Ronald Reagan was president, and he wouldn't even talk about it.

I needed to find a way to acknowledge all the lives that had been lost, so I passed out stacks of posterboard and markers to the gathering marchers, asking them to write the names of people they knew who had been killed by this new disease.

At first people were hesitant, but finally, they began writing out the names. We marched these placards down to United Nations Plaza and to the building that housed the federal Health and Human Services' West Coast office. We'd hidden ladders in the shrubbery nearby, and we climbed up the building's facade and taped the names to the wall.

A gentle rain fell, no speeches or music, just thousands of people reading these names on this patchwork of placards up on that wall. And I thought to myself: It looks like some kind of quilt.

I thought of my grandma and my great-grandma back in Bee Ridge, Indiana, and the quilts they once made—warm and comforting and middle American, traditional, a family-values sort of symbol. I knew it was the symbol we should take.

Everyone told me it was the stupidest thing they'd ever heard. I envisioned people sitting on living room floors or church basements and working with scraps of fabric of different textures and colors to create something, and I thought that, maybe, by telling our loved ones' stories and working with our hands, we could combat that sort of paralysis that comes when you're overwhelmed by too much grief, too much loss.

The AIDS Memorial Quilt is made up of 49,000 panels, each representing an individual lost to AIDS. Each panel is 3 feet by 6 feet, about the size of a grave. The last display of the entire quilt was in 2012, when it covered the National Mall from the steps of the Capitol building all the way to the Washington Monument.

People ask me if it was hard to learn how to be happy after losing so many friends at such a young age. I tell them I'm still learning. I think anyone who goes through that kind of experience, with that kind of—the enormity of the loss—you know, it's similar, I think, to being in a war. There are some days when it is so painful I can barely function, but I have to. And I do, and I find that I get my strength from my community and my friends. I am surrounded by people who went through that time with me, and we support each other. And we love each other and are grateful for every bit of laughter and joy that comes our way. We forged real families through it all, which brings me to gay marriage.

When I was young, marriage was just one of many things on a long list of rights and privileges that were denied us because of our sexual orientation. But many of us, influenced by early feminism, viewed marriage as a patriarchal institution conjuring the days when women were property. Many of us were skeptical of marriage, didn't view it as terribly important, and would dismiss it as just a piece of paper that was not needed to validate our relationships.

Then came AIDS, and suddenly, that little piece of paper meant insurance coverage, visitation rights in the hospitals, property rights. I can tell you stories about people who cared for their partners of 20 years, and then, after they'd passed away, the blood families swept into town and sold the furniture and threw the partner out in the street, because he had no legal rights. The AIDS epidemic gave us powerful evidence of how important the institution of marriage was, and how much that little piece of paper mattered in our ordinary lives.

There was another part to it after what we had been through and after what we had witnessed—people caring for their partners and sharing in that horrendous struggle against death. It's hard physically, it's hard emotionally, it's hard spiritually. There was this new attitude within the community: What do you mean, this isn't a marriage?! To hell with you! Out of all that misery and pain and suffering came a new understanding of ourselves, our families, our community—and a deeply felt demand for full equality under the law. ∎

Cleve Jones is the American AIDS and LGBTQ rights activist who conceived the NAMES Project AIDS Memorial Quilt, which has become, at 54 tons, the world's largest piece of community folk art as of 2016. In 1983, at the onset of the AIDS pandemic, Jones co-founded the San Francisco AIDS Foundation, which has grown into one of the largest and most influential AIDS advocacy organizations in the United States. Jones' book, *When We Rise: My Life in the Movement,* became an ABC TV series and was broadcast in February and March 2017. 🐦 *@CleveJones1*

JUST THE FACTS

1 OUT OF 137

AMERICAN
TEENAGERS
13 TO 17 YEARS OLD
IDENTIFY
AS TRANSGENDER.

—*THE NEW YORK TIMES*

This does NOT belong on the cover of National Geographic but rather on the cover of some psychology journal. I do not want this coming into my home where children can see and read it.

Kudos to @NatGeo for making #trans lives visible & sharing Avery Jackson's story.

Shame on anyone who blames this publication for promoting what is a very real biological evolution... My transgender son goes to a high School with at least ten other transgenders. It isn't weird science, they are born this way. Shame on parents who try to change or 'church' this out of their transgender kids.

This belongs on the cover... because it's a conversation taking place around the world, not just here at home. You're conflating sex with gender. They are not the same thing.

You people are sick... the youth and children shouldn't be exposed to this filth. This will breed hate!

Good grief! Life is getting complicated. Does anybody out there long for the days of Ward and June Cleaver. You know "Leave it to Beaver"... black and white TV?

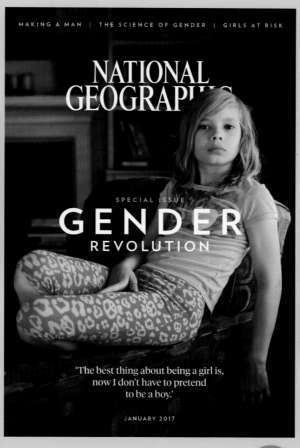

MAKING A MAN | THE SCIENCE OF GENDER | GIRLS AT RISK

NATIONAL GEOGRAPHIC

SPECIAL ISSUE

G E N D E R
REVOLUTION

'The best thing about being a girl is, now I don't have to pretend to be a boy.'

JANUARY 2017

You might want to actually get to know some folks who are gay, transgender. And better yet if you get to know... his/her loving family. It WILL change your entire view on these matters.

I am transgender and i just wanted to say thank you all for the kind words and understanding.

This is nothing but cruelty and child abuse. When I was a child I... wanted to be a dog. I even ate my food from a bowl. I knew of course it was fantasy. My parents, thankfully, never [took] me to a doctor for dog hormone therapy.

WHEN *NATIONAL GEOGRAPHIC* featured Avery Jackson, a 9-year-old transgender girl from Kansas City, to appear on the cover of its "Gender Revolution" issue, it sparked an online firestorm, with tens of thousands of passionate comments on Instagram, Facebook, and Twitter about the appropriateness of the magazine tackling this controversial topic. The groundbreaking issue showed that there is a global revolt against traditional boy and girl "buckets" that instruct boys and girls how to dress, how to play, how to look, and how to behave. Susan Goldberg, editor-in-chief of the magazine, explained, "Beliefs about gender are shifting rapidly and radically. That's why we're exploring the subject this month, looking at it through the lens of science, social systems, and civilizations throughout history."

Must not be anymore drowning polar bears, seal clubbing, starving children, foul water in third world countries, animal stories, or other REAL NatGeo interests any more. Please cancel my subscription forthwith!

NG just made a huge step forward to open minds. I just proudly subscribed. Thanks!

FIGHTING THE GOOD FIGHT

TIM COOK

As CEO of Apple, the world's most valuable company, Tim Cook has used his visibility to take a public stand on major issues including racial equality, privacy, protecting the environment, access to education, and LGBTQ rights. In October 2014, in *Bloomberg Businessweek*, Cook stated, "While I have never denied my sexuality, I haven't publicly acknowledged it either, until now. So let me be clear:

I'm proud to be gay, and I consider being gay among the greatest gifts God has given me. I believe deeply in the words of Martin Luther King, who said, life's most persistent and urgent question is, 'What are you doing for others?' I often challenge myself with that question, and ...... If hearing that the CEO of Apple is gay can help someone, then it's worth the trade-off with my own privacy."

NEW YORK, AUGUST 31, 1970.
In the late 1960s, when New York City's Stonewall Inn was the largest gay establishment in the United States, it had no liquor license. The New York State Liquor Authority had the power to refuse a license to an establishment it considered to be "disorderly," and according to the regulations in force at that time, any gay bar fit that description. Police raided the Stonewall on a regular basis but, in return for tip-offs well in advance of a raid, envelopes of cash were slipped by the inn's mobster owners to police to minimize disruptions. That was the rhythm of life at the Stonewall until an early morning raid on June 28, 1969, when things didn't go as planned. The Inn didn't get its usual tip-off, and

cops began to arrest the surprised customers. Patrol wagons scheduled to transport the arrested to jail were late, and that is when the mood turned ugly. Rowdy patrons fought with police who knocked several of them down, sending the crowd into a frenzy. Far outnumbered at that point, the police were forced to hide inside the Inn until members of the Tactical Police Force showed up to free them. For the gay community, that small taste of victory was heady and began a battle against the police that continued for several nights. The Stonewall protests were largely credited with giving birth to the Gay Liberation movement. Violent interactions like this one (opposite), during a confrontation in Greenwich Village after a Gay Power march in

New York in August 1970 continued, but soon gay rights organizations had formed in almost every major American city. The first Gay Pride parades took place in June 1970, and have continued every year since. In June 2017, Senator Chuck Schumer announced that Google was providing a million-dollar grant to Stonewall's legendary Christopher Street location to help preserve oral histories associated with the 1969 uprising. In a *New York Daily News* article, Schumer said, "With this money, they will translate the legacy of Stonewall from a physical landmark into a digital experience, so that the lessons of its history can reach tens of millions of people across the nation and across the globe."

NEW YORK, JUNE 13, 2016. Ever since the 1969 Stonewall uprising, which marked the birth of the modern gay rights movement, the Stonewall Inn has served as a gathering place for gays to mark events of major significance to the LGBTQ community. Here, a day after the massacre of 49 patrons by a heavily armed gunman at Pulse, a gay bar in Orlando, Florida, crowds gather (above) for a vigil at the Stonewall Inn in remembrance of the victims. Two weeks later, President Barack Obama designated the Stonewall Inn and nearby Christopher Park the first national monuments to the LGBTQ movement.
📷 PRINCE WILLIAMS

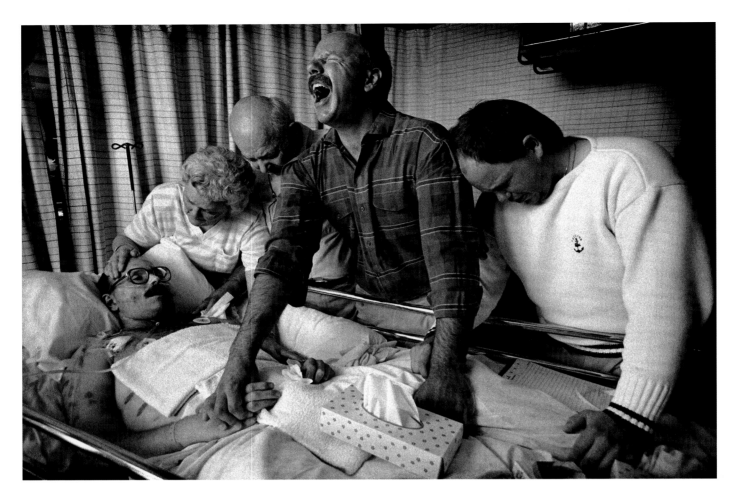

FOR THOSE WHO WERE DIAGNOSED with HIV in the 1980s, it was a death sentence. Today, a 20-year-old man or woman with HIV who begins treatment early can expect to live the lifespan of an average American. That is because the disease, which attacks the immune system, can be controlled by modern-day antiretroviral medications. It is estimated that 1.1 million Americans are currently living with HIV. Tragically, 1 in 5 are unaware they are infected. In this 1989 image (above), taken before antiretrovirals were discovered, the family of 33-year-old Tom Fox mourns at his bedside in his final moments of life. "I love you so much, son," says Doris Fox, moments after Tom has told her and his father, Bob, his older brother, Bob Jr., and his younger brother, John, that he can no longer breathe. "Just relax and let it go. You're almost there." On Tom's request, moments earlier, a doctor had withdrawn the ventilator that was forcing pure oxygen into his starving lungs. To date, more than 700,000 people in the United States have succumbed to the deadly disease.
📷 MICHAEL A. SCHWARZ

WASHINGTON, D.C. In the early years of the AIDS pandemic, the social stigma felt by surviving family members and the refusal of funeral homes and cemeteries to handle the remains of those who had died of the disease left no possibility for a proper burial or memorial service. So in 1987, Cleve Jones, an AIDS activist in San Francisco, encouraged relatives and loved ones from all over the country to contribute a colorful cloth panel, about the size of a grave and carrying the name of the deceased, to a commemorative quilt. Over the next decade, the AIDS Memorial Quilt grew to include nearly 50,000 panels covering more than half a square mile, making it the largest community folk art project in the world. To date, more than 14 million people worldwide have viewed this powerful reminder of

the AIDS plague, including a group of young men (below), who comforted each other in 1989 after seeing the quilt displayed on the National Mall in Washington, D.C. The AIDS quilt was laid out again on the Mall in 1992 (right), one of only five times it has been viewed in its entirety.
📷 MARY ELLEN MARK, BELOW

GOVERNOR DODGE STATE PARK, DODGEVILLE, WISCONSIN, JULY, 1993. Lizz Hall reaches for her girlfriend, Amy Grahn, as the couple sunbathe in a rental rowboat far from the eyes of other teens and families on the beach. "I felt more comfortable being close to her when we were by ourselves than with other people—so I could flirt with her, talk to her silly, or just be lovey," Grahn explained. 🖭 RITA REED

SAME LOVE
BY MACKLEMORE AND RYAN LEWIS

*When I was in the third grade I thought that
      I was gay,*
*'Cause I could draw, my uncle was, and I kept
      my room straight.*
I told my mom, tears rushing down my face
*She's like "Ben you've loved girls since before
      pre-K, trippin'."*
Yeah, I guess she had a point, didn't she?
Bunch of stereotypes all in my head.
*I remember doing the math like, "Yeah, I'm
      good at little league."*
A preconceived idea of what it all meant
For those that liked the same sex
Had the characteristics
The right wing conservatives think it's a decision
*And you can be cured with some treatment
      and religion*
Man-made rewiring of a predisposition
Playing God, aw nah here we go
*America the brave still fears what we don't
      know*
*And "God loves all his children" is somehow
      forgotten*
*But we paraphrase a book written thirty-five-
      hundred years ago*

...If I was gay, I would think hip-hop hates me
Have you read the YouTube comments lately?
"Man, that's gay" gets dropped on the daily
We become so numb to what we're saying

A culture founded from oppression

Yet we don't have acceptance for 'em

*Call each other faggots behind the keys of a
      message board*
*A word rooted in hate, yet our genre still
      ignores it*
Gay is synonymous with the lesser
*It's the same hate that's caused wars from
      religion*
*Gender to skin color, the complexion of your
      pigment*
*The same fight that led people to walk outs
      and sit ins*
*It's human rights for everybody, there is no
      difference!*
Live on and be yourself
*When I was at church they taught me
      something else*
*If you preach hate at the service those words
      aren't anointed*
*That holy water that you soak in has been
      poisoned.*

*...With a veil over our eyes we turn our back
      on the cause*
'Til the day that my uncles can be united by law
*When kids are walking 'round the hallway
      plagued by pain in their heart*
*A world so hateful some would rather die
      than be who they are*
And a certificate on paper isn't gonna solve it all
But it's a damn good place to start
No law is gonna change us
We have to change us
Whatever God you believe in
We come from the same one
Strip away the fear
Underneath it's all the same love
About time that we raised up...

In 2012, a year when many of hip-hop's big artists were singing about their money and sexual prowess, hip-hop duo Macklemore and his DJ and producing partner Ryan Lewis grabbed the spotlight with a stirring song about same-sex marriage rights.

Recorded in conjunction with a successful campaign to legalize same-sex marriage in Washington state, the song quickly became an anthem for supporters across the country.

Macklemore said he and Lewis wrote "Same Love" because they were fed up with hip-hop's chauvinistic and anti-gay tropes. "Misogyny and homophobia are the two acceptable means of oppression in hip-hop culture," Macklemore told a radio interviewer soon after the song came out. "It's 2012. There needs to be some accountability."

The evocative lyrics led to a Grammy nomination for Song of the Year in 2012 and, as of July 2017, the song's official video has had 171.9 million views on YouTube.

Following a sold-out concert in the Long Horn state, an exhausted Lewis shared his thoughts with *Out* magazine, "To perform that song in Texas and Idaho, in states that are classically conservative, and see a new generation of people sing as loudly as people were tonight, you're reminded of the power that a musician has to proactively use their craft to change culture."

Adds Macklemore, "Of course, we play it regardless of what we think the response is going to be. There's been such ground made in terms of acceptance in the hip-hop community. What Barack Obama did, and what Frank Ocean did, and what, hopefully, 'Same Love' did is start a conversation." ∎

ON JUNE 27, 2015, NEWSPAPERS nationwide featured the Supreme Court's ruling that guarantees the right to same-sex marriage. "No longer may this liberty be denied," Justice Anthony M. Kennedy wrote for the majority, in a decision that felt like the culmination of years of activism by LGBTQ groups, civil rights organizations, and the Anti-Defamation League. The high court's decision followed similar rulings by several state supreme courts, and brought U.S. law into line with public opinion polls, which showed that 64% of Americans approved of same-sex unions.

PHOTO ILLUSTRATION BY DAN MARCOLINA

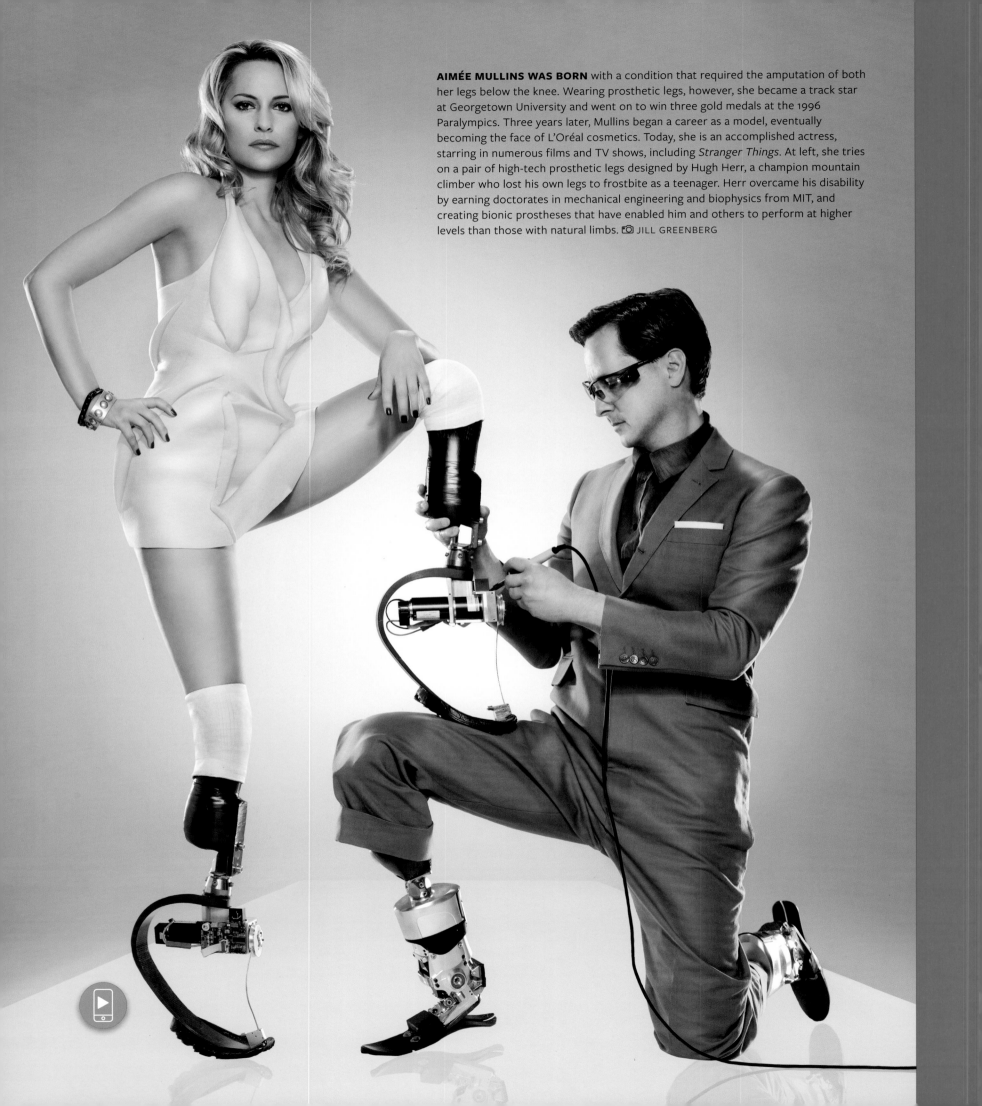

AIMÉE MULLINS WAS BORN with a condition that required the amputation of both her legs below the knee. Wearing prosthetic legs, however, she became a track star at Georgetown University and went on to win three gold medals at the 1996 Paralympics. Three years later, Mullins began a career as a model, eventually becoming the face of L'Oréal cosmetics. Today, she is an accomplished actress, starring in numerous films and TV shows, including *Stranger Things*. At left, she tries on a pair of high-tech prosthetic legs designed by Hugh Herr, a champion mountain climber who lost his own legs to frostbite as a teenager. Herr overcame his disability by earning doctorates in mechanical engineering and biophysics from MIT, and creating bionic prostheses that have enabled him and others to perform at higher levels than those with natural limbs. 🖾 JILL GREENBERG

DISABLED AMERICANS

THE TWENTY-FIRST CENTURY is both an exciting and a challenging time for people who are considered to have disabilities. And while disability has come out of the closet, so to speak, people who have atypical bodies and the objects and the trappings to match (such as mobility supports and hearing aids) are still perceived as not normal, in need of special treatment, or as objects of charity and discrimination.

For most of human history, many forms of disability were explained as divine, moral, or karma. And, in the not so distant past, human diversity and difference with those at the extremes engendered reactions ranging from fascination to revulsion. Beginning in the late 1860s (and ending only in the 1970s), many American states enacted "ugly laws," making it illegal for people whose appearance made others uncomfortable to appear in public.

In the twentieth century, modern medicine and technology transformed the concept of disability into a medical deficit and drove a newly emerging disability industry. While the advances of this medical industry improved longevity and functionality, it also continued to stigmatize the disabled, thus prolonging social, economic, and civic injustices and inequality.

This new social model set the intellectual scene for passage of the Americans With Disabilities Act (ADA) in 1990, prohibiting discrimination against individuals with disabilities in all areas of public life.

In the twenty-first century, a new perspective emerged from scholars who study disabilities, who posited that disability was an artificial or "socially constructed" category caused by intolerance. They suggested that the rigidity of the social and built environments was responsible for much of the injustice, rather than the medical conditions themselves.

It became increasingly clear that when barriers were removed, people with disabilities could be independent and equal in society. Much work remains to be done, but changes introduced in the past century bode well for the disabled community and for society. ∎

THE OPPORTUNITY OF ADVERSITY

BY AIMÉE MULLINS

SEVERAL YEARS AGO, while I was finishing up an article, I realized that I had never once in my life looked up the word "disabled" to see what I'd find. I always have a thesaurus handy, so I looked up the word.

The entry read: "Disabled, *adjective*: crippled, helpless, useless, wrecked, stalled, maimed, wounded, mangled, lame, mutilated, run-down, worn-out, weakened, impotent, castrated, paralyzed, senile, decrepit, laid-up, done-up, done-for, done-in, cracked-up, counted-out; see also hurt, useless, and weak. *Antonyms:* healthy, strong, capable."

I was reading this list out loud to a friend and at first I was laughing, it was so ludicrous, but I'd just gotten past "mangled," and my voice broke, and I had to stop and collect myself from the emotional shock and impact that the assault from these words unleashed.

Of course, this was my raggedy old thesaurus, so I'm thinking this must be an ancient print date, right? But, in fact, the print date was the early 1980s, when I would have been starting primary school and forming an understanding of myself outside the family unit, as I related to the other kids and the world around me. Needless to say, thank God, I wasn't using a thesaurus back then. From this entry, it would seem that I was born into a world that perceived someone like me to have nothing positive whatsoever going for them, when in fact, today I'm celebrated for the opportunities and adventures in my life.

So, I immediately went to look up the most recent online edition, expecting

MILTON, VERMONT, MARCH 2008. Special education teacher Paul Erena spends the afternoon with his son, James, who was born with a neurological disorder that severely limits his ability to move and speak. James' treehouse was built by Forever Young Treehouses and funded by the Make-a-Wish Foundation, which has awarded grants to more than 150,000 disabled and terminally ill children. 📷 JEB WALLACE-BRODEUR

to find a revision worth noting. Unfortunately, the updated version of this entry wasn't much better. The last two words, listed under *"Near Antonyms,"* were particularly unsettling: "whole" and "wholesome."

This is not just about the words, it's what we believe about people when we name them with these words. It's about the values behind the words and how we construct those values. Our language affects our thinking and how we view the world and how we view other people. In fact, many ancient societies, including the Greeks and the Romans, believed that to utter a curse verbally was very powerful, because to say the thing out loud brought it into existence. So, what reality do we want to call into existence: a person who is limited or a person who's empowered? By casually doing something as simple as naming a person, a child, we might be putting lids and casting shadows on their power. Wouldn't we want to open doors for them instead?

One such person who opened doors for me was my childhood doctor at the Nemours/Alfred I. duPont Hospital for Children in Wilmington, Delaware. His name was Dr. Peter Pizzutillo, an Italian American, whose name, apparently, was too difficult for most Americans to pronounce, so he went by Dr. P. He always wore really colorful bow ties, and Dr. P. had the perfect disposition for working with children like me.

I loved almost everything about my time spent at this hospital, with the exception of my physical therapy sessions. I had to do what seemed like innumerable repetitions of exercises with these thick, elastic bands in different colors to help build up my leg muscles, and I hated those bands more than anything—I hated them. I had names for them and I just hated them. Even though I was only a

WHERE WOULD YOU GO if you'd never been away from home? What would you do if you didn't have much time left? In 2005, Darius Weems, a 15-year-old from Athens, Georgia, living with Duchenne muscular dystrophy (DMD), set out with a group of friends on a 7,000-mile road trip to MTV headquarters in Los Angeles. The pretext was to ask the network to customize his wheelchair on the popular automotive program *Pimp My Ride*. But the real purpose was to make a documentary film about Weems' odyssey that would promote awareness of his fatal disease and raise money for a cure. In filmmaker Logan Smalley's 2007 documentary, *Darius Goes West: The Roll of His Life,* Weems touched the ocean for the first time, sat with his friends at the edge of the Grand Canyon, and advocated for greater wheelchair access in the United States. The film, which critics praised as both "life-affirming" and "heartbreaking," won scores of film festival awards and raised more than $2 million for DMD research. In 2016, the 27-year-old Weems died of complications from DMD.
⌖ DYLAN WILSON

5-year-old child, I was already bargaining with Dr. P. to try to get out of doing these exercises, unsuccessfully, of course. And, one day, he came into my session—exhaustive and unforgiving, these sessions were—and he said to me, "Wow, Aimée, you are such a strong and powerful little girl. I think you're going to break one of those bands. When you do break it, I'm going to give you a hundred bucks."

Now, of course, this was a simple ploy on Dr. P.'s part to get me to do the exercises I didn't want to do at the prospect of becoming the richest 5-year-old on the second-floor ward, but what he effectively did for me was to reshape an awful daily occurrence into a new and promising experience for me. Today, I often wonder to what extent his vision and his declaration of me as a strong and powerful little girl shaped my own view of myself as an inherently strong, powerful, and athletic person well into the future.

This is an example of how adults in positions of power can ignite the power of a child. But, as with the examples of those thesaurus entries, our language isn't allowing us to evolve into the reality that we would all want, the possibility that individuals can envision themselves as being fully capable. Our language hasn't caught up with the changes in our society, and many of these changes have been brought about by technology.

Certainly, from a medical standpoint, my prosthetic legs, like laser surgery for vision impairment, or titanium knees and hip replacements for aging bodies, allow me and other people to engage more fully with their abilities, and move beyond the limits nature has imposed on them. Meanwhile, social networking platforms allow people to self-identify, to claim their own descriptions of themselves, so they can align themselves with global groups of their own choosing. I'm convinced

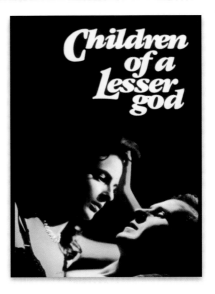

that technology is revealing more clearly to us now something that has always been true: that everyone has something rare and powerful to offer our society, and that the human ability to adapt is our greatest asset.

The human ability to adapt is an interesting thing. People have continually wanted to talk to me about overcoming adversity, and I'm going to make an admission: That phrase never sat right with me. I always felt uneasy trying to answer people's questions about it, and I think I'm starting to figure out why. Implicit in this phrase of "overcoming adversity" is the idea that success, or happiness, is about emerging on the other side of a challenging experience unscathed or unmarked by the experience. It's as if my successes in life have come about from an ability to sidestep or circumnavigate the presumed pitfalls of a life with prosthetics—or what other people perceive as my disability. But, in fact, we are changed. We are marked, of course, by a challenge, whether physically, emotionally, or both. And I'm going to suggest that this is a good thing. Adversity isn't an obstacle that we need to get around in order to resume living our life. It's part of our life. And I tend to think of it like my shadow. Sometimes I see a lot of it, sometimes there's very little, but it's always with me. And, certainly, I'm not trying to diminish the impact, the weight, of a person's struggle.

There is adversity and challenge in life, and it's all very real and relative to every single person, but the question isn't whether or not you're going to meet adversity, but how you're going to meet it. So, our responsibility is not simply shielding those we care for from adversity, but preparing them to meet it well. We do a disservice to our kids when we make them feel that they're not equipped to adapt. There's an important difference and distinction between the objective medical fact of my being an amputee and the subjective opinion of other people in society about whether or not I'm disabled. Truthfully, the only real and consistent disability I've had to confront is the world ever thinking that I could be described or somehow limited by those definitions.

In our desire to protect those we care about by giving them the cold, hard

HOLLYWOOD'S PORTRAYAL of people with disabilities began to change in the 1960s, beginning with *The Miracle Worker* (top, left), the true story of teacher Annie Sullivan (Anne Bancroft), who taught deaf and blind Helen Keller (Patty Duke), to communicate. *Rain Man* (top, right) in 1988, starring a self-absorbed Tom Cruise suddenly responsible for his older autistic savant brother (Dustin Hoffman), won universal acclaim for its portrayal of autism and won the Oscar for Best Film. *Children of a Lesser God* (1986) (above) revolved around the romantic relationship between a former student at a school for the deaf and a teacher (William Hurt), who have conflicting approaches to speech and deafness. The film earned Marlee Matlin an Oscar for Best Actress. She is the only deaf actress to win an Academy Award in any category.

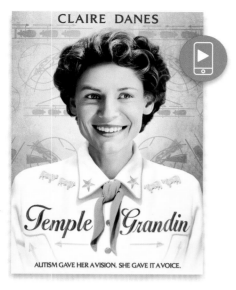

WHEN THE ENTERTAINMENT industry began featuring realistic portraits of people with disabilities, it had a demonstrable effect on public attitudes. In 2010, HBO's television biopic *Temple Grandin* (top), starring Claire Danes, told the story of an autistic woman who drew upon the methods she used to calm herself when she was under stress to revolutionize practices for the humane handling of livestock on cattle ranches and in slaughterhouses. In 2016, ABC followed suit with *Speechless* (above), a sitcom that follows the DiMeo family as it searches for a supportive educational environment for JJ (Micah Fowler), their high school-aged son, who has cerebral palsy. The 18-year-old, who began acting at 5 years old and appeared on television shows like *Sesame Street* and *Blue's Clues*, has cerebral palsy himself.

truth about their medical prognosis, or, indeed, a prognosis on the expected quality of their life, we must make sure that we don't put the first brick in a wall that will actually disable someone. Perhaps the existing model—of looking only at what is broken in you and how we are to fix it—is more disabling to the individual than the pathology itself.

By not treating the wholeness of a person, by not acknowledging his or her potency, we are creating yet another unfair obstacle, on top of whatever natural struggle the person may have. We are effectively grading someone's worth to our community. We need to see through the pathology and into the range of human capability. And, most importantly, there's a partnership between those perceived deficiencies and our greatest creative ability. It's not about devaluing, or negating, these struggles, as something we want to avoid or sweep under the rug, but instead to find the opportunities wrapped in the adversity. The idea I want to put out there is not so much about overcoming adversity as it is opening ourselves up to it, embracing it—grappling with it, to use a wrestling term. Maybe even dancing with it. Perhaps, if we see adversity as natural, consistent and useful, we're less burdened by the presence of it.

In 1859, when Charles Darwin first shared his groundbreaking theory of evolution, he illustrated a truth about the human character. To paraphrase: it's not the strongest of the species that survives, nor is it the most intelligent that survives; it is the one that is most adaptable to change. Conflict is the genesis of creation. From Darwin's work, we can recognize that the human ability to survive and flourish is driven by the struggle of the human spirit, through conflict, into transformation. So, again, transformation, adaptation, is our greatest human skill. And, perhaps, until we're tested, we don't know what we're made of. Maybe that's what adversity gives us: a sense of self, a sense of our own power. So, we can give ourselves a gift. We can reimagine adversity as something more than just tough times. Maybe we can see it as change. Adversity is just change that we haven't adapted ourselves to yet.

I think the greatest adversity that we've created for ourselves is this idea of normalcy. Now, who's normal? There's no normal. There's common, there's typical. There's no normal, and would you want to meet that poor, beige person if they existed? I don't think so. If we can change this paradigm from one of achieving normalcy to one of possibility—or potency, to be even a little bit more dangerous—we can release the power of so many more children, and invite them to engage their rare and valuable abilities with the community.

Anthropologists tell us that the one thing we as humans have always required of our community members is to be of use, to be able to contribute. There's evidence that Neanderthals, 60,000 years ago, carried with them their elderly and those with serious physical injury, and perhaps it's because the life experience of survival of these people proved of value to the community. They didn't view these people as broken and useless; they perceived them as rare and valuable.

A few years ago, I was in a food market in the town where I grew up in that red zone in northeastern Pennsylvania, and I was standing over a bushel of tomatoes. It was summertime: I had shorts on. I hear this guy, his voice behind me, saying, "Well, if it isn't Aimée Mullins!" And I turn around, and it's this older man. I have no idea who he is.

And I said, "I'm sorry, sir, have we met? I don't remember meeting you."

He said, "Well, you wouldn't remember meeting me. I mean, when we met, I was delivering you from your mother's womb."

This man was Dr. Kean, a man that I had only known about through my mother's stories of that day, because, of course, in typical fashion, I arrived late for my birthday by two weeks. My mother's prenatal physician had gone on vacation, so the man who delivered me was a complete stranger to my parents. And, because I was born without the fibula bones, and had feet turned in, and a few toes in this foot and a few toes in that, he had to be the bearer—this stranger had to be the bearer of bad news.

He said to me, "I had to give this prognosis to your parents that you would never walk, and you would never have the kind of mobility that other kids have, or any kind of life of independence. And you've been making a liar out of me ever since."

Then he said the most extraordinary thing. Throughout my whole childhood, he had saved newspaper clippings about me, whether it was when I won a second-grade spelling bee, marched with the Girl Scouts or in the Halloween parade, winning my college scholarship, or any of my sports victories. Dr. Kean had used these clippings and my story as part of his curriculum for teaching resident students, medical students from Penn State University's Hershey College of Medicine. He called my part of his course the x factor, the potential of the human will. No prognosis can account for how powerful this could be as a determinant in the quality of someone's life. And Dr. Kean went on to tell me, "In my experience, unless repeatedly told otherwise, and even if given a modicum of support, if left to their own devices, a child will achieve."

Dr. Kean made that shift in thinking. He understood that there's a difference between the medical condition and what someone might do with it. And there's been a shift in my thinking over time, too. If you had asked me at 15 years old whether I would trade prosthetics for flesh-and-bone legs, I wouldn't have hesitated for a second. I aspired to that kind of normalcy back then. But if you ask me today, I'm not so sure. It's because of the experiences I've had with them, not in spite of the experiences I've had with them. Perhaps this shift in me has happened because I've been exposed to more people who have opened doors for me than those who have put lids and cast shadows on me.

All you really need is one person to show you the epiphany of your own power, and you're off. If you can hand somebody the key to their own power—the human

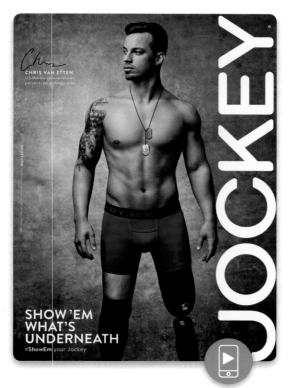

CHRIS VAN ETTEN
US Marine veteran shows
perseverance always wins

JOCKEY

SHOW 'EM
WHAT'S
UNDERNEATH
#ShowEm your Jockey

THE WORLD OF ADVERTISING is constantly looking for the next trend, and in 2015, advertisers turned their attention to something new, edgy, and unexpected: the disabled. The trend has been attributed in part to the more than 1,600 U.S. soldiers who have been wounded by improvised explosive devices, or IEDs, after 15 years of wars in Iraq and Afghanistan. Many amputees now proudly display custom prostheses as a show of their patriotism. Others point to the public's growing fascination with man/machine hybrids in films like *Ex Machina* and *RoboCop*, as leading indicators of how humanity is evolving.

Jockey featured Chris Van Etten (above), a former Marine who lost both legs to an IED, in its "Show 'Em What's Underneath" campaign. "Our goal was less about highlighting Chris' disability and more about shining a light on a true story of perseverance and endurance," Dani Simpson, president of PureGrowth, the consulting firm that created the Jockey campaign, told Campaign Live, an advertising industry publication. Toyota, Kenneth Cole, Nike, and Swiffer have also used both military amputees and Paralympians in their advertising campaigns. Several agencies now specialize in fulfilling corporate requests for disabled models.

spirit is so receptive—if you can do that and open a door for someone at a crucial moment, you are educating them in the best sense. You're teaching them to open doors for themselves. In fact, the exact meaning of the word "educate" is very close to the word "educe." It means "to bring forth what is within, to bring out potential." So again, which potential do we want to bring out?

There was a case study done in the 1960s in Britain, when they were moving from grammar schools to comprehensive schools. It was known as the "streaming trials." We call it "tracking" here in the United States. The idea is to separate and group students and rank them into A, B, C, D, and so on. And the A-level students get the tougher curriculum, the best teachers, etc.

The Brits did an extraordinary experiment, one that I think we should all consider today with all the debates about the best method to educate our children. Here is how it worked: over a three-month period, they took the D students, repeatedly told them they were bright and gave them all As, and at the end of this three-month period, the majority of them were actually performing at A level.

The heartbreaking, flip side of this study, is that they took the A-level students and told them they were Ds. And guess what happened at the end of that three-month period?

A crucial part of this case study was that the teachers were duped, too. The teachers didn't know a switch had been made. They were simply told, "These are the A students, these are the D students." And that's how they went about teaching them and treating them. The kids lived up or down to their own and to the teachers' expectations.

It goes without saying that the only true disability is a crushed spirit. A spirit that's been crushed doesn't have hope, it doesn't see beauty, it no longer has our natural, childlike curiosity and our innate ability to imagine. If instead, we can bolster a human spirit to keep hope, to see beauty in themselves and others, to be curious and imaginative, then we are truly using our power well. When a spirit has those qualities, we are able to create new realities and new ways of being.

I want to leave you with a poem by a fourteenth-century Persian poet, Hafiz, that my friend Jacques d'Amboise told me about. The poem is called "The God Who Only Knows Four Words": "Every child has known God, not the God of names, not the God of don'ts . . . But the God who only knows four words and keeps repeating them, saying: 'Come dance with me.' Come, dance." ∎

Aimée Mullins was born without fibulae in both legs, which were then amputated below the knee. By age 2, she had learned to walk with wooden legs and later won attention as a pioneering athlete, becoming the first person with a "disability" to compete in Division I in the NCAA. She set world records at the 1996 Atlanta Paralympics in the long jump, 100-meter, and 200-meter races and was the first person to wear carbon-fiber prostheses modeled on the hind legs of a cheetah. Mullins made her runway debut as a model for designer Alexander McQueen, signed a global beauty contract with L'Oréal, was named as one of *Sports Illustrated's* "Coolest Girls in Sport," and will be inducted into the National Women's Hall of Fame in 2017. As an actress, Aimée has collaborated with luminaries ranging from Matthew Barney to Steven Soderbergh. She tirelessly champions the idea that our human "difference" is in fact our strength. 🐦 *@AimeeMullins*

Courtesy of TED. Aimée Mullins, October 2009. Watch the complete TED Talk on TED.com

FRANKLIN DELANO ROOSEVELT (left) was the first president with a significant physical disability. In 1921, at the age of 39, he was diagnosed with polio, which resulted in his partial paralysis. At the time, disability was associated with weakness, something that Roosevelt, as a politician, could not afford to show, and so he went to great lengths to hide his infirmity from public view. As part of that effort, he designed his own wheelchair from a dining room chair fitted with bicycle wheels. The contraption allowed him to maneuver easily around tight corners and narrow hallways. Presidential aides and a compliant press kept Roosevelt's use of his wheelchair hidden from most of the public during his 12 years as the nation's leader. In a rare photograph taken in 1941, Roosevelt sat in his wheelchair on the porch of his Hyde Park, New York, home with his dog, Fala, and Ruthie Bie, the granddaughter of the Roosevelt family gardener.
⬜ MARGARET SUCKLEY

TAMMY DUCKWORTH (right) has a few significant firsts in her career. A U.S. Army helicopter pilot who was severely wounded when she was shot down in Iraq in 2004, she lost both her legs and became the first female double amputee of the war. Appointed by President Barack Obama to a top post at the Veterans Affairs Department, Duckworth, a retired lieutenant colonel, made caring for disabled veterans her first priority, establishing new programs for those with post-traumatic stress disorder (PTSD) and traumatic brain injuries. As one of the most recognizable disabled veterans in the country, Duckworth proudly stood on her prosthetic legs and addressed the 2012 Democratic National Convention in Charlotte, North Carolina, on its first day (right). In November that year, Duckworth became the first disabled woman elected to the U.S. House of Representatives. Since 2017, she's been representing the people of Illinois as the first disabled woman veteran in the U.S. Senate. Duckworth has told reporters: "I'm not ashamed I'm in a wheelchair. I earned this wheelchair. I've always insisted it's not something that we hide."
⬜ ALEX WONG

FIGHTING THE GOOD FIGHT

MICHAEL J. FOX

In 1991, at the age of 29, actor Michael J. Fox was diagnosed with Parkinson's disease, a long-term degenerative disorder of the central nervous system. He has since become the country's highest-profile advocate for research toward a cure for Parkinson's. His Michael J. Fox Foundation focuses on funding promising experimental paths, including embryonic stem cell research. In 2006, Fox starred in a powerful campaign ad in support of Missouri Democrat Claire McCaskill's Senate challenge to Republican incumbent Jim Talent. Fox, visibly shaking with Parkinson's, compared McCaskill's support for stem cell research with Talent's push to criminalize that science. "They say all politics is local, but that's not always the case," Fox said. "What you do in Missouri matters to millions of Americans, Americans like me." His advocacy earned him a place in 2007 on *Time* magazine's list of 100 people "whose power, talent or moral example is transforming the world." The recipient of numerous honorary degrees for his contributions to Parkinson's research, Fox and his foundation launched a raffle in 2016 to raise public awareness of the disease. It raised nearly $7 million.

WHEN **DANIEL KISH WAS** a year old, he lost sight in both eyes to retinal cancer. But he taught himself to navigate by clicking his tongue and listening for echoes—a method science calls echolocation. Today, Kish, 50, teaches echolocation—he calls it FlashSonar—to blind people people at the World Access for the Blind, the California nonprofit he founded in 2000. Kish and his organization have taught at least 500 blind children his technique, which uses sound and echoes to produce images similar to sight for the visually impaired. In 2009, Kish's research was used in a Spanish study that taught 10 sighted subjects basic navigation skills within a few days. In another study, MRI brain scans were taken of Kish and another echolocation expert, to identify the parts of the brain involved in echolocation. The study showed that the same areas of brain that process visual information in sighted people also process echo information in individuals using blind echolocation. In 2015, he demonstrates FlashSonar onstage (above) at the annual TED conference held in Vancouver, Canada. ◎ BRET HARTMAN

IN 2006, DEFENSE ADVANCED Research Projects Agency (DARPA) officials approached inventor Dean Kamen and asked him to develop an advanced prosthetic arm for the war-wounded and other amputees. Kamen, who holds almost a thousand U.S. and foreign patents, many of them for innovative medical devices that have expanded the frontiers of health care worldwide, was specifically charged with developing a prosthetic device that could perform movements with dexterity comparable to a natural limb. Only a year later, Kamen (far right) posed proudly with the "Luke Arm," named after the replacement limb worn by the *Star Wars* character Luke Skywalker. The modular prosthesis replicates most movements of the arm and hand and can pick up objects like a grape (right) without crushing them. Under its silicon skin are tiny actuators and sensors that can detect grip pressure and allow for simultaneous movement of

multiple joints. Kamen improved the design with feedback from user testing. Despite Kamen's speedy response to DARPA's request, it wasn't until 2014 that the Food and Drug Administration cleared the arm for commercial sale.
◎ SHAWN G. HENRY

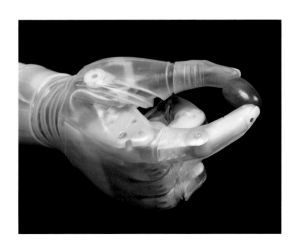

BORN THIS WAY
BY LADY GAGA

*It doesn't matter if you love him, or capital
    H-I-M
Just put your paws up
'cause you were born this way, baby*

*My mama told me when I was young
We are all born superstars
She rolled my hair and put my lipstick on
In the glass of her boudoir*

*"There's nothing wrong with loving who you
    are"
She said, "'Cause he made you perfect, babe"
"So hold your head up girl and you'll go far,
Listen to me when I say"*

*I'm beautiful in my way
'Cause God makes no mistakes
I'm on the right track, baby
I was born this way
Don't hide yourself in regret
Just love yourself and you're set*

*Oh there ain't no other way
Baby I was born this way
I'm on the right track, baby
I was born this way...*

*Give yourself prudence
And love your friends
Subway kid, rejoice your truth
In the religion of the insecure
I must be myself, respect my youth...*

*Don't be a drag, just be a queen
Whether you're broke or evergreen
You're black, white, beige, chola descent
You're Lebanese, you're orient
Whether life's disabilities
Left you outcast, bullied, or teased
Rejoice and love yourself today
'cause baby you were born this way*

*No matter gay, straight, or bi
Lesbian, transgendered life
I'm on the right track baby
I was born to survive
No matter black, white or beige
Chola or orient mad,
I'm on the right track baby
I was born to be brave...*

Same DNA, but born this way.

It took Lady Gaga a lifetime to learn how to cope with the bullying and taunting that comes with being different. It took her just 10 minutes to write the lyrics to "Born This Way," an anthem of acceptance and empowerment that millions around the world have adopted as their own, after experiencing persecution on account of their race, religion, ethnicity, sexual identity, or disability. Being the outsider is territory that Lady Gaga knows well, and "Born this Way" celebrates that it's OK—in fact, it's great—to be different. In an interview with the BBC, she described the song and the accompanying sci-fi-themed video as "the story about the birth of a new race, a race that bears no prejudice, a race whose primary ambition in life is to inspire unity and togetherness." "Born This Way" struck a powerful chord with a worldwide audience, selling more than a million copies within five days of its 2011 release. The song went on to become the fastest-selling single in iTunes history and a No. 1 hit in 23 countries. In 2015, the Anti-Defamation League presented its Making a Difference award to the Born This Way Foundation, created by Lady Gaga and her mother, Cynthia Germanotta, to honor their work in combating bigotry and hatred and promoting youth empowerment in schools. In her acceptance speech, Gaga said, "It takes just one story to inspire someone to be nicer in class. It takes just one story to inspire someone who wants to give up. It takes just one story to change somebody's life." Her message, celebrating what makes each of us unique, connected with a worldwide audience of over 150 million viewers in 2017, when she headlined the Super Bowl LI halftime show (right) in a performance that was the most viewed musical event in history. ∎

CHRISTOPHER POLK, RIGHT

NO PLACE FOR HATE

BY JONATHAN BRODER

IN LATE OCTOBER 2008, federal authorities—with the help of some highly regarded Jewish intelligence operatives—managed to thwart a white supremacist conspiracy to assassinate Barack Obama, only days before he was elected as the nation's first African American president.

The plot came to light when police in Jackson, Tennessee, arrested Daniel Cowart, a member of the racist Supreme White Alliance, and Paul Schlesselman, his neo-Nazi sidekick, after they shot out the windows of a local African American church. When the police discovered that the two had amassed a sizable stockpile of illegal weapons, they summoned federal authorities. Under their questioning, the pair confessed that they were about to execute one of the deadliest hate crimes in modern U.S. history: according to court documents, Cowart and Schlesselman planned to behead more than a dozen black schoolchildren, gun down scores more African American adults, and in a final flourish, kill candidate Obama with a high-powered rifle at one of his final campaign stops.

Faced with a conspiracy of this magnitude, the feds needed to know whether it involved others who still intended to carry out the murderous plan. And with only days to go before the election, they needed that information quickly.

TEMPLE, GEORGIA, APRIL 23, 2016. The neo-Nazi National Socialist Movement and several Ku Klux Klan groups gather for a cross and swastika burning. The ceremony was held to demonstrate cooperation and coordination between the white supremacist groups. With the increase in anti-Semitic and racist attacks since the 2016 election, the Anti-Defamation League has stepped up its monitoring of extremist organizations, sharing its intelligence with federal, state, and local law enforcement to prevent violence against Jews, Muslims, African Americans, and other minorities. 📷 ERIK S. LESSER

So, the authorities turned to the Anti-Defamation League, or ADL, a Jewish civil liberties organization widely respected among law enforcement professionals for the close but unobtrusive watch it keeps on extremist groups and individuals.

The authorities did not ask ADL to assume any law enforcement responsibilities. What they wanted to know was whether ADL already had information on these individuals from their active monitoring of public sources. Within a matter of hours, ADL produced a detailed 28-page dossier on Cowart and Schlesselman, their Supreme White Alliance group, and the names of other members and sympathizers. Armed with that information, federal officials quickly fanned out to question dozens of individuals and associates. They

BOSTON, APRIL 5, 1976.
Ted Landsmark, an African American lawyer and civil rights activist, was running late for a meeting at Boston's City Hall and wasn't paying attention when he rounded a corner in front of the building, where young anti-busing demonstrators were coming in the other direction. Among the protesters was Joseph Rakes, a teenager who had come to protest against court-ordered desegregation busing that would send half of his friends to another school. Their two worlds collided when one of the other protesters hit Landsmark, breaking his nose. A moment later, Rakes grabbed a flagpole and lunged toward Landsmark, missing his face by inches. Then the protesters moved on. The entire encounter lasted all of seven seconds. But the photo, which won photographer Stanley Forman his second Pulitzer Prize, freezes in time the anger, violence, and racial tensions that divided the country back then and which still divide black and white Americans in many cities today.
📷 STANLEY FORMAN

determined Cowart and Schlesselman were acting alone. In 2010, a federal court convicted the pair of conspiring to kill a major presidential candidate, along with a long list of gun crimes. Cowart is now serving a 14-year sentence in federal prison. Schlesselman is serving a 10-year sentence.

The FBI, as well as state and local police, often rely upon ADL for intelligence on extremists, because privacy laws forbid law enforcement from monitoring such groups and individuals without sufficient probable cause to believe they're about to commit a crime. ADL, however, faces no such restrictions. Acting much like a team of investigative journalists, the researchers and analysts of ADL's Center on Extremism are constantly gathering information on anti-Semitic, racist, and Islamic extremists, which they routinely share with state and federal authorities. And, as the foiled Obama assassination plot demonstrates, ADL wastes no time in filling critical gaps in knowledge.

In a 2014 speech, then-FBI Director James B. Comey hailed ADL as an essential resource for law enforcement. "Your leadership in tracking and exposing domestic and international terrorist threats is invaluable," Comey told a gathering of ADL's national leadership in Washington, D.C. "Your experience in hate crime prevention and investigations is essential. Your research has helped agents and analysts as they conduct threat assessments and prepare intelligence reports. And the training you voluntarily provide—at conferences, in classrooms, and at the community level—is eye-opening and insightful."

Comey added: "If this sounds a bit like a love letter to the ADL, it is, and rightly so."

Providing law enforcement with critical intelligence on hate groups is only one of the ADL's numerous civic services. Yet it is one for which the organization is uniquely suited. The many years ADL has spent fighting against anti-Semitism have served to hone the investigative methods it now utilizes to help law enforcement officials battle many other forms of intolerance and extremism.

The Anti-Defamation League qualifies as one of the nation's premier civil rights organizations. The organization has fought relentlessly for the civil rights not only of Jews, but of African Americans, Asian Americans, Latino Americans, women, Muslims, immigrants, members of the LBGTQ community, the disabled, and other oppressed minorities.

As the FBI, police and many other officials attest, ADL is a civil liberties organization like no other. Its experts have educated tens of thousands of federal, state, and local police about both domestic and international terrorist organizations. ADL and the United States Holocaust Memorial Museum also run a unique program called "Law Enforcement and Society: Lessons of the Holocaust" that brings law enforcement officers from all over the country and overseas to the museum in Washington. There the officers are encouraged to reflect upon their role in protecting society and reminded of what can happen when governments subvert laws and ethical codes. This program is now mandatory for every new FBI agent and an integral part of the Bureau's training programs for senior-level officers. To date, more than 130,000 law enforcement personnel and 30,000 teachers have participated in the training initiative.

The Anti-Defamation League's imprint also can be found in the curriculum of the U.S. Air Force Academy in Colorado Springs, Colorado, once a hotbed of evangelical proselytization. Today, all the academy's instructors, officers, and cadets are required to take an ADL-crafted course on the constitutional separation of church and state. Other ADL programs around the country educate teachers, parents, and students on how to become more attuned to the damage that hatred can inflict on people, property, and the country's fundamental values of mutual respect and equal treatment. ADL also produces regular surveys of anti-Semitic attitudes and audits of anti-Semitic incidents in the United States. Its trailblazing 2014 Global 100 study, a first-of-its kind survey of anti-Semitic attitudes in more than 100 countries, is widely respected as the most authoritative study on the prevalence of anti-Semitism around the world.

The Anti-Defamation League's work goes back more than a century. It was a major force behind laws in the 1950s that unmasked the Ku Klux Klan, forcing Klansmen to show their faces rather than hide under their hoods. Over the decades, the organization has played a vital role in numerous landmark civil rights cases, including *Brown v. Board of Education* in 1954, which outlawed segregated public schools, and *Obergefell v. Hodges* in 2015, which legalized gay marriage nationwide. ADL's efforts also have advanced a new category of legislation, known as "hate crimes law," which increased the penalties for crimes committed on the basis of a person's race, color, religion, national origin, ethnicity, gender, or sexual orientation. And in today's digital age, most states have added ADL-authored provisions against cyberbullying to their anti-bullying statutes.

But it hasn't waged these battles alone. One of the keys to ADL's influence has been the coalitions it has formed with other civil liberties organizations, such as the National Association for the Advancement of Colored People (NAACP), the Human Rights Campaign (HRC), the League of United Latin American Citizens (LULAC) National Council of La Raza, and the Interfaith, and the Interfaith Coalition on Mosques (ICOM), among many others. "There's strength in numbers," says Deborah Lauter, ADL's senior vice president for policy and programs. "When you're working in coalition with allies, it elevates our voices and sends a clear message of people of goodwill in civil society, banding together to stand up to hate."

AN UNPRECEDENTED MISSION

Founded in 1913 amid fierce nativist hostility toward the waves of immigrants arriving on America's shores, the Anti-Defamation League committed itself "to

BIRMINGHAM, ALABAMA, 1963. One image that brought the unspeakable brutality of the civil rights movement to the entire nation was Bob Adelman's photo (right) of protesters fighting to keep their footing against powerful fire hoses aimed at them by police. Adelman took great personal risks during the 1963 Freedom Summer to capture images like this one. The photographer once described Martin Luther King's reaction to seeing this picture. "I went up to Doc—which is what we called Dr. King—and gave him a print of the picture," Adelman told *The Guardian*. "He said he was startled that beauty could come out of so much pain." ⬡ BOB ADELMAN

stop the defamation of the Jewish people." But unlike other religious and ethnic defense organizations at the time, ADL included in its mission a pledge "to secure justice and fair treatment to all."

The organization based its philosophy on the words of Hillel, the first-century BC Jewish sage who famously asked, "If I am not for myself, then who will be for me? If I am only for myself, then what am I? And if not now, when?" In practice, says ADL's deputy national director, Kenneth Jacobson, the organization "turned those three questions into a code that says, 'First, be proud of who you are and fight the defamation of the Jewish people. But if that's all you're doing, then you're not a real civil rights organization. So you must stand up for others too. And don't dawdle.'"

By any measure, ADL, working with other civil rights groups and a well-worn copy of the U.S. Constitution, has made enormous strides over the past century. Today, the circumstances for Jews, African Americans, Latino Americans, Asian Americans, women, and the LGBTQ community in the United States are unquestionably better than they were in 1913. Laws now prohibit, at least in theory, much of the institutionalized discrimination that these minorities

faced in courts, voting booths, the workplace, schools, and housing. In today's United States, vastly more members of our population are able to embrace their own diversity, no longer fearful they'll be branded as outside the national mainstream. Independent scholars credit ADL as a major force in bringing about changes that have moved the United States closer to its founding principles of equal rights for all citizens.

Yet in the wake of the 2016 presidential election, the country is experiencing a resurgence of xenophobia, racism, and intolerance. ADL offices across the nation have been swamped with reports of threats and assaults against African Americans, Latinos, Muslims, and gays. Many now fear that the nation is facing the greatest threat to civil liberties in the past 40 years.

And in a wave of anti-Semitism not seen since the 1930s, the FBI has catalogued scores of incidents involving bomb threats against Jewish institutions, Nazi swastikas scrawled on the sides of synagogues, and headstones toppled in Jewish cemeteries. "Let's party like it's 1933," quipped white supremacist leader Richard Spencer at an election victory celebration for Donald Trump in Washington, referring to the year Adolf Hitler took power in Germany.

Driving this anti-Semitic wave is an energized "alt-right"—an Orwellian rebranding of white nationalists like Spencer, who regard the outcome of the 2016 presidential election as the vindication of their racist agenda.

Perhaps most chilling, the White House has said it won't rule out Trump's intention to register all Muslims already in the country as a necessary "security precaution." Some of the new president's aides cite the internment of Japanese

MARIETTA, GEORGIA, AUGUST 17, 1915. Leo Frank, the Jewish manager of an Atlanta pencil factory, was lynched (left) in one of the most notorious and highly publicized cases of anti-Semitism in the United States. Frank had been charged with the murder of a young girl who worked in his factory. With the public demanding swift justice, the jury hastily convicted Frank on flimsy evidence and sentenced him to death. After a review of the case, Governor John Slaton concluded that Frank was innocent and commuted his sentence to life imprisonment, confident that Frank's innocence would be established and that he would be set free. But Slaton's decision enraged the public, which had been whipped into an anti-Semitic fury by a populist newspaper publisher. Riots erupted in Atlanta. On the night of August 16, 1915, an angry mob burst into the prison where Frank was being held, hauled him away, and hanged him from an oak tree the next morning. More than any other incident, it was the lynching of Frank that awakened Jews to the physical threat posed by American anti-Semitism, giving the newly formed Anti-Defamation League even greater impetus to fight against a rising tide of prejudice.

SUPERMAN, CREATED IN 1933 by Jerry Siegel and artist Joe Shuster, two Jewish high school students living in Cleveland, Ohio, had a real world impact when the *Superman* radio show adopted a story that mocked and discredited the Klu Klux Klan. It all started with the work of the activist writer Stetson Kennedy, who in the late 1940s went undercover with the Klan as a self-appointed spy, and then reported what he'd learned to law enforcement officials. To his dismay, the officials were either sympathetic to the Klan or simply unwilling to confront them. So, instead, he provided his intelligence to the producers of *The Adventures of Superman.* Kennedy's timing was exquisite. With the Nazis defeated, Superman needed a new nemesis, and the Klan, with its hooded members, violent methods, and secret rituals, was straight out of central casting. In 1946, *The Clan of the Fiery Cross*, a 16-part series in which Superman defeats the KKK, made the group look comical. The Klan tried to organize a boycott of the show's sponsor, Kellogg's Cereal, but it went nowhere.

Americans during World War II as a legal precedent for such a move.

Recalling how Jews were forced to register in Nazi Germany in the prelude to the Holocaust, Jonathan Greenblatt, CEO and national director of the Anti-Defamation League, has sounded a defiant rallying cry for the battles against intolerance that lie ahead.

"If one day, Muslim Americans are forced to register their identities, then that is the day that this proud Jew will register as a Muslim," he told ADL's inaugural summit on anti-Semitism in New York shortly after Trump's election. "Because fighting prejudice against the marginalized is not just the fight of those minorities. It's our fight...that is the cause that ADL signed up for when we were founded a century ago."

A HUNDRED YEARS OF STRUGGLE

The Anti-Defamation League's lofty mission began with Sigmund Livingston, the German-born Chicago lawyer who founded the organization in 1913, at a time when anti-Semitism was woven into the fabric of American life.

On vaudeville stages and in newspapers, Jews were commonly caricatured as bearded, hook-nosed Shylocks. Jews were excluded from the senior ranks of major companies. In the run-up to World War I, a U.S. Army training manual portrayed Jews as slackers and cowards. After the war, they were often painted as communists, because many Jews fervently believed that a civilized society should provide a safety net for those less fortunate. Many neighborhood associations refused to sell or rent property to Jews, and resorts posted signs warning "No Dogs! No Jews!" One of the most prominent anti-Semites at that time was Henry Ford, founder of the Ford Motor Company, who used his newspaper, *The Dearborn Independent,* to reprint the infamous anti-Semitic forgery *The Protocols of the Elders of Zion*, in an early instance of "fake news."

But it was the case of Leo Frank, a young Jewish New Yorker, that awakened the Jewish community to the physical dangers posed by American anti-Semitism. In 1913, a Georgia jury convicted Frank on trumped-up evidence for the murder of a young woman at an Atlanta pencil factory and sentenced him to death. Though his sentence was commuted to life imprisonment, a vigilante mob chanting, "Hang the Jew!" stormed the jail where Frank was held, took him to the dead girl's hometown, and hanged him from an oak tree the next morning. Frank's brutal death became front-page news nationwide, and his conviction and lynching was portrayed as the result of anti-Semitism.

In response, many prominent American Jews threw their full support behind the then-fledgling Anti-Defamation League. Over the next three decades, ADL, under the sponsorship of the B'nai B'rith, marked the first inroads against anti-Semitism in the United States. In 1916, *The New York Times*' publisher, Adolph Ochs, who also served as a senior ADL executive, appealed to the nation's newspaper editors to stop their "objectionable and vulgar" depiction of Jews

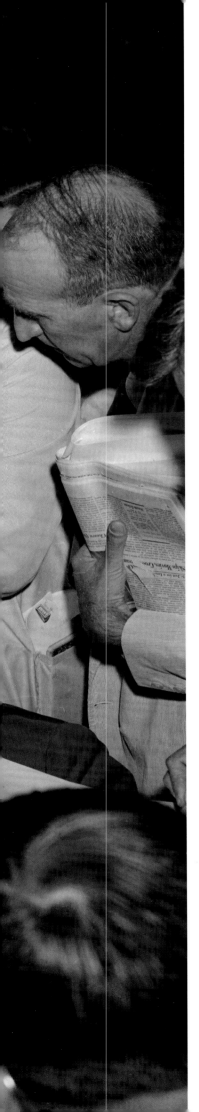

**WASHINGTON, D.C.,
SEPTEMBER 9, 1954.** Joseph
McCarthy (left, center, seated),
appears, surrounded by reporters,
after a hearing of his Permanent
Subcommittee on Investigations.
The Wisconsin senator used the
committee to flaunt unfounded
allegations accusing prominent
people of communist sympathies,
destroying the reputations of
hundreds. In 1953, President Dwight
D. Eisenhower attacked McCarthy's
methods at a dinner held by the
Anti-Defamation League. The
president's criticism, along with
ADL's accusations of anti-Semitism,
emboldened McCarthy's detractors.
Over the next year, CBS broadcaster
Edward R. Murrow publicly exposed
McCarthy as a fraud and a bully,
and his Senate colleagues formally
censured him over his smear tactics.
Powerless, McCarthy declined both
physically and emotionally, drinking
heavily until his death in 1957 at the
age of 48.

WASHINGTON, D.C., 1947.
Movie actor Humphrey Bogart
and his wife, actress Lauren Bacall
(above), lead a large group of
Hollywood stars to a hearing of the
House Committee on Un-American
Activities, which was investigating
the "Hollywood Ten," a list of actors,
directors and writers, for their
alleged communist sympathies and
influence on the motion picture
industry. Bogart and Bacall, along
with actor Danny Kaye and director
John Huston, organized the
Committee for the First Amendment
to protest the Congress's targeting of
the film industry.

ROY COHN, APPEARING on the
cover of *Esquire* magazine in 1978
(right), was the red-baiting chief
counsel for Senator Joseph McCarthy,
whose tactics became synonymous
with intimidation and demagoguery. In
an effort to blunt the Anti-Defamation
League's criticism of McCarthy, Cohn
tried to win a senior position in the
organization, but was rebuffed. Cohn
later counseled an aspiring young real
estate mogul named Donald Trump.
In business and legal matters, Cohn
advised Trump to always attack and
never apologize, honing the belligerent,
win-at-all-costs style that came to
define Trump's public persona.

NEW ORLEANS, NOVEMBER 14, 1960. Federal officials accompany first-grader Ruby Bridges to the William Frantz Elementary School in New Orleans, making her the first African American student to desegregate a Southern public school. The historic moment took place six years after the U.S. Supreme Court's 1954 ruling in *Brown v. Board of Education*, which stipulated that state laws establishing separate public schools for African American and white students were unconstitutional. Though many Southern whites objected to federally enforced school integration, the first-grader's walk, later immortalized in a painting by Norman Rockwell, represented a high-profile victory for the American civil rights movement.

in the press. By 1920, Livingston was gratified to report that the practice had virtually stopped. Also at ADL's urging, President Woodrow Wilson ordered the recall of the offensive Army training manuals and made a concerted effort to highlight Jewish contributions to the war effort in his speeches.

Yet these victories only served to underscore a painful irony that America's Jews faced at the time. Though they made up only about 2 to 3 percent of the U.S. population, Jews frequently found themselves scapegoated for many of the country's ills, largely because they were seen as easy and defenseless targets.

ADL confronted far more ominous challenges in the 1930s and 1940s, as Hitler rose to power in Germany. American fascist groups promoted anti-Semitic canards, attributing to the Jews responsibility for the Great Depression. Leading the charge was the pioneering aviator Charles Lindbergh, a national hero and leader of the isolationist "America First" movement, which sought to keep the United States out of World War II. In a 1941 speech in Des Moines, Iowa, Lindbergh, falling back on age-old anti-Semitic stereotypes, accused the Jews of using "subterfuge and propaganda" to manipulate the public into supporting the war. "Their greatest danger to this country lies in their large ownership and influence in our motion pictures, our press, our radio and our government," Lindbergh warned. Today, white supremacists are still disseminating Lindbergh's false accusations against the Jews.

But American Jews were not defenseless. Once the United States entered the war, ADL discredited Lindbergh and other anti-Semitic agitators, such as Father Charles Coughlin, his pro-fascist Christian Front, and the German American Bund, by exposing their ties to Nazi Germany. Moreover, ADL's ability to publicly shame anti-Semites prompted a rare apology from Henry Ford, who

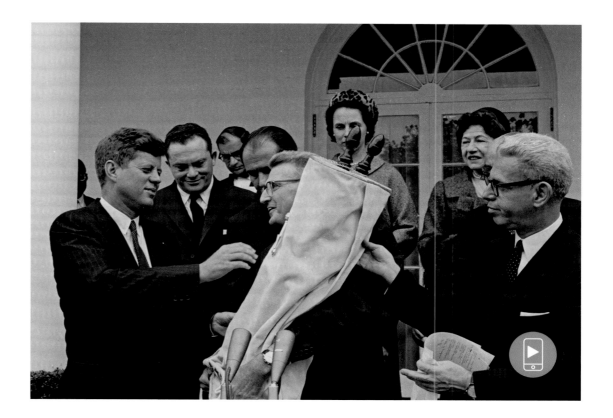

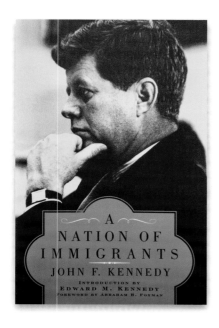

wrote to Livingston, ADL's founder, expressing his regret and the hope that "hatred of the Jew, commonly known as anti-Semitism, and hatred against any other racial or religious groups, shall cease for all time." The information-gathering techniques that ADL developed to unmask pro-Nazi organizations later served as models for its research on other extremist groups.

Up until the war, the Anti-Defamation League had been little more than a loose confederation of some 150 prominent volunteers. But once that conflict ended, ADL transformed itself into a professional organization, moving its headquarters to New York and establishing its civil rights and educational divisions, its research and investigative arm, the Center on Extremism, and more than two dozen branches across the country. ADL's regional leaders initiated frequent meetings with senators and congressional representatives to discuss the organization's work, which in turn bolstered ADL's political clout on Capitol Hill.

The postwar years also saw ADL throw itself into the second half of its original mission—defending the civil liberties of non-Jewish minorities. In one of the organization's first forays into these struggles, ADL mounted a fierce campaign against discriminatory practices against African Americans in housing, contributing an important amicus brief to the U.S. Supreme Court in the landmark 1948 case of *Shelley v. Kraemer*. Accepting the premise of ADL's brief, the justices held it was unconstitutional for courts to enforce restrictions that prohibited persons from owning or renting property based on their race or color. ADL also exposed discrimination in college admissions, which eventually eroded the unofficial quotas that limited the number of Jews and other minorities that many schools were willing to accept each year.

The Anti-Defamation League scored one of its most significant achievements in 1950, when it won passage of a law in the Georgia state Legislature that prohibited Ku Klux Klan members from wearing their hoods during their rallies and demonstrations. In arguing for the law, ADL was careful not to challenge the Klan's First Amendment right to demonstrate. Instead, the organization argued that the Klan used hoods to disguise their involvement in violent crimes, in much the same way criminals wore masks to conceal their identities while robbing a bank or committing other crimes.

When the anti-mask bill was introduced to the legislature, Georgia Governor Herman Talmadge, a staunch segregationist, contemptuously sent it to the Sewers Committee, presumably to die. But Alexander Miller, who oversaw ADL's regional offices at the time, convinced newspapers to editorialize in favor of the measure, framing it as a test of the state's authority over the Klan. The media campaign succeeded, and when the bill reached Talmadge's desk, public pressure forced him to sign it. The anti-mask law, later adopted by an additional five Southern states and some 50 communities, had far-reaching implications. "As a result of the successful campaigns to enact this legislation, public opinion and public officials aligned themselves against the Klan in the South," Miller said in ADL's oral history, *Not the Work of a Day*. "By the 1950s, the Ku Klux Klan had become a small, fragmented, largely powerless organization."

Today, in an echo of the anti-Klan effort, ADL is leading a campaign to pressure social media sites like Facebook and Twitter to take action against those who use the Internet to spread hatred against racial, ethnic, religious, and sexual minorities. In their 2013 book, *Viral Hate: Containing Its Spread on the Internet,* Abraham Foxman, the former ADL national director, and Christopher Wolf, the organization's resident expert on Internet law, point out that, due to the First Amendment's free speech guarantees, legal action is not always the most effective remedy. However, they note, the First Amendment does grant social media sites the right to decide "what is in or out of bounds for display on their Internet platforms." As the authors warn: "Words of hate can easily turn into acts of hate."

In the 1950s, ADL also proved to be one of the most effective opponents of Senator Joseph McCarthy, whose communist witch hunts destroyed the reputations of hundreds of innocent Americans. Because many of the targets of McCarthy's unsubstantiated charges were Jewish, ADL accused him of anti-Semitism and launched one of the first sustained efforts by a major civil liberties organization to discredit him. Until ADL took action, even President Dwight D. Eisenhower had been reluctant to criticize the powerful Wisconsin senator.

Some scholars credit ADL's 1953 decision to award Eisenhower its highest honor—the America's Democratic Legacy Award—as the catalyst that

THE ELECTION OF DONALD Trump left many progressives stunned and despondent. After a week of tears and despair, a small group of 10th-graders at Little Red School House, a progressive private high school in New York's Greenwich Village, decided it was time to demonstrate their opposition to Trump. In a move to attract other students to their cause, they created a Facebook page titled "NYC School Walkout, Love Trumps Hate" and announced they would walk out of class and march on Trump Tower at 10:30 a.m. the following Tuesday. Word of the demonstration spread to other groups, and by the time the march began, thousands had turned out. Despite a cold November rain, they packed the protest pen outside Trump Tower and then marched down Fifth Avenue. Though the protesters had no permit, police did not interfere and even directed traffic away from marchers as they chanted anti-Trump slogans all the way to Washington Square Park.
📷 ANDRES KUDACKI

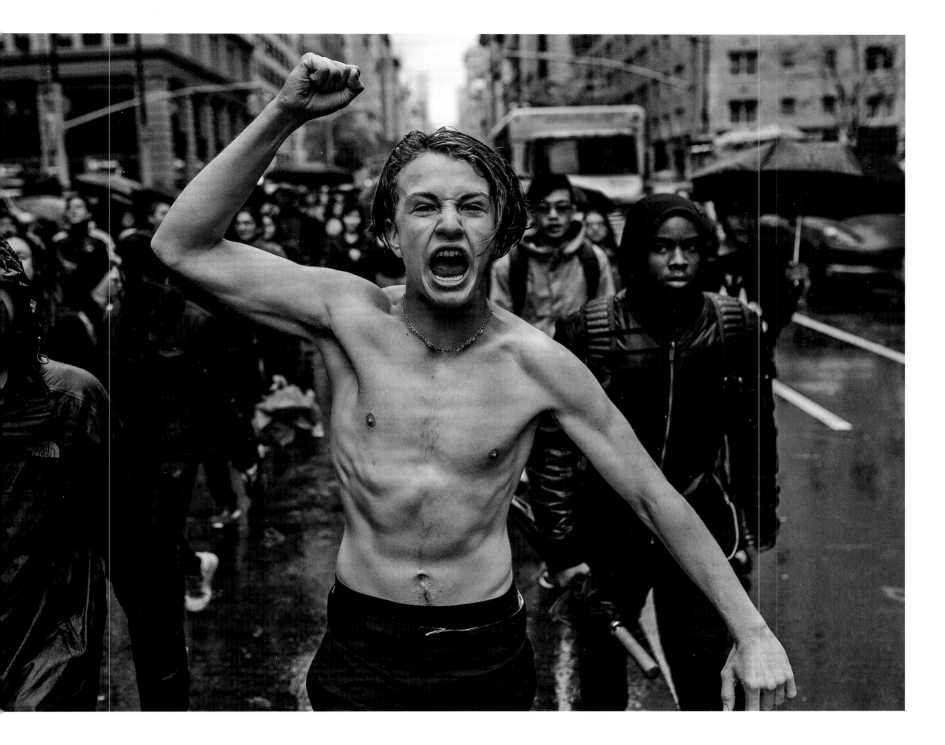

emboldened the president to publicly condemn McCarthy's methods for the first time. Eisenhower delivered his denunciation at ADL's 40th anniversary dinner in Washington. Standing at a lectern in the ornate ballroom of the Mayflower Hotel, he ditched his prepared remarks and instead spoke about the "code" of honesty and forthright behavior that his upbringing in Abilene, Kansas, had instilled in him. He then contrasted that code with the behavior of those in Washington who were going behind people's backs to smear them with innuendo and false accusations. "In this country, if someone dislikes you, or accuses you, he must come up in front," Eisenhower insisted. "He cannot assassinate you or your character from behind, without suffering the penalties an outraged citizenry will impose."

YOU'VE GOT TO BE CAREFULLY TAUGHT
BY RODGERS AND HAMMERSTEIN

You've got to be taught to hate and fear
You've got to be taught from year to year
It's got to be drummed in your dear little ear
You've got to be carefully taught

You've got to be taught to be afraid
Of people whose eyes are oddly made
And people whose skin is a diff'rent shade
You've got to be carefully taught

You've got to be taught before it's too late
Before you are six or seven or eight
To hate all the people your relatives hate
You've got to be carefully taught

When the musical *South Pacific* opened to rave reviews on Broadway on the night of April 7, 1949, Jewish composers Richard Rodgers and Oscar Hammerstein knew they had a hit on their hands, albeit a controversial one. The scene is set on a South Pacific island in World War II, and one of the plotlines involves an interracial romance between an American lieutenant and an exotic, dark-skinned Indo-Chinese woman. The soldier fears the social consequences he'll face if he marries and brings her back to his upper-class Philadelphia home. Reflecting on the source of his own prejudices, the lieutenant muses on the fact that racism "is not born in you. It happens after you're born." Southern legislators denounced *South Pacific* as having been inspired by Moscow. One Georgia representative commented, "Intermarriage produces halfbreeds. In the South, we have pure blood lines, and we intend to keep it that way." Hammerstein said he was surprised that "anything kind and humane" must necessarily originate from Moscow. But he agreed with the Georgia legislators on one thing: that the song was indeed a protest against racial prejudice. ■

GAINESVILLE, GEORGIA, 1986. A retired poultry inspector (right) at a Klan rally holds her 16-month-old great-granddaughter before attending an early evening cross-burning and then later marching with others in full Klan regalia through the African American sections of town. 📷 GERRIT FOKKEMA

PETAL, MISSISSIPPI, 2002. The young son of a Klansman (left) pauses momentarily, seeking his parents' approval after beating a doll hanging from a noose. 📷 CHRISTOPHER CAPOZZIELLO

Though Eisenhower never specifically mentioned McCarthy by name, there was no mistaking his target. "President Attacks McCarthy for First Time," blared the next day's headline in *The New York Times*. McCarthy's coup de grâce came when broadcaster Edward Murrow unmasked him on television as a bully and a fraud. Soon after, McCarthy's popularity dwindled, particularly in the Senate, where he had been its central figure. In 1954, the Senate took the rare step of censuring McCarthy, leaving him powerless.

MARCHING WITH MLK

Throughout the 1960s, ADL continued to play a prominent role in the fight for black civil rights. In June 1964, the organization joined with other groups to organize a major rally in Chicago. More than 70,000 people—black and white—gathered at Soldier Field to hear Reverend Martin Luther King Jr. demand that Congress pass President Lyndon B. Johnson's historic civil rights bill. "Asia and Africa are moving at jet-like speed toward political independence, but there are places in the United States where we are moving at a horse-and-buggy pace to get a hamburger and a cup of coffee," King told the crowd. Standing beside King was ADL's Midwest regional director, A. Abbott Rosen.

Within two weeks, the bill passed, and Johnson signed it into law. A year later, National Director Benjamin Epstein and ADL leaders walked alongside King as he led hundreds on what initially began as a peaceful march from Selma to Montgomery, Alabama, to secure voting rights for African Americans. When police brutally attacked the peaceful marchers with clubs, fire hoses, and dogs, a number of Jewish leaders and activists were left bleeding alongside King and his followers.

Of all the white civil rights groups at the time, ADL was one of the most active in the South. "We would go to places where there had been violent anti-black acts and investigate," Burnett Roth, a lay leader and member of the ADL's Civil Rights Committee, told the organization's oral historians. "We would be the ones interviewing the police on Klan activities directed not at Jews, but at blacks." He added that because ADL had such good sources in communities across the South, its network of sympathetic activists were often able to warn black communities before the Klan held a rally that might threaten their lives.

Because of the close ties that ADL had formed with King and other black leaders, white civil rights groups often turned to the organization to arrange introductions to their black counterparts. "Time after time," Roth recalled, "we caused meetings to be held between blacks and whites all over the South." Reflecting on his 50-year tenure at ADL, Roth called the lines of communication that developed between the white and black communities one of ADL's "most important achievements."

Another major part of the Anti-Defamation League's work over the past century has been its advocacy on behalf of Israel. In the 1980s, an annual program that brought hundreds of delegations of U.S. lawmakers and other

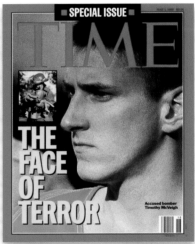

IN 1995, TIMOTHY MCVEIGH, a member of a white supremacist militia, blew up a federal building in Oklahoma City (top and above), killing 168 people in what remains the deadliest domestic terrorist attack in U.S. history. In response, the Anti-Defamation League helped craft legislation to outlaw militias from conducting military-style training exercises for the purpose of disrupting civil order. The legislation, enacted by only 21 states, also empowers law enforcement to investigate militia activity and prevent domestic terrorism before it occurs.

government officials to Israel to enhance their understanding of Israeli life and its challenges. The goodwill these study missions engendered proved invaluable after the 1973 Middle East War, when Arab producers halted oil shipments to the United States as punishment for its support for Israel. Amid a wave of anti-Semitic accusations at home that falsely blamed Israel and the Jews for the country's oil shortage, ADL fought back. With the support of its allies on Capitol Hill, ADL helped win passage of laws in 1977 and 1978 that prohibited American companies from complying with the Arab boycott of Israel.

Meanwhile, back home, ADL's Center on Extremism began tracking a new threat: the rise of heavily armed anti-government and white nationalist militias. Preaching hatred against blacks and Jews and contempt for government authority, these groups openly began conducting military training exercises in rural areas. Six months before the 1995 Oklahoma City bombing, ADL produced a detailed report that tried to alert the nation to the growing menace of such anti-government militia groups, but it received little attention.

The bombing of the Alfred P. Murrah Federal Building in Oklahoma City on April 19, 1995, by two militia movement sympathizers, left 168 people dead and

● e Anti-
...tion
...(ADL)
...he first
...ate
...aw.

...ongress
...he

...us
...sm

● **1990** President George H. W. Bush signs the **Hate Crime Statistics Act.** It requires the U.S. attorney general to collect **data** "about crimes which manifest evidence of prejudice based on race, religion, sexual orientation, or ethnicity."

● **1993 The Supreme Court** unanimously upholds the Wisconsin hate crime penalty enhancement law, in *Wisconsin v. Mitchell.*

● **1994 The Hate Crimes Sentencing Enhancement Act** is enacted into law. The act allows judges to impose harsher penalties for hate crimes, including those based on gender, disability, and sexual orientation.

● **1997** President Bill Clinton devotes one of his weekly radio addresses to hate crimes, specifically bias crimes against LGBTQ people.

● **1997** President Clinton hosts the first **White House Conference on Hate Crimes.**

● **1998** In June, three men, members of white supremacist groups in Texas, strip African American James Byrd Jr. naked and drag him behind their pickup truck for three miles. His body was dismembered.

In October, two men tie gay college student Matthew Shepard to a fence in Laramie, Wyoming, and leave him to die in the cold.

● **1999** The renamed **Hate Crimes Prevention Act** is again introduced into Congress.

In a Gallup poll, 75% of Americans believe that homosexuals should be covered by hate crimes laws.

● **2000** MTV airs a movie about the murder of Matthew Shepard.

50,000 people send emails urging President George W. Bush to support the hate crimes bill.

● **2001** Following the 9/11 attacks, the FBI documents a 1,700% increase in anti-Muslim hate-related incidents.

● **2007** President Bush threatens to veto a bill (on National Defense) if hate crimes legislation is attached to it.

The hate crimes part is stripped from the bill.

● **2008** The Anti-Defamation League initiates a series of nationwide education programs to teach acceptance, including "No Place for Hate."

● **2009** More than 13 years after its introduction, President Barack Obama signs the newly named **Matthew Shepard and James Byrd Jr. Hate Crimes Prevention Act** into law.

● **2015** FBI updates **...Crimes ...Collecti... ...Guidelin...** training to includ... informat... crimes d... against ... because ... gender, ... identity ... anti-Sikh ... Arab, an... Hindu ha... crimes.

In 2015, there were 7,121 hate crime victims. The reported number is low. Hate crimes are vastly underreported.

Here's why they were targeted ...

Race/ethnicity	59.2%
Religion	19.7%
Sexual orientation	17.7%
Gender identity	1.7%
Disability	1.2%
Gender	0.4%

... and here's who they were:

2,201 victims were African American (13% of U.S. population)

1,239 LGBTQ (3.8% of U.S. population)

789 White (62% of U.S. population)

731 Jewish American (1.4% of U.S. population)

392 Latino American (17% of U.S. population)
307 Muslim American (1% of U.S. population)

1,462 others (including Native American, Asian American, Arab American, and members of other races/ethnicities and religions)

CHARLESTON, S.C., JUNE 2015.
When 23-year-old Dylann Roof
walked calmly into the Mother
Emanuel church in Charleston,
South Carolina, the Bible study
group already in progress welcomed
him and handed him a sheet with
religious verses. He sat down in a
pew for 15 minutes and then, as a
dozen people stood for prayers with
their eyes closed, Roof pulled out a
Glock .45-caliber pistol and fired 70
rounds at the worshippers, killing
nine African American churchgoers
in cold blood. An unrepentant Roof
said during his trial that he hoped
his actions would inspire a race
war. Two weeks later more than
half a dozen black churches went
up in flames (right) in a spate of
arson attacks across the South. Two
months later, on February 16, 2017,
Benjamin Thomas Samuel McDowell,
29, a South Carolina man with white
supremacist ties, was arrested by the
FBI for planning commit a shooting
"in the spirit of Dylann Roof" on a
South Carolina synagogue. A federal
jury of nine whites and three African
Americans sentenced Roof to death
in December 2016 on 33 federal hate
crime charges. Roof appears (far
right) via video before a judge.

JUST THE FACTS

AS OF 2017,

5

STATES
(ARKANSAS, GEORGIA,
INDIANA,
SOUTH CAROLINA,
AND WYOMING)
ARE THE ONLY STATES
WITHOUT ANY STATE
HATE CRIME LAWS.

—2016 ANTI-DEFAMATION
LEAGUE

nearly 700 wounded in what remains the deadliest single domestic terrorist incident in U.S. history. Journalists desperate to understand the perpetrators and their ideology found answers in ADL's report, which was widely cited as a prescient and authoritative source on homegrown extremism. While Congress passed a law that increased penalties for convicted terrorists, ADL drafted another measure aimed at preventing domestic terrorist acts before they occurred. The law, adopted by 21 states, outlaws paramilitary training by militias for the purpose of civil disorder. According to Michael Lieberman, ADL's Washington counsel, who helped craft the legislation, the law also empowers state and federal authorities to investigate militia training sessions to determine whether members are exercising their Second Amendment gun rights, as their leaders claim, or preparing for RaHoWa, the acronym these groups use for a "racial holy war," one of their principal objectives. "Now the police have a tool to find out," Lieberman says.

Another of ADL's most important achievements has been its success in advancing hate crimes legislation, an undertaking that has broadened an emerging field of criminal law. ADL's relentless advocacy helped win passage of the 1990 Hate Crimes Statistics Act, which requires the Justice Department to keep a public record of all crimes committed against people on the basis of their race, religion, or ethnic background. That law paved the way for 45 states and the District of Columbia to pass hate crimes statutes, all of which are based on an ADL-crafted model that requires enhanced penalties for bias-motivated crimes. The five states that still have not passed any hate crimes laws are Arkansas, Indiana, South Carolina, Wyoming, and Georgia.

As part of its campaign against hate crimes, the Anti-Defamation League also led an eight-year struggle to win enactment in 2009 of the Matthew Shepard and James Byrd, Jr., Hate Crimes Prevention Act. For the first time, the measure, named after Shepard, a gay student beaten to death in 1998 by homophobes in Laramie, Wyoming, and Byrd, an African American dragged to death behind a truck the same year by two white supremacists in Jasper, Texas, expanded existing federal hate crimes law to include crimes motivated by a victim's sexual orientation.

Who decided to run the "jews people" segment on @CNN and what steps are being taken to remove them from that position?

So the banner was out of line, but having neo-Nazis on CNN was a-ok? Gotcha.

They don't have to give voice to what every racist troll says, that just legitimizes hate. Don't feed the trolls

We need to stop allowing Jews to pretend they're people until we figure out what's going on

Hey @CNN. 1. You gotta call alt-right what it is—white supremacist. 2. Just b/c some idiot says it doesn't mean you put it on the chyron.

Awful

Made me so sick to see that. Please push for public apology.

WHEN CHYRONS ATTACK

THE TRUMP TRANSITION
ALT-RIGHT FOUNDER QUESTIONS IF JEWS ARE PEOPLE
LIVE CNN
S&P ▲ 16.28

Why does CNN give him a platform?

Pinches self I'm real! I'm a person!

Encourage you to study media in the early days of Hitler

Which editors are routinely replacing the terms "Neo-Nazi" and "racist" with "alt-right" and "racially charged?"

I believe "Jews are people" infers that it's a matter of opinion. It's not a debate and shouldn't be treated as such

IN NOVEMBER 2016, CNN received waves of criticism after running an onscreen banner for nearly three minutes with the phrase, "Alt-right founder questions if Jews are people." During the segment, guest-hosted by Jim Sciutto, two media correspondents, Rebecca Berg of Real Clear Politics (center) and Matt Viser of *The Boston Globe* (right), were interviewed about statements made the day before by Richard Spencer, founder of a neo-Nazi organization, the National Policy Institute. The backlash was swift and widespread, with many viewers noting that it was inappropriate for CNN to feature such an anti-Semitic statement onscreen and objecting to CNN's propagation of the fringe group's hateful rhetoric. During the interview, Sciutto characterized Spencer's rhetoric as "hate-filled garbage," and the rest of his panel also expressed disgust at Spencer's remarks. Sciutto later apologized for the graphic, which not only gave voice to Spencer's neo-Nazi views but also appeared to identify Globe correspondent Matt Viser as Richard Spencer (sparking a second online furor). Sciutto said, "The banner—which we don't write from the chair—was out of line."

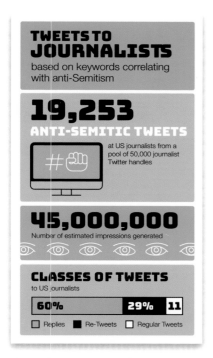

TWEETS TO JOURNALISTS
based on keywords correlating with anti-Semitism

19,253
ANTI-SEMITIC TWEETS
at US journalists from a pool of 50,000 journalist Twitter handles

45,000,000
Number of estimated impressions generated

CLASSES OF TWEETS
to US journalists

60%	29%	11
☐ Replies	■ Re-Tweets	☐ Regular Tweets

The October 19, 2016, Anti-Defamation League. *Task Force Report on Harassment and Journalism*

NEW YORK, FEBRUARY 4, 2017.
On a late, cold winter evening, passengers bundled in heavy coats boarded the No. 1 subway only to find Nazi swastikas and anti-Semitic hate speech scrawled over every ad and window in their car. On one subway map, a person had written "Jews belong in the oven" with a swastika (above, middle). Gregory Locke, one of the shocked passengers, reported what happened next in a posting on his Facebook page, "The train was silent as everyone stared at each other, uncomfortable and unsure what to do. One guy got up and said, 'Hand sanitizer gets rid of Sharpie. We need alcohol.' He found some tissues and got to work." Locke added, "I've never seen so many people simultaneously reach into their bags and pockets looking for tissues and Purel. Within about two minutes, all the Nazi symbolism was gone." In 24 hours, more than 518,000 people had seen his post on Facebook, and shared it more than 354,000 times.
📷 GREGORY LOCKE

And in 2014, when the country faced a rash of police shootings of unarmed black men, the White House turned to the professionals who run ADL's extensive law enforcement training courses for new approaches to strengthen the relationship between police and the communities they serve. "If they forget that when people do not trust them, if they are feared, they have failed," ADL's director of national law enforcement initiatives, David Friedman, told the President's Task Force on 21st Century Policing. "The only real safeguard we have from abuse is the conscious decision that each officer makes to act according to the profession's core values, which revolve around his or her role as a protector of the people—all people."

UNFINISHED BUSINESS

For more than 100 years, the Anti-Defamation League's triumphs have helped bend the arc of the nation's history toward greater social justice. ADL has accomplished this, first and foremost, by recognizing the need to speak up in the face of intolerance.

Today, as President Trump's nativist "America First" rhetoric stokes fears of sinister "others," the need is now greater than ever. From suspicion of Syrian war refugees and animosity toward undocumented Latino laborers to the bomb threats and violence against Jewish institutions and the burning of more than a dozen mosques, a host of dark impulses all seem to be bubbling up at the same time. And ADL is rising to confront them once again.

Only days after the White House issued a travel ban on Muslim immigrants and refugees, ADL filed an amicus brief with the U.S. Court of Appeals for the Ninth Circuit in support of the state of Washington's challenge to the executive order. The brief reminded judges of shameful anti-immigration orders of the

past—such as Washington's refusal to accept a boatload of Jewish refugees fleeing from Hitler in 1939—that left an indelible stain on the United States' image as a sanctuary country. "America has always been at its best when it opens its doors to refugees and immigrants," the brief noted. "Sometimes the nation has risen to the challenge," it argued, but at other times, "when prejudice and fear predominate over reason and compassion, we falter, often with devastating consequences." ADL protested a similar crackdown ordered by the White House on the estimated 11 million undocumented immigrants already in the country. Under the executive order, authorities have swept up both criminals and law-abiding people for immediate deportation, sometimes separating children from their parents, which the government claims is "for their own safety."

Following the desecration of Jewish cemeteries in St. Louis and Philadelphia and threats against Jewish community centers around the country, ADL has been out front with public statements, Op-Ed by the organization's legal experts, and TV appearances by ADL's top leaders to insist that the White House speak out more forcefully against such threats.

Not content to wait for a White House response, ADL has issued security bulletins to the Jewish community nationwide, providing them with a manual on how to respond to threats. In February 2017, ADL organized a conference call in which Jewish community leaders could discuss additional security precautions with senior FBI special agents. Though the call was arranged at just one day's notice, some 700 representatives of Jewish institutions around the country called in. Regional ADL offices also have weighed in, providing security training for synagogues, Jewish schools, and community centers in their areas.

As threats have grown against mosques and other minority religious and ethnic communities, ADL has adapted its security manual to address their specific needs as well. Meanwhile, on the advocacy front, ADL professionals have been meeting with Muslim, Sikh, and Latino coalition partners to develop common strategies for legislative action to protect those communities. In the wake of the White House's order rescinding executive protections that allow transgender people to choose the bathroom of their choice, ADL and its LGBTQ partners have been brainstorming on legal briefs for what many experts see as a looming constitutional showdown over equal protection in the Supreme Court. "It's been intense," says Deborah Lauter. "We're being overwhelmed on all fronts."

ADL is also pressing on with its signature programs. Its Center on Extremism continues to monitor hate speech on the Internet, issue warnings, and provide law enforcement with intelligence on dangerous groups and individuals. ADL experts also continue to provide the media with background briefings on extremist websites such as the *Breitbart News Network*, which has become a platform for white supremacist screeds. The Center is now working with Hispanic coalition partners on a report that will explore how online hate speech affects the Latino community.

ADL also has been closely tracking white supremacists' utilization of the Internet and social media to spread their message of hate. One example of this was an echo symbol—three sets of parentheses—that in 2016, suddenly began to appear on the Internet and social media sites such as Twitter and Instagram, bracketing Jewish names. ADL identified this symbol as the work of white supremacists who had created databases containing both common Jewish names and those of prominent Jewish figures, and who then developed software that added the echo symbol around the names whenever they were found on a web or social media site. Many Jewish figures whose names were tagged, such as

Gabe Ortíz ✓
@TUSK81

Syrian refugees were among the St. Louisans who united to clean a desecrated Jewish cemetery.

m.riverfronttimes.com/newsblog/2017/...

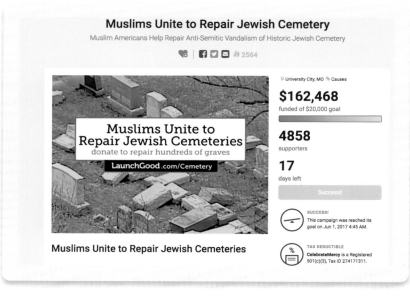

Muslims Unite to Repair Jewish Cemetery
Muslim Americans Help Repair Anti-Semitic Vandalism of Historic Jewish Cemetery

❤ 6 | 🇫 🔵 ✉ | 👥 2564

📍 University City, MO 👥 Causes

Muslims Unite to Repair Jewish Cemeteries
donate to repair hundreds of graves
LaunchGood.com/Cemetery

$162,468
funded of $20,000 goal

4858
supporters

17
days left

Success!

SUCCESS!
This campaign was reached its goal on Jun 1, 2017 4:45 AM.

TAX DEDUCTIBLE
CelebrateMercy is a Registered 501(c)(3), Tax ID 274171311.

Muslims Unite to Repair Jewish Cemeteries

ST. LOUIS, MISSOURI, FEBRUARY 21, 2017. Jewish and Muslim communities supported each other when both groups experienced a rise of hate crime incidents after the November 2016 election. After anti-Semitic vandals desecrated headstones in a local historic Jewish cemetery (above), the Muslim community in St. Louis used crowdfunding (left) to raise over $160,000 to help restore the cemetery. "Through this campaign, we hope to send a united message from the Jewish and Muslim communities that there is no place for this type of hate, desecration, and violence in America," the fundraising page on the site LaunchGood read.
📷 TOM GANNAM, ABOVE

VICTORIA, TEXAS, FEBRUARY 1, 2017. Only hours after President Donald Trump signed his executive order barring refugees from seven Muslim-majority countries, arsonists set a fire that completely engulfed the 16-year-old Victoria Islamic Center mosque. The fire was one of hundreds of recent attacks against Muslims and their mosques across the United States since the 2016 election began, according to the study "When Islamophobia Turns Violent." The town's response to the devastating fire grabbed international headlines including CNN's (right) when the local Jewish congregation gave the mosque's imam the keys to their synagogue to enable followers to worship. Donations from around the world via an online crowdfunding campaign to aid in the cleanup and rebuilding of the mosque exceeded $1.1 million. Here, Eman Ibrahim (top, left) and Amani Ramadan (top, right), are comforted by Sister Amata Hollas. 🄾 ANA RAMIREZ

**MAPLEWOOD, NEW JERSEY,
JANUARY 27, 2017.** It has been
shown in study after study that
empathy doesn't develop in a
vacuum. Prejudices and assumptions
based on race, religion, or gender
quickly melt when people from
different backgrounds actually spend
time together. When Governor Chris
Christie decided to withdraw New
Jersey from participating in the U.S.
refugee resettlement program, Kate
McCaffrey and Melina Macall, both
members of the Bnai Keshet
synagogue in Montclair, New Jersey,
took things into their own hands.
"When the governor said that no
Syrian refugee should be allowed in
because even a 5-year-old was a
terrorist risk, he didn't speak for
me—or for many of us," Macall told
The Times of Israel. So she and
others created a weekly "Syrian
Supper Club," and invited Syrian and
Iraqi refugees to their homes to meet
other members of their community
and to cook Middle Eastern meals
together. Guests pay a modest fee to
attend the dinner, which helps
provide these new members of their
community with spending money.
Maplewood's Jewish community,
remembering the struggles their
ancestors had as immigrants seeking
safety in the United States, is one of
several across the United States that
are actively welcoming Muslim
refugees. Here Haydar Al-Qaysi (left,
center), who fled Baghdad with his
mother and sister, raises his glass to
toast his hosts. 🄾 MATT KATZ

journalists Jonathan Weisman of *The New York Times* and Julia Ioffe, with *The
Atlantic*, became the targets of vicious anti-Semitic online threats.

Meanwhile, ADL's Education Department is updating two highly acclaimed
school programs under "A World of Difference" initiative that seek to create
a positive, hate-free culture. "No Place for Hate," which emphasizes ethnic
and religious tolerance, is now taught in some 1,700 middle schools and high
schools nationwide. Amid the current wave of anti-Semitic threats, ADL
educators are providing new materials for teachers and parents that instruct
them how to speak to young students in the face of hate incidents. The second
program, "Words to Action," is intended for Jewish high school and college
students, teaching them how to respond to anti-Semitism on campus. ADL
recently released a new current events classroom curriculum on anti-Semitic
incidents, with suggestions on how students can participate in the fight against
anti-Semitism. "Essentially, it's what we've done all along, but it's really at a
heightened level right now," Lauter says.

Abraham Foxman, ADL's storied national director from 1987 to 2015,
shares a parable that illustrates the ethos that has guided the organization
since its founding. One day, the story goes, a teacher overheard one of his
young students ridiculing an odd-looking classmate. Rebuking the boy for his
churlish behavior, the teacher ordered him to go outside, pick a dandelion,
and blow its seeds into the wind.

The student returned to report he had dutifully done as the teacher
instructed. "Now," the teacher ordered, "go back and collect the seeds."

"But that's impossible!" the student cried. "The wind carried them off in
every direction. I can't go get them."

NEW YORK, NOVEMBER 18, 2016.
The national director and CEO of the Anti-Defamation League, Jonathan Greenblatt (above), has spent a career in public service. Prior to heading ADL, he co-founded Ethos Water (acquired by Starbucks), which helped finance clean water programs in developing countries, and then served in the White House as Special Assistant to President Barack Obama. In his opening remarks at the 2016 inauguration of the ADL Center on Technology & Society in Silicon Valley, Greenblatt spoke about ADL's ongoing battle to combat cyberhate and the spread of anonymous online anti-Semitism: "Fifty years ago they were hiding behind their white hoods, now they are hiding behind their cell phones."
⌖ MICHAEL KOVAC

CHICAGO, ILLINOIS, JUNE 18, 2013.
The Anti-Defamation League's "No Place for Hate" program helps middle and high schools combat bullying, bias, and hatred directed at black, Latino, Jewish, Muslim, and LGBTQ students, including discussions about the consequences of bullying and prejudice. Students are also taught how to support someone who is being bullied, and are encouraged to keep a journal to record instances of bullying and to create poems or raps that break down stereotypes and promote respect for diversity. Since the program began, students at more than 1,700 schools across the United States, including these high school students in Chicago (above, right), have participated in the program, measurably reducing incidents of bullying at the schools. In June 2017, Harvard University withdrew acceptance letters from 10 incoming freshmen because they had posted racist and sexist comments on an online student messaging group. Had they participated in the "No Place for Hate" program, they might have retained their places.

"Neither can you undo the damage you've done to your classmate," the teacher admonished. "Your words are out there now, and all you can do is hope for his forgiveness."

Foxman adds: "We at the ADL do our utmost to prevent the inception of hate, to stop the seeds before they settle across the landscape. Or, at the very least, we work every day to minimize the damage hate can cause."

Despite ADL's current efforts and past triumphs, its struggle against bigotry, intolerance, and injustice is far from over. Indeed, even for an organization like ADL that has kept close tabs on extremists for nearly 80 years, it's a challenge of an entirely different magnitude when to combat hatred in a political environment where intolerance has been normalized and mainstreamed.

In a speech given shortly after 2016's unsettling election outcome, ADL CEO Greenblatt noted that it was the Jewish people who invented the phrase "Never again," the now-iconic words that first appeared on handmade signs held by Jewish inmates of Buchenwald shortly after U.S. forces liberated the concentration camp in April 1945.

"So let me just say—never is now," Greenblatt declared. "We must not be silent. We must raise our voices. We must act. We know why ADL was created. It was founded for moments just like these." ▪

Jonathan Broder is an award-winning journalist whose career has spanned more than four decades. As a foreign correspondent for the *Chicago Tribune,* he covered stories in more than 50 countries in the Middle East, Africa, South Asia, and Far East. Since returning to the United States, Broder has worked as an editor at *NPR* and *Congressional Quarterly* and a senior writer for *Newsweek.* His writing also has appeared in *The New York Times Magazine, The Washington Post, Salon,* and *World Policy Journal.* Based in Washington, D.C., Broder is a regular commentator on *C-SPAN, BBC Radio, PRI's "To the Point," Al Arabiya Television,* and *Voice of America.* 🐦 *@BroderJonathan*

F AMERICANS HAVE LEARNED anything from the struggle against bigotry and hatred over the past century, it's that the rights they've fought so hard to secure cannot be taken for granted. The arc of history will bend toward justice only so long as people remain vigilant and ready to defend those rights. This lesson is especially important for young people to absorb so they can carry on the struggle. Every year, some 50,000 high school students of all races, religions, and economic backgrounds visit the United States Holocaust Memorial Museum in Washington, D.C., to learn what happens when a society loses its moral compass. In this picture, a group of students stand in the museum's Tower of Faces, a three-story-high atrium lined with family photographs from the Jewish community of Eisiskes, a small town in Lithuania where Jews had lived for nearly 900 years. Over the course of two days in September 1941, Nazi SS troops and their Lithuanian auxiliaries massacred almost the entire Jewish population of the town, some 3,500 people. Only 29 Jews escaped the slaughter. The comments of one Cleveland student confirmed that the museum's message of "Never Again" had registered. "After visiting the Holocaust Museum today, I've become more aware of the discrimination going on around us," she wrote to her mother. "Also, I've promised myself to always stand up to hatred and discrimination. I learned that what I do can make a difference."

CREDITS AND THANKS

Rick Smolan, Project Director
Jennifer Erwitt, Project Director
Katya Able, Chief Operating Officer

DESIGN DIRECTOR
David Griffin

SENIOR EDITORIAL ADVISOR
Todd Brewster

CAPTION WRITER
Jonathan Broder

INFOGRAPHICS
Nigel Holmes

EDITORIAL DIRECTION
Mark Rykoff

IMAGE MANAGEMENT
Caroline Cortizo

COVER ARTIST
Tim O'Brien

RESEARCH DIRECTOR
Olivia Huffman

VIDEO RESEARCH
Elizabeth Cowperthwaite

CONTENT MANAGER
Alexandra Able

BUSINESS DEVELOPMENT
Barry Reder

SENIOR ADVISORS
Phillip Moffit, Life Balance Institute
Jane Friedman, Open Road
   Integrated Media

UNDERWRITERS
Eric & Linda Horodas

Make a difference

Please join us in fighting the good fight:
www.TheGoodFightBook.org

IMAGE PROCUREMENT
Karen Mullarkey
Jonathan Klein, Getty Images
Elodie Mailliet, Getty Images
Jeffrey Smith, Contact Press Images
Robert Pledge, Contact Press Images
Shelby Coffee, The Newseum
Colleen Bernhard, The Newseum
Carrie Christoffersen, The Newseum
Jordan Tannenbaum, United States
   Holocaust Museum
Miriam Lomaskin, United States
   Holocaust Museum
Kai Sabo, United States Holocaust
   Museum
Jean-Pierre and Eliane Laffont
Eric Meskauskas
Misha Erwitt
Bill Hunt
Charles Isaacs
Peter Menzel
Faith D'Alusio
Mike Davis
Deb Davis
Sasha Erwitt
Elizabeth Krist
Michael O'Brien
Don Winslow

IMAGE REPRODUCTION
Leslie Smolan, Carbone Smolan
   Associates
Daniel Marcolina, Illustration
Mike Lappin, *National Geographic*
Eric Luden, Digital Silver Imaging
Michael Marquand
Mio Nakamura
Michael Rylander
Kim Shannon

EDITORIAL
Stephen M. Anstey
Christian Bergland
Elizabeth Depoy
Stephen Gilson
A.J. Jacobs
Kim Kennedy
Katherine Lanpher
Alex Newman
Curt Sanburn
Margaret Low Smith, *The Atlantic*
Joy Solomon
Rabbi Dr. Jay Michaelson

DESIGN SUPPORT
David Whitmore

COPY EDITORS/ PROOFREADERS
Michele C. Anderson
Victoria Elliott
Angela Frucci
Anna Mantzaris

CHALK+CHISEL VIDEO APPLICATION
Marta Chell
Kelly Driver
Chris Kidd
Garrett Levy
Ben Slavin
Brian Thompson

VIDEO SOURCING AND PROCUREMENT
Ken Hertz, Hertz Lichtenstein &
   Young LLP
Jon Kamen, @Radical Media
Rich Miner, Google Ventures
Sandy Smolan, VR Microtheaters
Brian Storm, MediaStorm
Max Worrin

MUSIC CURATION
Michael Gore
Ty Roberts, Universal Music Group
Edgey Pires, The Last Internationale
Delila Paz, The Last Internationale
Lois Sasson

TRAVEL COORDINATOR
Maureen Sabino, Travel Destinations
   Unlimited

ACCOUNTING & FINANCE
Ally Merkeley, Bookkeeper
Denise Courtney, Accountant
Arthur Langhaus, KLS Associates
Joe Callaway, KLS Associates
Eugene Blumberg, Blumberg &
   Associates

**EMBASSY GRAPHICS
(PRE-PRESS)**
Brian Payne
Don Sourisseau
Lee Wilcox
Les Williamson

1010 PRINTING
Eliane Liu
Ellen Zhang

TRANSCONTINENTAL PRINTING
Mathieu Liboiron
Manon Poulin

STERLING PUBLISHING CO.
Adria Dougherty
Jennie Jewett
Sari Lampert Murray
Fred Pagan
Lauren Tambini

ADVISORS
Josh Baran, *Baran Communications*;
Dawn Barber, *Civic Hall*; Ivy Barsky,
*National Museum of America Jewish
History*; Sunny Bates, *Sunny Bates
Associates*; David Bigelow, *J.P.
Morgan Private Bank*; Jeffrey Bleich,
former Ambassador to Australia;
Lonnie G. Bunch III, *National Museum
of African American History and
Culture*; Rob Carter, *FedEx*; Sandy
Climan, *Entertainment Media
Ventures*; David Elliot Cohen; Cady
Coleman, *Astronaut*; Steffi Czerny,
DLD Media; Michael Donaldson,
Donaldson + Callif, LLP; John de
Lancie, *Actor*; Eric Ellestad, *Local
Roots Farms*; Rex Ellis, *National
Museum of African American History
and Culture*; Dan Farber, *Salesforce*;
Diana Farrell, *JP Morgan Chase
Institute*; Jessica Eve Goldfarb,
Civic Hall; Brian Grazer, *Imagine
Entertainment*; Robert Guinsler,
Sterling Lord Literistic, Inc.; Josh
Haner, *The New York Times*;
Jonathan Hart; Bruce Heavin; John
Hendricks, *CuriosityStream*; Mike
Hawley, *EG Conference*; Ken Hertz,
Hertz Lichtenstein & Young LLP;
Clare Hines, *Ogilvy & Mather*; Marc
Hodosh, *Co-Creator TEDMED*; Linda
Holiday, *Citia*; Tony Hsieh, *Zappos*;
Arianna Huffington, *Thrive Global*;
Zem Joaquin, *EcoFabulous*; James
Joaquin, *Obvious Ventures*; Holly
Jacobus, *Citia*; Melinda Janko, *100
Years*; Yasmine Delawari Johnson,
Youth Policy Institute; Matt Johnson,
Ziffren Brittenham LLP; Barbara
Kinney, *Emerson Collective*;
David Kirkpatrick, *Techonomy*;
Jon Levy, *The Influencers*; Deray
Mckesson, *Pod Save the People*;
Charles Melcher, *Melcher Media*;

Doug Menuez, *Fearless Genius*;
Walt Mossberg, *Recode*; Elizabeth
Hendricks North, *CuriosityStream*;
Juliana Olsson, *National Museum of
Natural History*; Lakshmi Pratury, *INK
Conferences*; Andrew Rasiej, *Personal
Democracy Forum*; Tom Rielly,
TED Conferences; Allan Ripp, *Ripp
Media*; Jane Rosch, *EG Conference*;
Simone Ross, *Techonomy*; Christina
Romero; Paul Sagan, *ProPublica*;
Swan Sit, *Revlon*; Richard Sergay;
Samuel Sinyangwe, *Campaign Zero*;
David Smith, *Kilpatrick Townsend
& Stockton LLP*; Greg Steltenpohl,
Califa Farms; Kelly Stoetzel, *TED
Conferences*; Charlie Szoradi,
Independence LED; Kara Swisher,
Recode; Selma Thomas, *National
Museum of African American History
and Culture*; Ellen Goldsmith-
Vein, *Gotham Group*; Jon Vein,
MarketShare; Lynda Weinman; Billie
Whitehouse, *Wearable Experiments*;
David J. Wittenstein, *Cooley LLP*;
Michael J. Wolf, *Activate*; Esther
Wojcicki, *Class Badges*; Richard
Saul Wurman; Tom Yellin, *The
Documentary Group*; Moses Znaimer,
IdeaCity

SPECIAL THANKS
James Able, Zachary Able, Sophia
Able, Martin Baldessari, Zoli Balog,
Heather Beaven, Yousry Bissada,
David Burnett, Ken Carbone, Sammy
Chadwick, Carrie Christoffersen, Turk
Cobell, Laurent Compagnon, Diana
Campuzano, Daniel Daley, Ebro
Darden, Connie Diletti, Gene Driskell,
Sean Dugan, Susan & Ben Durham,
Nusrat Durrani, Marianne Engle,
Amy Erwitt, C.J. Erwitt, David Erwitt,
Ellen Erwitt, Elliott Erwitt, Erik
Erwitt, Gabor Farkas, Ola Fleming,
Travon Free, Michael Gilbert, Brooke
Guthrie, Corey Hajim, Joseph P.
Harris, Colleen & Hunter Hancock,
Suzanne Horn, Samuel Irvine, Kamil
Kaluza, Athena Kangelos, Sheldon
Kasowitz, Bruce Kinlin, Hillary &
Cameron Lester, Karpra Li, Sonny
& Cara Blessley Lowe, Asa Mathat,
Tereza Machado-Menuez, Kiley and
Chris Manetta, Melvin Monette, Julia
Mosconi, Kim O'Dell, Jon O'Hara,
Dean and Anne Ornish, Kal Penn,
Tony Peyser, Natasha & Jeff Pruss,
Sydney & Evan Pruss, Silka Quintero,
Lori Reese, Debbie Donnelly
Robinson, Lily Rutherfurd, Trinity
Sambolin, Daniela Sbrisny, Marcia
Schiff, Joelle Sedlmeye, Tracey Lynn
Shifflett, Lisa Shufro, Tom & Beth
Sibley, Brigitte Sion, Ph.D., Iva Spitzer,
Trudy Styler, Sheri Sarver, Savannah
Smith, Jesse Smolan, Lily Smolan,
Phoebe Smolan, Reed Smolan, Adam
Szabo, Brad Takei, Drew & Sue
van Niekerk, Shari & Eric Warezak,
Jacquin K. White, Kay Woodcock,
Sam Worrin, Ariel Zambelich

SPONSORS
Getty Images
Digital Silver Imaging
Refinery29
YouTube
SAP

**SPECIAL THANKS TO THE
ANTI-DEFAMATION LEAGUE STAFF**
Marianne Benjamin, Amy Blumkin,
Steven Freeman, Jonathan
Greenblatt, Todd Gutnick, Daniel
Kelley, Kenneth Jacobson, Deborah
Lauter, Michael Lieberman, Jen
Liseo, Bonnie Mitelman, Marvin
Rappaport, Harry Reis, David
Robbins, Aaron Sussman, Clifford
Schechter, Oren Segal, Miriam
Spectre, Jillian Weintraub

FURRY MASCOTS
Bella, Felix, Leo, Luna, Mia, Minou,
Mr. Mookie, Ruby

INSTITUTIONAL SUPPORT
Anti-Defamation League
LBJ Presidential Library
The Library of Congress
The Osage Nation Museum
Oklahoma Historical Society
National Museum of America Jewish
   History
National Museum of African
   American History and Culture
National Museum of the American
   Indian
The Newseum
The Smithsonian Institute
United States Holocaust Memorial
   Museum

FOR SPEAKING OPPORTUNITIES
info@againstallodds.com

 PO Box 1189
Sausalito CA 94966-1189

THE GOOD FIGHT: AMERICA'S ONGOING STRUGGLE FOR JUSTICE is a registered
trademark of Against All Odds Productions II, Inc.

© 2017 Against All Odds Productions II, Inc.

ISBN 978-1-4549-2734-1

Distributed in the U.S. by Sterling Publishing Co., Inc.

1166 Avenue of the Americas, New York, NY 10036, USA

For information about custom editions, special sales, and premium and
corporate purchases, please contact Against All Odds Productions II, Inc.
at ablekatya@mac.com.

Manufactured in China

10 9 8 7 6 5 4 3 2 1

10/17

www.AgainstAllOddsProductions.com

PRAISE FOR *THE GOOD FIGHT*

"This book recounts a story both gripping and sacred." —DAVID WOLPE, MAX WEBB SENIOR RABBI, SINAI TEMPLE

"The LGBTQ community is as diverse as the fabric of this nation. We are women. We are Muslim. We are Jewish. We are black, white, Latinx, Asian American, and Native American. We are immigrants and we are people with disabilities. This important history illustrates our combined struggle for full equality, and is testament to the deeply held American belief that dissent is the highest form of patriotism." —CHAD GRIFFIN, PRESIDENT, HUMAN RIGHTS CAMPAIGN

"There has always been a gap in America between our ideals and our institutions. The beautiful essays and images in *THE GOOD FIGHT* remind us that only one thing has ever closed that gap: people power, organized tirelessly and applied relentlessly. Justice for all is worth fighting for." —ERIC LIU, CEO, CITIZEN UNIVERSITY

"*THE GOOD FIGHT* boldly offers up what the shared passion for justice looks like. This is both a timely and timeless book that is essential in understanding the movements for greater rights and acceptance from multiple perspectives. For those who relentlessly envision and fight for the world as they wish to see it and what it will take to get there, this volume's rousing testimonies and exquisite images will embolden you to continue onward with the tools of justice, innovation, and idealism as you fight the good fight." —CHERYL L. DORSEY, PRESIDENT, ECHOING GREEN

LEON L. LEWIS
National Director, 1913-1931

Stemming from a clear need to create an organization with a mission to "stop the defamation of the Jewish people and to secure justice and fair treatment to all," Sigmund Livingston of Chicago launched the Anti-Defamation League with only two desks and $200. ADL, an arm of the B'nai B'rith organization, was then founded in 1913 with Leon Lewis as its first National Director.

Negative stereotypes about Jews abounded as WWI broke out. ADL distributed a memo discouraging "objectionable and vulgar" media references to Jews.

BENJAMIN R. EPSTEIN
National Director, 1947-1979

Ben Epstein personified the dual mission of ADL, speaking to the continuing need for full individual rights. He led the way in combating forms of non-official institutional anti-Semitism, such as quotas in universities, housing, and employment. Epstein marched alongside Martin Luther King Jr. in Selma, upholding ADL's mission. He was joined by Sheldon Steinhauser, Denver Regional Director, and Oscar Cohen, Director of ADL's program division, among other ADL and civil rights leaders.

"Your tireless pursuit of equality of treatment for all Americans has made a lasting and substantial contribution to our democracy."

John F. Kennedy
President of the United States, 1961-1963

1913

1947

1931

FOR OVER 100 YEARS, ADL HAS BEEN A FORCE FOR CHANGE, A CHAMPION OF

RICHARD E. GUTSTADT
National Director, 1931-1947

With the country in the grip of the Depression and Hitler rising in Germany, American nativists and fascists—some with direct ties to the Nazis—spread anti-Jewish hatred freely. Alarmed that these groups not only threatened Jews but American democracy, ADL established a fact-finding operation aimed at monitoring and exposing extremism.

ADL spoke out against Father Charles Coughlin and his radio broadcasts that spewed anti-Semitic diatribes and pro-German propaganda over the airwaves.

ADL
Anti-Defamation League®

NATHAN PERLMUTTER
National Director, 1979-1987

ADL developed advertisements speaking out against anti-Israel propaganda, expanded its impact outside the U.S., and established an office in Israel.

ADL began conducting its annual Audit of Anti-Semitic Incidents. The League also published its first model hate crime law.

"Your efforts have benefitted both Jew and non-Jew alike and have served to strengthen our democratic ideal... you have my best wishes for... every continued success in your very important work."

Ronald Reagan
President of the United States, 1981-1989

JONATHAN A. GREENBLATT
CEO and National Director, 2015-Present

Advancing the organization quickly into the digital age, ADL opened a Silicon Valley-based Center on Technology and Society and inspired a landmark report by a specially created Task Force on Harassment and Journalism.

ADL also launched a groundbreaking annual summit on anti-Semitism that brought together leaders from across the business, technology, and religious communities to discuss ways to combat contemporary anti-Semitism, Never Is Now.

Protecting civil rights for all, Jonathan speaks out against anti-Muslim and other forms of discrimination. He launched "50 States Against Hate" to promote passage of comprehensive hate crime laws in every state in the U.S.

1979

2015

OUR NATION'S VALUES, AND A SHIELD AGAINST HATE AND EXTREMISM.

1987

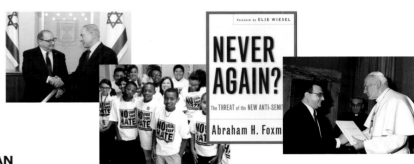

ABRAHAM H. FOXMAN
National Director, 1987-2015

Under Abe Foxman's leadership, ADL increased advocacy for Israel and new education initiatives took center stage. ADL's "A World of Difference" program, launched in New England, became ADL's flagship educational program, later complemented by the No Place for Hate® initiative.

At the request of Charles Ramsey, Washington, D.C.'s Chief of Police, ADL, in partnership with the United States Holocaust Memorial Museum, created Law Enforcement and Society, a unique training program for police that examines the Holocaust and its implications for law enforcement today. Since it was launched in 1999, more than 130,000 law enforcement personnel, including every FBI New Agent since 2000, have participated in the program, which is now in eight cities.

Recognizing growing concern about anti-Semitism and hate online, Abe co-authored Viral Hate and backed efforts to initiate partnerships with major tech companies to combat cyberhate. During Abe's tenure, the Matthew Shepard and James Byrd Jr. Hate Crimes Prevention Act (HCPA), the most comprehensive federal law enacted in the past four decades to protect against hate crimes, was signed by President Barack Obama.

OUR COMMITMENT RUNS DEEP
ADL STAFF AND LEADERSHIP

OFFICERS OF THE NATIONAL COMMISSION

NATIONAL CHAIR
Marvin D. Nathan

CEO AND NATIONAL DIRECTOR
Jonathan A. Greenblatt

PAST NATIONAL CHAIRS
Barbara B. Balser
Howard P. Berkowitz
Kenneth J. Bialkin
Barry Curtiss-Lusher
Burton S. Levinson
Glen S. Lewy
Melvin Salberg
David H. Strassler
Robert G. Sugarman
Glen A. Tobias

VICE CHAIRS
Martin L. Budd
Meyer Eisenberg
Esta Gordon Epstein
James Grosfeld
Charles Kriser
Steven Lyons
Ruth Moss
George Stark
Mark Wilf
Christopher Wolf

HONORARY VICE CHAIRS
Rudy Boschwitz
Yossie Hollander
Geri M. Joseph
Bernard Marcus
Cynthia Marks
Samuel H. Miller
Haim Saban
Michael Steindhardt
Gerald Stempler

TREASURER
Milton S. Schneider

HONORARY TREASURER
Robert H. Naftaly

SECRETARY
Thomas C. Homburger

ASSISTANT SECRETARY
Stanford Baratz

ANTI-DEFAMATION LEAGUE FOUNDATION PRESIDENT
Glen S. Lewy

STANDING COMMITTEE CHAIRS

ADMINISTRATION
Lawrence Rosenbloom
Pamela Schwartz

ADVOCACY & ENGAGEMENT
Michael Sheetz

AUDIT
Shelley Parker

BUDGET
Mitchell Weseley

CIVIL RIGHTS
Elizabeth A. Price

DEVELOPMENT
Ben Sax

EDUCATION
Miriam Weisman

FUNDING FOR THE FUTURE
Lawrence Miller

INFORMATION TECHNOLOGY
Arthur Reidel

INTERNATIONAL AFFAIRS
Eric Horodas

LEADERSHIP
Tracey Grossman
Tracy Treger

MARKETING & COMMUNICATIONS
Joseph Goldblum

OUTREACH & INTERFAITH AFFAIRS
Martin L. Budd

PLANNING
Milton S. Schneider

REGIONAL OPERATIONS
Esta Gordon Epstein

SENIOR MANAGEMENT TEAM

DEPUTY NATIONAL DIRECTOR
Kenneth Jacobson

CHIEF OF STAFF
Emily Bromberg

GROWTH
Frederic L. Bloch, SVP

LEADERSHIP
Shari B. Gersten, SVP

FINANCE & ADMINISTRATION
Michael A. Kellman, SVP

POLICY & PROGRAMS
Deborah M. Lauter, SVP

TECHNOLOGY
Rafail Portnoy, SVP

TALENT & KNOWLEDGE
Tom Ruderman, SVP

GENERAL COUNSEL, PRIVACY & SECURITY
Steven C. Sheinberg, SVP

BRAND & MARKETING
Amy Aronoff Blumkin, VP

LAW ENFORCEMENT, EXTREMISM & COMMUNITY SECURITY
David Friedman, VP

COMMUNICATIONS & DIGITAL
Betsaida Alcantara, VP

EDUCATION
Lorraine Tiven, VP (Interim)

REGIONAL OPERATIONS & ADVANCEMENT
David S. Waren, VP

NATIONAL DIRECTOR EMERITUS
Abraham H. Foxman

With enormous respect and gratitude, ADL thanks Eric and Linda Horodas for their foresight, generosity, and dedication to our mission and to making this book a reality.

Adam Jacobs photography

ABOUT THE AUTHORS

Rick Smolan, CEO of Against All Odds Productions, is a #1 *New York Times* best-selling author with more than 5 million copies of his books in print. A former *Time*, *LIFE*, and *National Geographic* photographer, Smolan is best known as the co-creator of the "Day in the Life" book series. Today, he and his partner, Jennifer Erwitt, orchestrate global projects that combine creative storytelling with state-of-the-art technology. Their projects each generate hundreds of millions of media impressions and are often featured on the covers of *Fortune, Time, GEO,* and similar publications around the world. Their books include *The Human Face of Big Data, Inside Tracks: Alone Across the Outback, America at Home, Blue Planet Run, The Obama Time Capsule, America 24/7, One Digital Day, 24 Hours in Cyberspace, Passage to Vietnam,* and *The Power to Heal.* More than a million people have watched Smolan's "Natasha's Story" on TED.com (www.NatashaStory.com). *Fortune* magazine describes Against All Odds Productions as "one of the 25 coolest companies in America." www.AgainstAllOdds.com

"PART OF SOCIAL PROGRESS IS UNDERSTANDING THAT A PERSON IS NOT DEFINED ONLY BY ONE'S SEXUALITY, RACE, OR GENDER." —TIM COOK

"FRANKLY, I'M BOTH PROUD AND ENVIOUS THAT THESE YOUNG PEOPLE ARE GROWING UP IN AN AGE WHERE THEY'RE FREE TO LOVE WHO THEY WANT." —GAIL SHISTER

"IF ALL MUSLIMS ARE TERRORISTS BECAUSE A SINGLE DIGIT PERCENTAGE OF TERRORISTS HAPPEN TO BE MUSLIM, THEN ALL MUSLIMS ARE PEACEMAKERS BECAUSE 5 OUT OF THE PAST 12 NOBEL PEACE PRIZE WINNERS (42 PERCENT) HAVE BEEN MUSLIMS." —OMAR ALNATOUR

"HATE CRIMES, COMMITTED SOLELY BECAUSE THE VICTIMS HAVE A DIFFERENT SKIN COLOR OR A DIFFERENT FAITH OR ARE GAYS OR LESBIANS, LEAVE DEEP SCARS NOT ONLY ON THE VICTIMS BUT ON OUR LARGER COMMUNITY. THEY ARE ACTS OF VIOLENCE AGAINST AMERICA ITSELF." —PRESIDENT WILLIAM JEFFERSON CLINTON

"PEOPLE SAY THAT SLAVES WERE TAKEN FROM AFRICA. THIS IS NOT TRUE: PEOPLE WERE TAKEN FROM AFRICA, AMONG THEM HEALERS AND PRIESTS, AND WERE MADE INTO SLAVES." —ABDULLAH IBRAHIM

"OUR LIVES BEGIN TO END THE DAY WE BECOME SILENT ABOUT THINGS THAT MATTER." —MARTIN LUTHER KING JR.

"YOU CAN BE PRO-COP *AND* PRO-BLACK. WHICH IS WHAT WE SHOULD ALL BE STRIVING FOR." —TREVOR NOAH

"IF YOU'RE NOT CAREFUL, THE NEWSPAPERS WILL HAVE YOU HATING THE PEOPLE WHO ARE BEING OPPRESSED, AND LOVING THE PEOPLE WHO ARE DOING THE OPPRESSING." —MALCOLM X

"WHAT WE SHOULD CELEBRATE MORE THAN DIVERSITY IS WHAT WE DO WITH IT. HOW DO WE BRING EVERYONE IN THE TENT AND CREATE SOMETHING TOGETHER? IN A TWENTY-FIRST CENTURY WAY THAT ACTIVATES OUR TRUE POTENTIAL, WE ALL NEED TO BECOME SWORN-AGAIN." —ERIC LIU